Jeffrey Otto

CAN MICROFINANCE WORK?

Can Microfinance Work?

HOW TO IMPROVE ITS ETHICAL BALANCE AND EFFECTIVENESS

Lesley Sherratt

Oxford University Press is a department of the University of Oxford.
It furthers the University's objective of excellence in research, scholarship,
and education by publishing worldwide. Oxford is a registered trade mark
of Oxford University Press in the UK and in certain other countries

Published in the United States of America by Oxford University Press
198 Madison Avenue, New York, NY 10016, United States of America

Library of Congress Cataloging-in-Publication Data
Names: Sherratt, Lesley, author.
Title: Can microfinance work? : how to improve its ethical balance and effectiveness / Lesley Sherratt.
Description: Oxford ; New York, NY : Oxford University Press, [2016] | Includes bibliographical references and index.
Identifiers: LCCN 2015035120 | ISBN 9780199383191 (alk. paper)
Subjects: LCSH: Microfinance. | Financial institutions—Moral and ethical aspects.
Classification: LCC HG178.3 S536 2016 | DDC 332—dc23
LC record available at http://lccn.loc.gov/2015035120

9 8 7 6 5 4 3 2 1

Printed in the United States of America on acid-free paper

For Christine

In memoriam

Contents

Preface

MY INTEREST IN microfinance was first sparked when the UN declared 2005 the "Year of Microcredit" and made microcredit central to its Millennium Development Goals, particularly that of halving extreme world poverty by 2015.

At the time, I was an investment manager running $1 billion in portfolios dedicated to investing in financial stocks for a large fund management firm. I had nearly twenty years' experience of investing in banks and financial institutions, but, being publicly traded commercial enterprises, very few of them indeed ever reached the poorest in society—and some of those that did had the roughest reputations.

So the idea that a form of banking existed that could lift the poorest out of poverty was something I wanted to know more of. It was not (then) an investable idea, so instead I explored it in a private capacity, as a donor and through sitting on the advisory board of a UK MFI operating in sub-Saharan Africa.

Ten years on, has microcredit helped deliver the Millennium Development Goals? The answer to that, sadly, is no. The proportion of people in extreme poverty in the world *has* reduced,[1] but much of that improvement has come from China's development, and without the involvement of microcredit. Many of the early studies that trumpeted microcredit's success have been discredited. The most recent and thorough randomized

[1] See, for example, the World Bank Poverty Overview at www.worldbank.org/en/topic/poverty/overview, where the number of people living on less than $1.25 per day is expected to have about halved between the 1990 baseline used there and 2015. (The *proportion* of people below this line has fallen more sharply, from 43% to 17%, but that owes part of its success simply to a rising global population).

evaluations, conducted across a wide range of contexts and continents, have failed to find any significant ability of microcredit to change the lives of the poorest.

Does that mean, then, as one commentator[2] suggested in jest, that "At this point, it is clear that any responsible policymaker must support the end of public subsidies for microcredit, social entrepreneurs should redirect their energies to some better cause, and this multi-billion dollar industry must wind down. Rigorous impact evaluation has proven that it was all built on a myth"? Well, that might indeed be a more rational response than the reviewer gives it credit for. But there are those who have invested many development-minded dollars, who will want to know more before abandoning the effort. Is microcredit following an intellectually and morally bankrupt model that is beyond repair, or is there anything left that can be done to make it "work"?

For it is not just that microfinance is now understood not to have much impact in reducing poverty. Its original promise had an additional strong ethical message as well—that it could empower the world's poorest women, as well as enrich them. Yet in practice it has been seen to exploit, coerce, and overindebt, with disastrous results for borrowers at times. We need to know not just if there is anything that can be done to make microfinance "work" in terms of poverty alleviation, but also if there is anything that can be done to ensure that it is practiced ethically. Indeed, we need to know if it is the case that practicing microfinance more ethically is necessary just in order to stand a chance of delivering the hoped-for economic benefit.

This book is primarily addressed to these questions. I hope and believe that interested citizens who wonder where their development tax dollar is going will find it useful; that students of public policy and applied political and moral philosophy will find it an extended working example of how, when the implementers of a development policy lose sight of the moral moorings behind it, they can achieve the opposite of the original intention; and that ethically confused practitioners who struggle with the idea that their efforts to enrich and empower the poor may have ended up exploiting instead, might find some guidelines within on how to restore their purpose.

But this book is most of all addressed to those funders of microfinance who have the opportunity not just to tweak the microfinance model, but to radically change it into one of several rather different forms: subsidized savings vehicles, small- to medium-sized enterprise [SME] funding, and commercialized microfinance more or less as we know it—but *regulated*. Any of these, I suggest, may stand a better chance of helping to deliver on what will be the Sustainable Development Goals going forward, than microcredit. Some practitioners have already begun to take up this challenge; many more could do so. The non-commercial funders of the microfinance movement—the development agencies in the United States, United Kingdom, and Continental Europe; the World Bank; the great philanthropic donors—can steer them on their way. If this book helps move some to do so, it will have achieved its purpose.

---

[2] Justin Sandefur, "The Final Word on Microcredit?" *Views from the Center Blog*, Centre for Global Development, January 22, 2015.

Acknowledgments

I WOULD LIKE to thank the many people I have learned from in the academic and financial worlds: this book has drawn heavily from both. I was fortunate enough to read politics, philosophy, and economics at New College Oxford at a period of extraordinary strength in its teaching across all these fields, and, happily for me, at a time when it had (just, after six hundred years) started to admit women. In business I was lucky to work for and learn from one of the best research-driven investors of his generation, Chris Tracey, and to run portfolios specializing in the financial sector during a couple of decades of extraordinary growth – and collapse. On returning to academia twenty-five years later, I benefitted tremendously from having as PhD supervisor and then colleague, Leif Wenar at King's College, London. Though Leif must have heard more about microfinance than he could ever have thought he wanted to know, he never ran out of patience with my struggle to unpick the intricacies of the ethics of its practices.

I'm very grateful to the volunteers, loan officers, social performance managers, fundraisers, CFOs, and CEOs of a number of microfinance firms I have worked and explored investment with. I do not name them not because I am unappreciative of the time they have given me, but because this book is, in part, rather critical of a number of practices that some of them employ. I do not wish this book to be seen as a hatchet job on any individual microfinance institution: where a practice is inexcusable, it is usually so for the many rather than the one. The point is not to name and shame any particular MFI, but to change the practices of the industry.

To my husband and young adult daughters, Katharine, Laura, and Peter, my profound thanks for your loving support in motivating me to get this book finished after the unexpected and early death of my beloved twin sister as final drafts were being prepared.

Most of all, I acknowledge my huge debt to the writing, teaching, and example of Professor Jonathan Glover. He writes so as to be understood; teaches with a cool rationality that freeze-dries, then blows away, the cobwebs of mind; and sets an example of compassionate humanity to us all.

Introduction

> If we had not been obsessed with the romantic idea of microcredit then maybe there would have been an earlier realizing of what microcredit does and what it can't do. . . . The crisis in microfinance was the result of the 3 C's: credulity, cupidity and corruption. The politicians were corrupt, we were all credulous, and the microfinance people were greedy. Put them all together and you get the crisis.[3]

This book is about the ethics of microfinance, the making of small loans to poor borrowers who lack access to mainstream financial services. Over the past thirty years, microfinance has become a major developmental tool. It now reaches around two hundred million borrowers,[4] the vast majority of whom are women and among the world's poorest people. Microfinance has made strong claims. It has claimed to foster development through the extension of credit, creating a process of enrichment for its borrowers. And it has further claimed that it not only enriches its borrowers, but simultaneously empowers them. The cast of its advocates has been glittering.

It is endorsed by the UN, which made microfinance a key tool in delivering on a number of its Millennium Development Goals. One of its leading proponents, Muhammad

[3] Abhijit Banerjee and Esther Duflo in conversation with Tim Ogden; see www.philanthropyaction.com/articles-an_interview_with_banerjee_and_dufllo_part_2.

[4] Larry Reed, with Jesse Marsden, Amanda Ortega, Camille Rivera, and Sabina Rogers, *Resilience: The State of the Microcredit Campaign Report*, Microcredit Summit Campaign (MCS) 2014, 8. Number is 204 million microfinance borrowers as of the end of 2012.

Yunus, and the bank he founded, Grameen Bank, were jointly awarded the Nobel Peace Prize in 2006. At the Microcredit Summit Campaign held in Halifax, Canada, that year, microfinance was hailed as "the vaccine for the pandemic of poverty."[5] Its appeal to help others help themselves has enlisted development agencies, philanthropists, celebrities, and royalty in its cause. It has managed to combine making some individuals' fortunes with a powerful moral vision. Microfinance providers that began as small, donor-funded nongovernmental organizations could a few years later float shares at extraordinary valuations on stock markets. Their CEOs could write autobiographies with titles such as *A Fistful of Rice: My Unexpected Quest to End Poverty through Profitability*,[6] and as late as 2012, the outgoing director of the Microcredit Summit Campaign could speak of his vision for microfinance as a force for "redemption," by which giving a poor woman a loan would somehow reveal her hidden honor and worth.[7]

But the bubble has burst. Academic studies have found the impact of microfinance on poverty to be, at best, neutral. Widespread overindebtedness is believed to have led to the repayment crisis in Bolivia, Mexico, Cambodia, Nicaragua, Morocco, and, most dramatically, the Indian state of Andhra Pradesh. Yunus has been forced out of the bank he founded by his government. Some (including Yunus himself) question whether, in moving from being provided by small-scale NGOs to being provided by fully commercialized banks driven by the profit motive, microfinance has lost its soul. It has become an industry that instead of empowering and enriching so many of the world's poorest women has instead ended up accused of exploiting, coercing, and, even further, impoverishing some of them instead.

Where does the truth about the ethics of microfinance lie in all of this? It was perhaps inevitable that an industry whose leading practitioners made such extensive use of ethical claims in their fundraising and promotion should suffer some sort of backlash. And at the very least, the industry has claimed far more for itself than it could substantiate, and shied away from evidence that has suggested a darker side. But what are the facts? Chapter 2 will investigate microfinance's claim to reduce poverty and empower women and find that it is overblown. Given that, is it sufficient to simply cease promoting and funding microfinance, leaving it as just a commercialized service to the poor of no inherent ethical merit or demerit? Or are there ethical issues bound up in the way that microfinance provides its service that mean it should either seek to change itself, or have change forced upon it through regulation?

In this book, I argue that microfinance's working practices have evolved to subvert the industry's largely benign intentions and create the conditions for exploitation and

---

[5] Peter Mackay (the then Canadian minister of foreign affairs), quoted by Ananya Roy in *Poverty Capital: Microfinance and the Making of Development* (New York: Routledge, 2010), 90.

[6] Vikram Akula, *A Fistful of Rice: My Unexpected Quest to End Poverty through Profitability* (Boston: Harvard Business School Press, 2010).

[7] Sam Daley Harris speech to Microcredit Summit Campaign in Valladolid, November 2012.

coercion to occur. Indeed I argue that they subvert what should be (but is not) the ethical principle at the heart of microfinance, a recognition of a duty of care to borrowers.

I do not argue that all, or even most, microfinance practitioners set out intending to exploit or coerce their borrowers, or understand that they owe, but deliberately choose to ignore, a duty of care to those borrowers. I argue rather that the industry employs working practices that tend toward these moral hazards being incurred, but that practitioners, meantime, remain so certain of their own good intentions that they are blinded to these risks.

The book proceeds as follows.

To understand how these risks are undertaken and realized, it is necessary to first understand the core of the most widely used microfinance model, how that model has come about, and the extent to which it "works" or not. Part I seeks to provide that empirical understanding. The first chapter provides a brief history of how microfinance and its practices have evolved, so that the reader can see, in later chapters discussing microfinance's ethics in depth, how far some dilemmas have always been there, how far some are new, and how far commercialization has exacerbated preexisting tendencies. This chapter will cover some of the central ethical debates—the subsidy versus sustainability debate, mission drift, private capture of arguably public profits. But these debates do not exhaust the range of ethical issues in microfinance. Rather, they express differences of opinion on how extensive the role of markets should be in providing services to the poor: an important issue, but one it might be conceivable that all could agree upon without touching the deeper issues of whether exploitation, coercion, and a breach of a duty of care are inherent in the practices of microfinance, whoever provides it.

Chapter 2 examines whether microfinance does in fact achieve its aims of enriching and empowering its borrowers, and finds little substantiation of these claims. This matters in the ethical equation, for if microfinance really did deliver on these goals, the risks of exploitation and coercion taken along the way might, at least by those who include a broadly consequentialist approach to their ethics, be thought more worth taking.

Parts II and III are the ethical heart of the book. Chapters 3, 4, and 5 are the most conceptual and take the ethical notions of exploitation, coercion, and paternalism and examine the extent to which they are prevalent—and possibly are not, but should be—in the relationship between the microfinance institution (MFI) and the borrower.

Chapter 3 explores whether microfinance does in fact exploit its borrowers, principally but not only through the level of interest charged. I explore the concept of exploitation and resist the idea that exploitation should always be deemed wrongful: but do conclude that microfinance does in fact wrongfully exploit its borrowers. It does so by taking advantage of their exclusion from formal financial services to charge rates which are multiples of those in the formal sector; through imposing group lending conditions and compulsory "savings"; and by insisting on inflexible loan terms that in some circumstances will foreseeably result in hardship in repayment, or the use of child labor to make it possible. Chapter 3 covers the theory of exploitation, but in chapter 9 I lay out explicitly what a nonexploitative rate of interest would be—one that does not take advantage of borrowers' exclusion from formal financial services—and argue that any higher rate is wrongfully exploitative, regardless of whether it is charged by a for-profit, commercialized bank, a not-for-profit NGO, or indeed a moneylender.

In chapter 4 I show how the practice of lending to groups with mutual liability can turn borrowers from a self-helping source of solidarity to a coercive force for loan collection. I reject the idea that the offer of microfinance itself is coercive: that goes too far. But making group liability a condition of the offer of a loan foreseeably creates the circumstances where coercion is used (whether by the loan officer, an agent of the MFI, or the group itself) for loan collection in practice. I illustrate the chapter with examples of coercive loan collection practices, particularly from Bangladesh and India—from bullying, humiliating, and shaming (in societies where shaming can quickly lead to divorce and destitution), to the theft of a defaulting borrower's possessions and *ghar bhanga*, housebreaking, where the defaulting borrower's house is sold off, literally piece by piece.

I consider the argument that this can be *justified* coercion and reject it—at least when it comes to coercive loan collection. Confiscation of savings to cover a default, however, *would* arguably be an example of justified coercion. In some instances, the coercive pressure is applied not by the MFI itself, but on a borrower behind in her payments by her own borrowing group. This is so at least in part because the other members of the group will not otherwise have their own loans renewed until payment is made, or will have their savings confiscated to make good the default. Again examples from the field will be given. I also consider the extent to which the MFI bears responsibility for the coercive behavior of a borrowing group, when it has essentially exerted coercive pressure, justified or otherwise, on *them*.

In chapter 5 I consider whether there is a duty of care in microfinance and what, in this context, that would mean. MFIs most commonly present their relationship with borrowers not as patriarchal, exploitative, or coercive, but as one of gentle and justifiable paternalism—requiring the borrower to undergo basic business training, make compulsory savings, take out life insurance. Classically, Grameen and the Bangladesh Rehabilitation Assistance Committee (BRAC) originally imposed the social goals of the "Sixteen Decisions" and "Seventeen Rules." This chapter examines which of these impositions on the borrower are genuine justifiable paternalism, and which are in fact not paternalistic at all, as being not so much for the benefit of the borrower as for the benefit of the MFI itself. Although some practices *are* found to be justifiably paternalistic, more are not. Most worryingly, the one practice that *would* be justifiable paternalism if used, the exercise of a duty of care from the MFI to the borrower, is notable by its absence.

The duty of care referred to here is the legal responsibility of a seller of a potentially harmful product to a purchaser who is unable to ascertain the risk of that harm for herself. In such circumstances, the seller has a duty not to sell it unless reasonable care has been taken to be sure that it will *not* harm this particular purchaser. Evidence of exercising such a duty of care would be, for example, logging whether the profit the borrower anticipated making from the proposed business is actually enough to pay the true—properly calculated—interest rate on the loan. I examine the implosion of microcredit in Andhra Pradesh as an example not just of a woeful failure by the industry to meet that duty of care, but as an example of a terrible breach of it in helping to overindebt, with some disastrous consequences, so many of its clients.

Chapter 6 through 8 throw the focus wider again from the close focus on MFI and borrower and look at the ethical detail of microfinance at the industry level. Chapter 6 examines what we know—and, unfortunately, the very great deal we do not know—about how the distribution of the benefit and burdens of microfinance is spread. It acknowledges the amount that we do not know about the downside of microfinance, and is critical of the industry's failure to find out, which results from the industry's knowing failure to measure the subsequent fate of its dropouts. Nonetheless, what we *do* know, and the extent to which we know it, is laid out, and, though sketchy, it is an unhappy picture for proponents of microfinance seeking to help the poor: the very poorest do the worst from engaging with it, but there are some gains for the least-worst-off 5% of borrowers. It is a picture of the worst off losing, the majority seeing little difference made or incurring many small negatives, and a very few actually alleviating their poverty and becoming the success stories the marketing of the industry is built upon.

This chapter also discusses what distribution of the benefits and burdens of microfinance is acceptable. Can any amount of general good offset harm to any one particular person? How many lives going worse from engagement with microfinance are acceptable for each life that goes better? The chapter suggests that the current distribution is likely to be ethically unacceptable and that focus is needed on how to reduce the numbers who do worst from microfinance.

Chapter 7 looks at the underbelly of microcredit: what it means to run a small enterprise in the informal economy. Although the prevalent story of petty trading in microfinance is selling foodstuffs, the more significant margins lie in less ethically comfortable areas, such as the borrower arbitraging the MFI's lower-than-moneylender interest rates to become a moneylender herself. This chapter explores the ethical issues raised by the fact that most of the microfinance-funded borrowers operate within the "informal" sector and much of their activity is illegal or illicit. Businesses are not registered, they do not pay tax, they ignore health and safety standards normal in the formal sector. Loan uses can be for illegal activities—funding illegal migration, making housing improvements on illegal settlements, or the production and sale of "moonshine"—high ethanol alcohol. The use of child labor is not uncommon. This chapter, then, looks at the more ethically challenging practices of the microfinance borrowers themselves, and the extent to which MFIs are complicit in them.

The issues here are complex. The MFI and borrower are typically complicit together in illegal activity. From the MFI's point of view, some of these illegal/illicit businesses carry the highest margins and are the most successful, giving the MFI the best chance of not only this borrower repaying but also her being able to cover the defaults of others. To the borrower, the illegal activity may seem to the best option she has available. If necessity means that a child needs to earn enough to cover the cost of its existence, using it in a microenterprise may be a better alternative than sending it out to work for another family. Those harmed by the illegal activity may not always be obviously apparent, and certainly do not necessarily include the MFI or borrower, but individuals in the wider community. Yet difficult as the issues are, boards of MFIs need to face them. Lines can be drawn between supporting some illegal or illicit loan uses and not others, and I suggest boards adopt John Stuart Mill's harm principle as a guide to how to do so.

Chapter 8 widens the focus to examine the macro impact of microfinance on economies. Chapter 2 examined the evidence for microfinance making individuals better off; Chapter 8 examines the evidence for microfinance aiding in the development of whole economies—and finds it similarly lacking. It also examines the ethics of the extent to which microfinance can or should be seen as a substitute for state provision of public goods.

Part IV of the book pulls the first three parts of the book together and looks at the lessons we can draw about microfinance and the role it has played in development.

Chapter 9 tries to answer the question, what are the things we need to do to ensure that microfinance is practiced ethically? Five major recommendations are made: (1) establish what a nonexploitative interest rate would be; (2) drop the use of group liability; (3) tailor loan terms and conditions to individual client needs and specify and implement serious client protection measures; (4) establish clear policies on what uses of loan capital, and uses of child labor, are permissible (outlawing harmful child labor, at least as defined by local laws); and (5) build a mindfulness of externalities, of microfinance institutions being alert to the consequences of their actions en masse, not just individually.

These recommendations are no guarantee, sadly, of making microfinance *work* in terms of raising many out of poverty: but, if implemented, they would improve the ethical balance of microfinance's practices and tend toward a better net result, overall, than, on average, zero impact, by limiting some of the harms microfinance causes.

All five are linked by the need for very much greater transparency in the sector: regarding what interest rates are actually charged, on loan collection policies, on impact. The chapter considers mechanisms by which the industry might achieve these things voluntarily, and it is not impossible that it could clean up its own ethical act. But I conclude with a proposal to development agencies that the impact of their funding to microfinance might be much enhanced if a portion of it were shifted from financing microfinance directly, or through microfinance investment vehicles, to the facilitation of savings (albeit these might need to be subsidized); to provide credit to SMEs rather than individual entrepreneurs; and finally to fund the support of local regulation of the industry, to help it to achieve more net good by reducing the harm of some of its practices.

Chapter 10 serves as an epilogue to consider the wider lessons microcredit can offer antipoverty development efforts generally, and indeed the central lessons microcredit can take from development theory. It outlines the dangers of hubris, particularly in leading to a failure to evaluate properly; the classic dangers of the principal-agent problem; the paradox involved in trying to help others to help themselves; the dangers posed by lack of transparency, feedback, and accountability; and the risks, in focusing too much on micro solutions, of missing the macro picture.

Finally, I return to the central dilemma of microfinance—its Faustian bargain to exchange its control over the price at which credit is extended to the poor, for the wide-scale outreach made possible by sustainability or profitability. To become ethical, and more effective, the bulk of microfinance needs to change direction from where it is. It could refocus on savings and financial inclusion with only a minimal offering of credit, but it is unlikely it would be able to do so on a large scale without subsidy. It could scale up away from the myth of all individuals being potential entrepreneurs to embrace SME lending, which could be sustainable. Or it can stay on its current territory, but with much tougher controls to prevent the current working practices again subverting the generally benign intentions of practitioners. But if it does stay in this current comfort zone, although strong self-regulation could achieve a lot, it seems unlikely that microfinance can buy its soul back now. It is likely that if it is to be practiced nonexploitatively and ethically, good intentions will not suffice: tough and detailed external regulation will be required.

CAN MICROFINANCE WORK?

I Empirics

> The understanding of mathematics is necessary for a sound grasp of ethics.
>
> —SOCRATES

1 The Double-Edged Sword

THE MICROFINANCE MODEL AND THE MORAL HAZARDS INHERENT WITHIN IT

THIS CHAPTER BEGINS with a summary of what is the most common standard operating model for microfinance institutions. It is not, of course, the only one, but it is the model at the core of the majority of microfinance institutions that have grown up over the past forty years. Having set this out, the chapter then backtracks to see how this model of "best practice" has evolved, and how the changing extent to which market forces have played a role in delivering microfinance has shaped that evolution. It finishes by comparing the elements of the original microfinance model of the 1970s to "best practice" today, suggesting that while some ethical doubts regarding the model are of recent origin, arising as microfinance commercialized, others are deep-rooted.

1. The Microfinance Model: A Summary of Current "Best Practice" and Ethical Issues It Raises

The vast majority of what is termed microfinance today is, more simply, microcredit. Microcredit is the provision of very small size loans to poor borrowers, typically at higher interest rates than a traditional bank charges, but below those of a moneylender. Classically, it is offered to women, in groups, because women are seen as safer credit risks. It is extended on the basis that it will be used to support a small-scale business, the profits of which generate the cash flow to make the interest payments and eventually repay the loan, although it is known that many loans are actually used for consumption.

The loan is made without collateral, but with the commitment of the group to repay the loan on behalf of an individual if one defaults, the so-called "group liability" model. Individual lending is growing, but lending to groups (predominantly with group liability, sometimes with no formal group liability but a practice that no fresh loans are made until someone in the group has covered any defaults of others) is still the dominant form. Repayment levels are very high—97% and above[1]—but as they need to be if the model is to function either without further capital injection or without still higher interest rates than those already being charged. This high, 97%-plus number has often been taken as indicative of the fact that microcredit must be of benefit to its borrowers, or they would not be repaying and coming back for more. It will be seen in chapter 4 that this should not be assumed.

The wider term "microfinance" subdivides into microsavings, microcredit, and, recently, some microinsurance. Microsaving is the provision of savings accounts as a way of smoothing the financial flows of the unbanked. Microsaving itself raises few ethical issues beyond the cost of the provision and the risk of the provider absconding with the savings. The vast majority of the expansion in microfinance in the last few decades has been in microcredit, which is frequently offered alone, as the regulatory hurdles to offer microsavings are typically much higher. The growth rate of microsavings has increased sharply in recent years, but off a very small base. Following industry practice, microfinance will be the term most commonly used here, but it should be borne in mind, and the context will attempt to make clear, that this generally means microcredit. Although there are certainly issues of financial exclusion among the poorest in developed countries, microfinance has predominantly grown in developing countries, particularly in Asia, South America, Eastern Europe after the fall of the Berlin Wall, and, more recently, Africa. This is not to suggest that it does not exist in developed countries, but the practices discussed in this book have generally been developed in emerging economies.

The operating model of a standard microfinance institution today is that it is at least "sustainable," if not a fully commercial, for-profit institution: that is, that it makes enough money to cover its operating costs and does not require subsidy to continue as a going concern. This makes for an attractive pitch to those who fund MFIs, for it means that the money given to be lent out is constantly recycled, being repaid by one borrower before being lent to another, without leakage into covering any operating losses of the MFI. Thus the donation of a given amount of money for lending can then be used many times and, in theory, achieve many multiples of good.

The unchallenged assumption that the microfinance industry has made as it has evolved, at least until very recently, is that the provision of credit to the poor is an unqualified good for them: that is precisely why many practitioners will have become involved in the first place. But there is an ambiguity at the heart of microfinance, simply because

---

[1] For the global-level average repayment rate, MIX Market, see www.themix.org/about-microfinance/FAQ.

credit—debt—is a double-edged sword. Credit can both empower the borrower by enabling her to start a business whose profitability alleviates her poverty, and exacerbate that poverty if the business entered into with the credit fails to flourish and the interest rate payments become burdensome or even unmanageable. Used unsuccessfully, it can lead to a debt spiral ending with the borrower worse off than she began or, in worse cases, ostracized from her society or even, as has been reported in the 2010 crisis in microfinance in Andhra Pradesh, resorting to suicide.

These elements of the microfinance model that have evolved as "best practice" raise a number of additional ethical issues to those inherent even in the original model. The principal charges that can be leveled against microcredit are that the offering of it is, or can be, exploitative; that loan collection practices are, or can be, coercive; and that the way in which it is typically practiced is paternalistic—although it will also be argued that in some instances it is not paternalistic enough, and, indeed, that a fundamental duty of care from MFI to borrower is being either ignored or breached. These are some of the issues examined in depth in Parts II and III.

This model of a typical MFI today is thus one that lends overwhelmingly to women, in groups, with group liability in very many cases, with pressure to keep growing the loan portfolio, pressure to keep costs down, and low tolerance of any repayment problems.

The operational model of the industry was not always thus. What follows is a necessarily simplified account of how it has developed. A full history of the creation of microfinance and all the different strands of credit provision to the poor would fill a book in itself. At the cost of ignoring some of these strands in the interest of space, and because the central model that exists today is what concerns this book the most, the following account focuses on how the elements of best practice in modern microfinance today have evolved.

2. How Today's "Best Practice" Evolved

THE EARLY GRAMEEN BANK MODEL

The history of the provision of short-term credit to the poor is as long as the history of moneylending, which is pretty much as long as monetized economies have been around. What is distinctive about the microfinance model is that it is funded, at least initially, from sources outside the community in which lending occurs, often from overseas; that there is a strong emphasis on credit rather than savings; and that there is a drive for operational sustainability, if not full commercial profitability. The origins of that model lie predominantly in South Asia in the 1970s. Arguments for a longer lineage for microfinance can be made: some trace it back to eighteenth-century philanthropists and the German cooperative movement of the nineteenth and early twentieth centuries.[2] But if there is a

[2] For example, see David Roodman, *Due Diligence: An Impertinent Inquiry into Microfinance* (Washington, DC: Center for Global Development, 2012), 36–64.

modern-day descendant of nineteenth-century European cooperative movements today, a closer relative than microfinance would be rotating savings and credit associations (ROSCAs)[3] or the self-help groups of India, which like the cooperatives remain essentially based on local savings rather than foreign investment, donations, or borrowings, as do the village savings and loans associations (VSLAs).[4]

Part of the distinctiveness of the microfinance model has been its (at least initial) reliance on funding from outside the local community lent to. This is how it was for two of today's largest microfinance institutions, BRAC and Grameen Bank.[5] They were forged in the early, desperate days of Bangladesh as a nation, recovering from famine and its war of independence and receiving development aid to kick start recovery.

BRAC—originally Bangladesh Rehabilitation Assistance Committee, now simply known by its acronym—was founded in 1971 by Fazle Hasan Abed in response to the tropical cyclone that had killed between three hundred thousand and five hundred thousand in November 1970 and left millions bereft of homes and livelihoods that had been swept away, and food and drinking water in short supply.[6] Credit provision was part of

---

[3] ROSCA is a method of collective saving and borrowing, wholly financed by the group that does it. A group decides to save a fixed amount each week for a set period, with one member (taking it in turn) borrowing all the group's savings each week. So in a standard ROSCA of, say, fifteen people, each member puts a fixed amount into a pot every week for fifteen weeks (say, 10 units a week) and each week a different member is allowed to take the whole pot (150). For someone who gets the pot in week 1, he essentially has a loan that he then repays over the next fifteen weeks. For the person who gets the pot in week 15, he has essentially been saving for it for fifteen weeks. ROSCAs are common, very simple, and do not require outsiders or outside finance. Because the group itself retains no money, no record-keeping (other than remembering whose turn it is to have the pot next) is necessary. Members select each other, and the length of time for which the ROSCA will operate is agreed in advance. ROSCAs' limitation is that they are very rigid—everyone has to save/borrow the same amount, whereas they may have different needs, and so the scope of ROSCAs is likely to remain small. But they are efficient within the limitations of what they do. Guilds provided this sort of function in medieval Europe. ROSCAs disappeared in Europe in the seventeenth century as "friendly societies" began to take their place, but remain common in developing countries.

[4] These also go back deep into history, but in recent decades CARE has helped spread them to two million borrowers in Africa. VSLAs operate by members of a group regularly saving into a pot, usually for a fixed period of time like six months, then borrowing variable amounts from it as needed. Interest is charged on loans, and more organization is needed than with ROSCAs in terms of the record-keeping of how much each has saved or borrowed, so a higher standard of literacy from at least three members is necessary. The box for the savings is triple-locked, with three different keyholders to reduce fraud. At the end of the agreed period, all outstanding loans have to be repaid, and then the proceeds of the box (including interest that has built up) are distributed to the members of the group: so VSLAs can be more flexible than ROSCAs and act as saving as well as borrowing vehicles. The only outside help needed is the provision of the strongbox and some explanation of how to work the scheme (which CARE has provided): otherwise, it is a recycling of a community's own money between themselves, which, as with ROSCAs, makes it very cheap and efficient, but also limits its size.

[5] The third large Bangladesh microfinance institution, ASA, was also founded in the 1970s, but did not turn to microcredit until the 1990s, although once it did, it made up fast for lost time, now having over four million borrowers (see http:mixmarket.org/mfi.asa).

[6] Ian Smillie, Freedom from Want: The Remarkable Success Story of BRAC, the Global Grassroots Organization That's Winning the Fight against Poverty (Sterling, VA: Kumarin Press, 2009), 18.

BRAC's attempts to provide relief across many fronts, but was not central to it, and did not become a major focus for some years. It is thus that Muhammad Yunus, who in 1976 founded Grameen Bank, which focused much more explicitly on credit provision alone, has come to be regarded by many as the founding father of modern microfinance.

Microfinance has an ability to overdwell on personalized stories and mythologize its heroes, but it is nonetheless worth examining the story of Yunus's creation of Grameen Bank, for the model he developed became the model that was replicated over the next thirty years: and it is worth observing the differences between the original, simpler, model and the predominant microfinance model of today.

In 1974, Professor Muhammad Yunus was head of the economics department at Chittagong University, and Bangladesh was in the grip of famine. Yunus had "started to dread my own lectures. What good were all my complex theories when people were dying of starvation on the sidewalks and porches across from my own lecture hall?"[7] Yunus began to study poverty from the bottom up, in the rural village of Jobra, close to the University. The key moment for him came in 1976 when he met Sufiya Begum, who wove bamboo baskets for a profit of two cents a day, on which she tried to feed her family. The amount of money she made was determined by the *paikars*, the middlemen who supplied bamboo at its cost price of twenty-two cents on the condition that the completed basket was sold back to them at twenty-four cents. Begum did not have enough capital of her own to buy her own bamboo and believed that the cost of borrowing from the local moneylenders to do so (at interest rates that could vary from 10% a week to 10% per day) was even more prohibitive than the deal with the *paikars*.

It was the fact that Begum could only make two cents a day that shocked Yunus.[8]

> In my university courses, I theorized about sums in the millions of dollars, but here before my eyes the problems of life and death were posed in terms of pennies. Something was wrong. Why did my university courses not reflect the reality of Sufiya's life? I was angry, angry at myself, angry at my economics department and thousands of intelligent professors who had not tried to address this problem and solve it. It seemed to me that the economic system made it absolutely certain that Sufiya's income would be kept perpetually at such a low level that she would never save a penny and would never invest in expanding her economic base. Her children were condemned to live a life of penury, of hand-to-mouth survival, just as she had lived it before them, and as her parents did before her. I had never heard anyone suffering for a lack of twenty-two cents. It seemed impossible to me, preposterous. Should I reach into my pocket and hand Sufiya the pittance she needed for capital?

---

7 Muhammad Yunus, *Banker to the Poor: Micro-lending and the Battle against World Poverty* (New York: PublicAffairs, 1999), viii.

8 Yunus, *Banker to the Poor*, 48.

> That would be so simple, so easy. I resisted the urge to give Sufiya the money she needed. She was not asking for charity. And giving one person twenty-two cents was not addressing the problem on any permanent basis.

Yunus gathered data on all those in the village who, like Begum, needed access to credit to facilitate selling their produce at full retail price rather than at a rate set to give them just enough to survive, but which reserved all of the margin for a middleman. Twenty-seven dollars was enough to provide all the capital necessary for forty-two people. Yunus's original intention was not to set up a bank himself: he went to his local bank to see if they would lend to the poor in their own area and was laughed away with the objections that the bank could not possibly lend to the destitute: the interest earned on the small amounts required would not even cover the cost of filling in the loan documentation, the borrowers were too illiterate to fill in any forms, and, most of all, they had no collateral.

Out of this experience came Grameen Bank, the essence of which has been to view the poor as trustworthy to repay small loans, regardless of collateral, especially when these loans have been made in small village groups, creating peer pressure, and when future credit will not be extended until the first loan is repaid. For Yunus, an important part of the provision of microcredit has been not just for women to begin to move out of poverty, but that in the process of doing so for themselves, by their own efforts, they become empowered socially as well as economically. Their own access to credit and therefore the means to make a living was thought to strengthen their position in a society that had traditionally denied them this access. A further important part of this model is, of course, that the capital lent is in fact repaid, and is then recycled to new borrowers, so that the one unit of capital lent can have multiple effects over the years in helping borrowers out of poverty.

Note too in this very early model of Grameen Bank that the aim is very limited and very simple. It is to take an *existing* entrepreneur, someone who is already running some small subsistence business, and replace the middleman, who extracts all the inherent profit in the operation, with a cheap line of credit (it is not clear if Yunus charged any interest at all on these original loans). In chapter 8, the problem is raised that microfinance is frequently offered to borrowers to start *new* businesses, which may simply undercut existing petty trading businesses and drive them out of business, making microfinance seemingly appear to work for the individual microcredit borrower, but not for the community as a whole. The original Begum loan did not do this: microcredit was used to undercut the middlemen and moneylenders, not other businesses.

Note also that the social, as well as financial, empowerment of women was an important part of this early model of microfinance. As will be seen in later chapters, Grameen Bank had its "Sixteen Decisions" and BRAC its "Seventeen Rules"—which aimed at social development for women, albeit they largely extended to issues of health, discipline, and mutual support rather than more radically challenging the place of women in Bangladesh society. Grameen Bank's decision to commit to neither giving nor receiving dowry went furthest in challenging cultural practice, but it is unclear that despite borrowers being required to recite this among the other Decisions at meetings, that it was ever much adhered to in practice.[9]

The parts of this early model that are recognizable today are that loan repayments are frequent and small and that lending takes place to small groups of people who form peer groups that can give mutual support, but could also exert pressure for repayment. Initial group size was usually five, and groups then joined into centers that then held the weekly meetings for requests for loans, approval of them, and repayment.[10]

The model quickly evolved. Yunus persuaded the Bangladesh central bank to let him test his model on a large scale in the Tangail district, near Dhaka, in 1979. It was at this stage that the emphasis on lending only to women developed: according to Todd's account of Grameen Bank,[11] this was because there was a serious repayment crisis in Tangail in the mid-1980s, which led to this change, among others. The percentage of borrowers who were women doubled between 1981 and 1985 from 31% to 65% and thereafter kept rising toward 100%.[12] The theory is that women are better repayers than men because they are more responsible financially and do not drink or waste away the loan or invest all of it in a high-risk, not immediately cash-generative project. The extent to which those reasons are wholly explanatory, as opposed to the possibility that in a highly patriarchal society, women are much more easily coerced into repayment than men, is explored in chapter 4.

For now, note that the emphasis on group lending, with group liability, has been present from the start but, as shall be explored in depth later, is not devoid of ethical problems. At least part of the motivation for lending in groups was to increase a sense of solidarity and empowerment among borrowers, but lending collectively (with group liability) immediately transfers the interest of the MFI from being in the outcome for the individual borrower, to being in the collective outcome for the group. At this point, concern that the MFI should properly have, that an individual borrower can make enough at her chosen business to cover interest payments on the loan, is replaced with concern only that someone in her lending group will make enough to cover her payments if necessary. The interests of the MFI (through its loan officers) and the individual borrower become

[9] See Helen Todd, Women at the Center: Grameen Bank Borrowers after One Decade (Dhaka: Westview Press, 1996), 202–205; Aminur Rahman, Women and Microcredit in Rural Bangladesh: An Anthropological Study of the Rhetoric and Realities of Grameen Bank Lending (Boulder, CO: Westview Press, 1999), 93; and Lamia Karim, Microfinance and Its Discontents: Women in Debt in Bangladesh (Minneapolis: University of Minnesota Press), 83–84. Karim's observations not only confirm Todd's and Rahman's that there were either very few or no dowry-free marriages among the Grameen borrowers they studied but go further: that loans were taken out from Grameen Bank precisely to pay dowry.

[10] Todd, *Women at the Center*, 20.

[11] Todd, *Women at the Center*, 20.

[12] Grameen Bank Historical Data Series, available at www.grameen.info.org/index.php?option=com_content&task=view&id=177&Itemid=182.

misaligned. It also means that if an individual borrower is struggling to repay, those called on in her group to make good her payment—who will be among the poorest in society themselves, this being the target group of MFIs—may react to being required to make good the payment less with solidarity than with desperation. The coercive methods of an impoverished group desperate to get something back from a borrower whose missed payment they have made good may be worse again than those of a loan officer or agent of an MFI.

As the Grameen Project morphed into the Grameen Bank (Yunus obtained a banking charter in late 1983, the Project having initially been funded by the Ford Foundation, the UN International Fund for Agricultural Development, and the governments of Bangladesh, the Netherlands, Norway, and Sweden),[13] the following essential model had been evolved, eventually to be replicated globally:

1. Lend only, or predominantly, to women, in groups of five to twenty.
2. Require the women to play a leading role in the formation of the group, on the assumption that they will know the most likely successful microentrepreneurs-to-be in their society, at any rate better than a loan officer from outside the immediate village will.
3. Employ a simple, standardized loan product with regular, small repayments, which is renewable once repaid. Typically, once a few cycles of successful repayment have been achieved, larger loans (and sometimes a better rate) are provided by the MFI.

The interest rate charged varies enormously around the world, from Grameen's approximately 20% to well in excess of 100% with all additional charges included. It is the interest rate charged that is the main (not only) cause of microfinance being accused of exploitation. This charge is explored in depth in chapter 3.

4. Provide basic business training in advance of a loan being made. Groups would typically have to wait for some eight weeks from formation of a group to the first loan disbursement, to ensure that this had occurred, and to build the solidarity of the group. There is generally a stress on loans only ever being used for investment/working capital, never for consumption. In practice, money being fungible, this is far from guaranteed, but nonetheless it has been an important principle in training.
5. Weekly or fortnightly repayment meetings where the group meets together for repayment, possibly for training, and to raise any issues with the loan officer.

[13] Beatriz Armendáriz and Jonathan Murdoch, *The Economics of Microfinance* (Cambridge, MA: MIT Press, 2007), 12.

6. The group liability model. Groups take collective responsibility for loans. Classically, this is through explicit joint liability, where each borrower in a group undertakes to make the repayments of any other member of the group if she fails to. It can also work informally whereby no one in the group is extended a new loan after the first cycle if any one member of the group has defaulted during it.[14] This is regarded as essential for high repayment rates and also acts as a peer screening process. It can, of course, also be seen as potentially coercive.

The potential for coercion is explored in depth in chapter 4. I will argue, however, that the use of the group liability model, while originally well intended to enhance group solidarity, is the cause of a second moral hazard in microfinance, on top of the risk of coercion. This is that it fundamentally undermines the MFI's duty of care to the borrower. This is explored in chapter 5.

In the 1980s, microfinance began to seriously develop in Central and South America as well. The aid agency Accion hired Jeffrey Ashe to find what forms of aid worked and he concluded that microfinance was the answer. With USAID hiring Accion to explore methods of supporting small business in poor countries, funding began to flow into microfinance.[15] In 1986 USAID funded the NGO PRODEM in Bolivia, which established a separate private commercial microfinance bank for urban clients, BancoSol. It quickly became the most profitable bank in Bolivia. These successes gave impetus to the "new wave" movement, which required that MFIs aim to achieve at least operational sustainability.

For although Grameen Bank was promoted on the basis of viability through high repayment rates and low costs, many microfinance NGOs in the 1980s were not explicitly aiming at operational sustainability: they believed that a constant subsidy drip was justified as the price of keeping the interest rates they charged down. Tolerance of that was about to run out.

THE "FINANCIAL SYSTEMS" MODEL

By the 1990s, the attitude of donors to constantly providing subsidies had changed. MFIs had, in the 1980s, been seen as a considerable improvement as a way of achieving financial inclusion for the poor, certainly an improvement on government-implemented rural credit assistance programs, which were regarded as having failed to reach the poor, and had faced problems of large-scale default.[16] But as the 1980s moved into the 1990s, the

[14] Grameen Bank shifted toward individual lending when it launched its Grameen II model for lending (details follow). Others have followed, so borrowing is now a mix of individual and joint liability, with the latter still larger. Where, of course, individual lending is disbursed through groups and individual loans are not renewed until all in the group have repaid, there is still group sanction, although not explicit joint liability.

[15] Roodman, *Due Diligence*, 81–82.

[16] See, for example, Thankom Arun et al., "Finance for the Poor: The Way Forward?" in *Microfinance: A Reader*, ed. David Hulme and Thankon Arun (London: Routledge, 2009), 7.

development community moved toward the view that while microfinance might be better than inefficient government agricultural subsidy, development subsidy to microfinance should not itself be indefinite. MFIs should aim, first, for break-even ("sustainability"), and in due course straight commercial profitability began to be seen as acceptable. Advocates of microfinance divided into two camps: those who believed in the "poverty lending" approach, and those who believed in the "financial systems" approach.[17]

The poverty lending—or subsidized—approach was, broadly, the original Grameen Bank model described above: provision of credit alongside some social services, subsidized by donors or governments to keep the interest rate charged down or, at any rate, to provide the additional social services without these having to be paid for through increasing the interest rate.

The emphasis of the financial systems—or sustainable—approach was on institutional self-sufficiency. It was argued that the unmet need for microcredit was so great, government and donor funding could never satisfy it on a global scale. Thus microfinance had to become profitable enough to not only cover costs, but produce an earnings stream that would fund its expansion into ever deeper areas of unmet need. Robinson argued that this was "the only possible means to meet widespread client demand for convenient, appropriate financial services."[18] Grameen Bank was seen as a leading advocate of the poverty lending approach, while "the microbanking division of Bank Rakyat Indonesia (BRI),[19] BancoSol in Bolivia, and the Association for Social Advancement (ASA) are at the forefront of the financial systems approach."[20] Attractive as it is to donors, there is a flip side to the emphasis in current best practice on, at a minimum, sustainability, but frequently profitability. This emphasis creates a constant pressure to keep growing the loan portfolio. This is because costs have a high fixed element, and so increasing the loan portfolio reduces the unit cost of each loan. This pressure to keep growing the loan portfolio can lead to insufficient time being taken by the loan officer to form a solid base for the borrowing group being lent to. It also creates pressure to increase the number of borrowers each loan officer serves, which, unless met by technological intervention, is likely to reduce the quality of each loan officer-borrower interaction.

The emphasis on at least sustainability if not profitability also of course leads to what has been termed a "zero tolerance of delinquency"—pressure on loan officers to ensure very regular repayment by clients, in order to minimize the possibility of default and either loan write-off or the expensive process of enforcing group liability. This is explored

---

[17] See, for example, Marguerite Robinson, "Supply and Demand in Microfinance," in *Microfinance*, ed. Hulme and Arun, 46.

[18] Robinson, "Supply and Demand," 55.

[19] The then-state-subsidized BRI in Indonesia set up an independent profit center in microfinance, BRI-UD, which charged market rates. It grew rapidly and by 2004 had 30 million savers and 3.1 million borrowers, becoming the leading example of a financially sustainable rural microfinance program.

[20] Robinson, "Supply and Demand," 55.

in much greater depth later, but at the very least it can lead to oppressive and coercive action being taken against borrowers by loan officers.

Grameen Bank itself began to move away from its original subsidized model of microfinance to a sustainable or profitable one after it ran into a further set of repayment difficulties. Borrowers' attendance at repayment meetings had dropped, and defaults risen—in some areas, repayment rates had fallen below 75% from the 98% advertised rate.[21] Morduch later noted: "Grameen's repayment rates have never been as good as they claimed [but] because Grameen has been so well-known, nobody has wanted to risk undermining the reputation of the idea."[22] Whether rising defaults would have proved terminal for Grameen Bank and its early model is unclear: the disastrous floods of 1998 then provided a face-saving way of writing off bad loans, only some of which may have originated with the floods.

Out of this came Grameen II, which was followed by an extraordinary resurrection of the bank. In terms of the models above, Grameen II moved from the "poverty lending" approach to the "financial systems" approach. Joint liability was formally dropped, but not the collective pressure of group meetings. A single, one-year loan term and inflexible weekly payments were replaced with a mix of loan terms. Rates moved closer to market rates. Savings came to substitute for international donor and Bangladesh government funds. Yunus rewrote his own goals from creating a poverty-free world where the only place poverty could be seen would be in "poverty museums"[23] to the somewhat less demanding (if still worthy) "bringing financial services to the poorest people—particularly the poorest women."[24] Grameen Bank became profitable. Members were no longer required to borrow, and it turned out that what many wanted to do was simply save (or a mix). Since it began offering savings, Grameen Bank has boomed. "Grameen took 27 years to reach 2.5m members—and then doubled that number in the three years following the full establishment of Grameen II."[25] Savings have become a crucial part of Grameen Bank's funding mix for providing loans. Between 2002 and 2005, Grameen tripled the deposits it held (from 8,952 million taka to 31,771 million taka) and doubled the loan portfolio (from 13,400 million taka to 28,897 million taka). Loan repayment levels were restored, at least on a reported basis – but as under Grameen II many overdue loans were

---

[21] Daryl Collins, Jonathan Morduch, Stuart Rutherford, and Orlanda Ruthuen, *Portfolios of the Poor: How the World's Poor Live on $2 a Day* (Princeton, NJ: Princeton University Press, 2010), 154.

[22] Quoted by Daniel Pearl and Michael Phillips in their article "Grameen Bank, Which Pioneered Loans for the Poor, Has Hit a Repayment Snag," published in the *Wall Street Journal* on November 27, 2001.

[23] Yunus, Nobel lecture on receiving the 2006 Nobel Peace Prize, available at www.nobelprize.org/nobel_prizes/peace/laureates/2006/yunus-lecture-en.html.

[24] Yunus interview with *USA Today*, April 25, 2013, online at http://www.usatoday.com/story/opinion/2013/04/25/muhammad-yunus-microcredit-column/2112371/.

[25] Stuart Rutherford, with Md Maniruzzaman, S. K. Sinha, and Acnabin and Co., "Grameen II—The First Five Years: 2001–2006," 5, *Grameen II Briefing Notes*, for MicroSave, http://www.microsave.net.

recast as 'flexible' loans and thus no longer overdue, the underlying basis may not have been as strong. Profits rose from 60 million taka in 2002 to 442 million taka in 2005.[26]

It appears that in this move toward profitability and away from subsidy, Grameen Bank moved away from serving its poorest clientele to the somewhat less poor. Economist David Hulme believes that the average Grameen client is now less poor than in the 1970s and 1980s. They would only be nonpoor or moderately poor by Bangladesh's official poverty line. A far smaller proportion are extremely poor: in 2005, Hulme believes, Grameen Bank had fifty-six thousand extremely poor clients (known as the "struggling members program)," against twenty-five million extremely poor people in the country. The "struggling members program appears to be either failing or tokenistic."[27]

THE FULLY COMMERCIALIZED MODEL

In the 1990s the World Bank moved into microfinance, especially through its International Finance Corporation (IFC) arm. It established the Consultative Group to Assist the Poor (CGAP), which produced the "Pink Book," *Micro and Small Enterprise Finance: Guiding Principles for Selecting and Supporting Intermediaries* on how microfinance should be practiced. CGAP set the guidelines for the evolving, 'sustainable' financial model for microfinance[28] MFIs would only get funded if credibly promising sustainability.

"New wave" became "best practice." Despite the fact that Yunus was no longer running Grameen Bank as he had originally planned, using the "poverty lending" approach, but rather in line with the "financial systems" approach, his reputation as a champion for alleviating female poverty took off. Some worried that microfinance was beginning to suffer "mission drift": that it was slipping too far away from its original focus on lending small sums to the poorest to alleviate their poverty, to a world of financial targets—that growth of the MFI was replacing the good of the borrower as the focus of the mission. But these voices were not dominant.

Microfinance started to attract celebrity endorsement in the 2000s. The Microcredit Summit Campaign was launched in 1997, initially a nine-year campaign to make microcredit available to one hundred million women in developing countries. In the first decade of the new century, the Gates Foundation made the first of a number of donations of millions of dollars to microfinance projects; in late 2005 eBay founder Omidyar gave

---

[26] See Grameen Bank, "Past Seventeen Years in BDT," at http://www.grameen-info.org/index.php?option=com_content&task=view&id=38&Itemid=87. At end 2013, deposits were 148,546 million taka, loans were 87,707 million taka, and net profit was 1,333 million taka.

[27] David Hulme, "The Story of the Grameen Bank: From Subsidized Microcredit to Market Based Microfinance," in *Microfinance*, ed. Hulme and Arun, 169.

[28] See Milford Bateman, *Why Doesn't Microfinance Work? The Destructive Rise of Local Neoliberalism* (London: Zed Books, 2009), 17.

$100 million to Tufts University to establish a microfinance fund.[29] The apotheosis was reached in 2006, when the Nobel Peace Prize was awarded jointly to Grameen Bank and Yunus. The concept of the gift that keeps on giving, which sustainability implies, was attractive not just to the very wealthy, but to those on modest incomes: Kiva was established by Matt Flannery and Jessica Jackley as an online portal to provide peer-to-peer lending for direct lending from individuals of modest income to individual borrowers (although in practice it is a way for individuals to lend to an MFI, which then on-lends to individual borrowers). Leleux and Constantiou suggest that in the two decades from 1984, the industry grew from an estimated base of $200 million 'to reach an estimated $30 billion in outstanding microfinance loans'.[30] It became an attractive investment opportunity to institutional investors as well: if the poor always did pay back, the returns were extremely attractive and the lack of correlation between microfinance and other debt instruments or equity indices made it appear a very attractive portfolio diversification for some institutional investors such as Deutsche Bank, Citi, HSBC, or Commerzbank.

The first microfinance investment vehicle (MIV), Profund, had started in 1995 to provide loans to MFIs. Profund did well enough over the next decade to attract many more MIVs to the table: by the end of 2009, there were over one hundred.[31] According to CGAP, the portfolios they managed amounted to two billion in 2007[32]. CGAP calculates that by the end of 2009, donors and international investors had invested at least $21.3 billion in microfinance institutions, with public entities putting in just shy of $2 billion in 2009 alone and individuals and institutional investors over $1 billion.[33]

With capital flooding in from philanthropists, the international development community, institutional investors, and private equity, saturation, over-indebtedness and ultimately repayment crises became possible. But first came two stock market flotations[34] of MFIs, which whilst not the first initial public offerings (IPOs) of MFIs, were the first to bring microfinance into public controversy.

The 2007 Compartamos IPO contained details in its prospectus that demonstrated to the world that it was charging poor women borrowers rates sometimes in excess of 100%, indeed, fully costed, up to 195%.[35] Salaries and bonuses for staff were high, and some in the development community took serious exception to the personal windfall the IPO gave Compartamos cofounder Carlos Danel, given that initial funding had come

---

[29] "Tufts Is Getting Gift of $100 Million, with Rare Strings," *New York Times*, November 4, 2005.

[30] Benoit Leleux and Dinos Constantiou 'An analysis of microfinance business models' in Benoit Leleux and Dinos Constantinou, eds., *From Microfinance to Small Business Finance: The Business Case for Private Capital Investments* (Basingstoke: Palgrave Macmillan, 2007), 49

[31] Roodman, *Due Diligence*, 235.

[32] Microfinance Investment Vehicles. *CGAP Brief April 2007*. Washington, DC: CGAP

[33] Roodman, *Due Diligence* 240–241

[34] Flotation, or "going public," being the process by which a privately owned company becomes a publicly owned company by selling shares in itself to the public.

[35] David Roodman, "Does Compartamos Charge 195% Interest?" *MicroFinance Open Book Blog*, January 31, 2011.

from donor agencies. Yunus called it "the end of microfinance": that microfinance institutions, having been created to fight the moneylender, had in fact become the new loan sharks.[36] Not all agreed: Accion, which had provided much of the subsidy to Compartamos, also made substantial profits from the IPO, which were intended for future microfinance funding.

The criticisms should perhaps be separated out: between those that found the extraordinary sums senior management made on the flotation of the company distasteful per se, and those that found elements of them distasteful because of where they had originated from.

Because of its fast growth and high margins, and—hard as it is to believe now, after the 2008 financial crash—because banks were "flavor of the month" among investors at the time, Compartamos both attracted a very high price/earnings ratio (of 24) and price/book multiple (an extraordinary 12.8 times book value)[37] on launch, allowing some to make four times their original stake. But it would be harsh to blame management or indeed Compartamos's early investors for taking a profit that reflected investor overexuberance for the pricing of the stock: management does not set what multiples markets trade stocks on.

Where the criticism hits home is that as an NGO, Compartamos had received public grants, but was still charging very high interest rates to the poorest. It was *those* resources—derived from public grants and high interest rates on the poor—that were now being converted into private individual fortunes. It was an extraordinarily unequal redistribution of assets and perhaps reset the balance between a microfinance world where positive social impact and profitability were at least dual objectives, to one where fresh profit-seeking capital only rushed into the sector.

The stock market flotation of what were previously NGOs also presents the concern that in the run-up to an IPO, a microfinance institution may be tempted to try to grow too aggressively. The IPO provides an incentive to grow as quickly as possible just in order to achieve a high price/earnings multiple but risks having loan standards drop in the rush and overindebting clients. This criticism is particularly pertinent to the SKS Microfinance (SKS) flotation.

SKS floated in 2010. It had expanded very rapidly, using its for-profit status to attract investment from private equity firms and venture capitalists such as Sequoia Capital and Blue Orchard. In April 2000, SKS served 695 members and had disbursed some $25,000 in loans.[38] By March 2004 it had grown to 200,000 members; by August 2006, 300,000 members and nearly $75 million loans disbursed. And then from 2006 things really

[36] Muhammad Yunus, "Yunus Blasts Compartamos," *Business Week*, December 2007.

[37] Ratios taken from *The Banco Compartamos Initial Public Offering*, Accion Insight no. 23, available at http://centerforfinancialinclusionblog.files.wordpress.com/2011/10/the-banco-compartamos-initial-public-offering.pdf.

[38] Akula, *A Fistful of Rice*, 99.

exploded. Between April 2006 and March 2008, 1,456,504 new clients were added and the gross loan portfolio grew by $241 million; in the run-up to the IPO, between April 2008 and March 2010, another 4,165,554 clients and just under $700 million of gross loans were added.[39] The adding of this frenetic growth to the sustainable model could only lead to lax loan quality checks and overindebtedness of clients. Markets tend to reward fast growing companies with higher price to earnings multiples, on the assumption that the growth rate can be extrapolated in to the future. It has to be doubted if SKS would have felt the pressure to grow at the dangerous pace at which it did, if the prospect of a lucrative IPO had not been before it.

It is only fair to note, however, that SKS was not alone in its extraordinary growth during this period. In the Indian state of Andhra Pradesh, the extension of credit overall had exploded from 40 billion rupees made to eight million borrowers in 2007, to 225 billion rupees made to twenty-five million borrowers in 2010. This expansion was fueled first by a government program to provide cheaper finance to borrowers and second by commercial MFI expansion. These figures show total loans quintupling in Andhra Pradesh whilst the number of borrowers 'only' tripled, indicating not only that loan size was getting larger, but that clients were taking on multiple loans. The Andhra Pradesh government became increasingly concerned about the level of client overindebtedness and abusive loan collection practices. Fresh reports of suicides among those unable to service all the debt prompted Andhra Pradesh's chief minister to pass an ordinance imposing new conditions on loan collection (less frequently and from locations near to local government premises), which prompted a collapse in loan repayments and threatened the future viability of some MFIs. One set of authors and industry practitioners, observing that the 2010 crisis was on a different scale from previous crises, concluded rather comprehensively: "The causes were complex and involved MFI management's pressure for growth at all costs, promoters' and investors' greed, bankers' folly, clients' overborrowing, journalists' frenzy, bureaucrats' inertia and politicians' irresponsibility."[40]

The ordinance, promulgated as a law in December 2010, did not allow MFIs to approach clients to seek repayment, and defaults rose to close to 100%. Microfinance in Andhra Pradesh came to a complete halt, but even elsewhere it had been turning into something of a slow car crash since the global financial crisis of 2008. Funding to the industry was reduced. Some major funders, such as the Norwegian government, withdrew from the sector. The flow of private equity into microfinance slowed sharply, and providers of development aid generally have become increasingly skeptical.

[39] Ramesh S. Arunachalam, *The Journey of Indian Microfinance: Lessons for the Future* (Chennai: Aapti Publications, 2011), tables 5.8 and 5.9, 86–87.

[40] Malcolm Harper, Lalitha Iyer, and Jane Rosser, eds., *Whose Sustainability Counts? BASIX's Long March from Microfinance to Livelihoods* (Sterling, VA: Kumarian Press, 2011), 37–38.

Doubts had begun to be raised about the efficacy of microfinance before the Andhra Pradesh crisis. Mordoch and Roodman[41] overturned the positive results of a previously highly influential study in Bangladesh.[42] Two highly respected teams of academics reported almost zero impact with regard to the effect of two major microcredit programs on poverty.[43] And as will be examined closely in chapter 2, in 2010 Duvendack and coauthors surveyed 2,643 publications offering analysis of microfinance's impact on poverty, and found that "there is no good evidence" for the belief that microfinance actually works and that the microfinance phenomenon had been based on "shifting sands."[44]

Following the Andhra Pradesh crisis, microfinance shrank—but not for long. Total clients, according to the Microcredit Summit Campaign, having peaked at 205 million, fell to 195 million—but recovered to 204 million by the end of 2012.[45] Outreach to poorer clients, however, has not recovered—having peaked at 138 million, it fell to 125 million and has now fallen further to 116 million. Commercialized microfinance has made up its mind about poorer clients and is focusing on the "less" poor. Returns from microcredit have fallen post its repayment crises, but its popularity survives with investors: perhaps less because its returns are still so high than because the returns on alternative asset classes, particularly in fixed interest, have been so low.

THE SMART CAMPAIGN

One effect of microfinance becoming a largely for-profit activity has been for development organizations and investors who were more interested in social impact to begin to look elsewhere for pro-poor interventions to support. Some nonprofits, but particularly Accion, have remained very committed to the sector (Accion of course remains a shareholder in Compartamos) and these have become anxious to restore the reputation

---

[41] David Roodman and Jonathan Morduch, "The Impact of Microcredit on the Poor in Bangladesh: Revisiting the Evidence," Working Paper 174, Center for Global Development.

[42] In their *Microfinance Banana Skins 2014* report, Lascelles, Mendelson, and Rozas put it rather more strongly than this, claiming the Roodman and Morduch study "brought down the edifice on which microfinance has stood for over a decade. It sought to replicate one of the landmark 1990s studies in Bangladesh, and found that the methodology for its most prominent claim—that 5% of Grameen Bank's clients get out of poverty every year—was based on faulty methodology. Instead, it found that these same clients' well-being has been essentially unchanged by their affiliation with Grameen." It is certainly true that Yunus and microfinance advocates generally had marketed microfinance on that particular result extensively. David Lascelles, Sam Mendelson, and Daniel Rozas, *Microfinance Banana Skins 2014: Facing Reality*, Center for the Study of Financial Innovation, http://www.citi.com/citi/microfinance/data/2014_microfinance_banana_skins.pdf.

[43] Dean Karlan and Jonathan Zinman, "Expanding Credit Access: Using Randomized Supply Decisions to Estimate the Impacts," *Society for Financial Studies* 23, no. 1 (2009): 433–464; and Esther Duflo, Abhijit Banerjee, Rachel Glennerster, and Cynthia G. Kinnan, "The Miracle of Microfinance? Evidence from a Randomized Evaluation," NBER Working Paper No. 18950, May 2013, available at http://www.nber.org/papers/w18950.

[44] Maren Duvendack, Richard Palmer-Jones, James Copestake, Lee Hooper, Yoon Loke, and Nitya Rao, "What Is the Evidence of the Impact of Microfinance on the Well-being of Poor People?" EPPI-Centre, Social Science Research Unit, Institute of Education, University of London, 2011, 75.

[45] Reed et al., *Resilience*, 8.

of microcredit and prevent it from slipping into representing simply institutionalized for-profit moneylending.

In 2008, the Center for Financial Inclusion (a unit of Accion International) came together with industry leaders to launch the Smart Campaign, which provides a set of "client protection principles" (CPPs) covering appropriate product design and delivery, respect for clients, privacy of client data, and mechanisms for complaint resolution.

The problem with the Smart Campaign was that the CPPs were left unspecified. Just what does fair and respectful treatment of clients require? What level of interest rates would "responsible pricing" disallow? Second, they are not enforced. Rather, an MFI can send the Smart Campaign a statement that it endorses these principles and then state on its publicity materials, websites, and so on, that it is signed up to the client protection principles of the Smart Campaign, and make no changes to its behavior whatsoever. No one from the Smart Campaign need come to see if any of the principles are followed or how they are interpreted. If this is self-regulation, it is self-regulation with the regulation left out.

Recognizing that there was little confidence that MFIs would follow the CPPs, in 2010 Smart began work on a Client Protection Certification Programme. This allows MFIs to apply to rating agencies, for a fee, to certify that they do indeed comply with CPPs. But the standards required to be met are still woeful. At a meeting of the UK Microfinance Gateway Club on November 27, 2012, Beth Rhyne, co-creater of the Smart Campaign, stated that these standards would, on a scale from "wrong/criminal" through "unsavoury" to "fit & proper" to "excellent," sit on the borderline between "unsavoury" and "fit & proper." It is obviously good that an industry leader thinks that the industry should pitch itself above the "wrong/criminal" scale, but something of a pity that "fit & proper" should not be regarded as an absolute minimum.

This is disappointingly unambitious. For the Smart Campaign, for an interest rate to count as "fair," it need only be roughly the same as that which everyone else charges: so if everyone else is charging 70%–100% per annum, 70% is "fair," regardless of what the formal rate is.

The full program launched in January 2013, and at the time of writing, few MFIs (around twenty) have been certified, even on this weak basis. But as of September 2014, the main Mexican subsidiary of Compartamos obtained Smart Campaign certification. Compartamos, as we saw above, charges extremely high interest rates: but others charge even more, so certification was possible. Whether Compartamos's certification is the starting bell or death knell for confidence in the CPPs and self-regulation within microfinance remains to be seen.

Since the Andhra Pradesh crisis, the industry has been moving on at a pace to redefine its mission from "microfinance" to "financial inclusion," as it once did from "microcredit" to "microfinance." Nonetheless, while the industry has certainly indulged in a period of soul searching, the operating model for "financial inclusion" is not a departure from the "financial systems best practices" described above, but rather just adds other elements to it (particularly the availability of savings). There is an increasing emphasis on "social performance measurement" and core codes of conduct, but it may be that these are just sticking plasters over a gaping wound if it is the core operational model of microfinance itself that gives rise to unethical practices.

3. The Original, Subsidized versus Fully Commercial Models of Microfinance: Where the Ethical Challenges Lie

Jonathan Morduch notably described the divide between the subsidized and sustainable models of microfinance as the "microfinance schism."[46] From the point of view of those believing in the subsidized model, the whole point of microfinance is to enable the poor to borrow enough to run a business whose profits can lead them out of poverty. The bigger the subsidy, the lower the interest rate that could be offered, and the better their chance of doing so. If the point of lending is to help the poor, making money from it *oneself* was anathema, a reversal of the original values. BRAC and Grameen had not required the profit motive to expand: their mission to serve the poor in their country was motive enough.

Unsurprisingly, advocates of the sustainable approach, or, now, of the fully commercialized approach, as not-for-profit nongovernmental organizations (NGOs) have moved to corporate status, do not see it this way. They argue that the poor should not be seen as "beneficiaries," objects of charity, but clients. They argue that by being sustainable, microfinance institutions can grow independent of donors' budget constraints: and once fully commercial, can go to international markets to borrow to drive even further expansion. It has been described as the "Walmart" model: "Walmart makes enormous profits but provides low-cost goods to millions of people and employment to the millions more who make and sell the goods. Selling financial services to the poor is no different from selling low-cost clothes or groceries, and only high profits, high share valuations, and high salaries can attract investors and talented people to initiate and lead MFIs."[47]

The enormous growth in microfinance over the past decade has largely come at the commercialized, for-profit end of the spectrum. The NGOs that exist now operating purely on a subsidized basis do not have significant assets. The next layer above, originally subsidized NGOs that moved to a "dual mission" of striving to reach their social goal while becoming sustainable, perennially struggle with the question of mission drift—the dilemma that achieving sustainability is made easier by serving a less poor, more profitable client base. Some in this group, of course, have transformed their corporate structure

[46] Jonathan Morduch, "The Microfinance Schism," in Hulme and Arun, *Microfinance*, 17–36.

[47] Harper, Iyer, and Rosser, eds., *Whose Sustainability Counts?* 221.

in order to become fully commercialized, regulated, and able to take deposits. Mission does not so much drift here as favor firmly the financial over the social mission.

It has been the microfinance funds raised in search of profit that have driven the growth of what is now regarded as an industry.

The major ethical challenges that the "best practice" model of microfinance faces now, which will be explored in depth throughout this book, have been highlighted as the use of group liability, potentially exploitative interest rates, coercive loan collection practices, and excessive loan growth overindebting clients. In terms of how far the commercialization of the original subsidized model has created these challenges, we can note that group liability is part of the model going back almost to the start; commercialization has not changed that. The move to at least cover costs—to become sustainable—did however lead, especially outside Asia, to much higher interest rates becoming acceptable.

But if the move to the commercialized model has led to the challenges of high rates, a zero tolerance attitude toward delinquency and an increase in the emphasis on loan growth in order to reduce the unit cost of lending, the aspiration toward IPOs has exacerbated the pressures still further. For a successful IPO, strong earnings growth, low write-offs, and high margins are required, each one increasing the chances of loan growth being prioritized over the risk of client overindebtedness.

An additional concern raised by advocates of the subsidized model against the fully commercialized model is that many, if not all, of the NGOs that have converted to fully commercial status had received subsidy or loans that were intended to get the institution up and running but were ultimately for the *borrowers'* good, by providing an assumed valuable service. For individuals on incorporation and sale to take share stakes and then sell them for very considerable personal enrichment is an abuse of that original trust. As Harper, Iyer, and Rosser put it, "Those who make personal fortunes by selling their shares are using public purpose funds to generate private profits."[48] Defenders of the commercial model would argue that this is irrelevant. The end of benefiting the poor justifies the means of achieving high profits for shareholders and personal fortunes for founders. Such defenders, however, do need to show that the *degree* of personal fortune acquired is truly necessary to motivate the founders; and of course the whole defense fails if the benefit to the poor is in fact only minimal or does not exist.

Although the ethical debates of subsidy versus sustainability and mission drift have been the principal ones tackled in the microfinance literature, the vehemence with which they have been conducted has to an extent hidden how much common ground they actually shared. Both assumed microfinance was in fact a force for good, for poverty alleviation. Both accepted that interest rates had to be set so as to cover a substantial portion of costs, differing only in how *much*. Both accepted, at least implicitly, that what the poor needed was *access* to credit, that what price that credit was offered at was a determinant

[48] Harper, Iyer, and Rosser, eds., *Whose Sustainability Counts?* 221.

of loan size, outreach, local employment costs—but not an independent ethical question in itself. The debate turned on the extent to which market forces should set borrowing terms for the poor: the question, was it ethical to offer these terms to the poor *at all*, regardless of whether it was done profitably or with subsidy, did not get asked much. Parts II and III make good this lacuna.

The debate over whether microfinance should be provided by subsidized or commercialized institutions has been won on the ground by the profitable model. The winning of the debate has wrought some changes to the "best practice" model of microfinance: obviously the aim of profitability, the willingness to base the interest rate charged on whatever is necessary to achieve profitability, rather than a realistic assessment of the client's ability to pay, but also the pressure to keep growing the loan portfolio, incentivizing loan officers by setting high repayment rate targets, and the downgrading of the social empowerment goal. But other aspects of the model have stayed much the same from original days: most lending is still in groups, with group liability, to women, with no formal collateral.

Commercialization has brought additional problems to microfinance, then; and the very notion of "profiting from the poor" will be distasteful to some, and individual executives personally profiting from funds originally sourced from development aid, equally distasteful to others. But some of the ethical issues—the risk of the group-lending model making the loan group itself become a coercive force against fellow borrowers, the use of the group-lending model obscuring and supplanting a duty of care from MFI to borrower—go back to the original model. All the ethical issues of microfinance's practices are explored in depth in Parts II and III. But first, as suggested in the introduction, a picture is needed, of whether microfinance *does* in fact deliver on its original aims to enrich and empower. If it did, some would regard the ethical risks as worth running. The next chapter examines that evidence.

If to do were as easy as to know what were good to do, chapels had been churches, and poor men's cottages princes' palaces
—SHAKESPEARE, The Merchant of Venice

2 Poverty's Panacea, or Snake Oil Salesmen

DOES MICROFINANCE WORK?

THE CLAIMS OF poverty reduction and empowerment that the industry has made have been large. Leading MFIs advertised themselves as offering a solution to global poverty. One of the strongest claims came from Muhammad Yunus in 2006: "58% of the poor who borrowed from Grameen are now out of poverty. There are over 100 million people now involved in microcredit schemes. At the rate we're heading, we'll halve total poverty by 2015. We'll create a poverty museum in 2030."[1]

Claims for empowerment have been as ambitious. Accion, the Foundation for International Community Assistance (FINCA), the Grameen Foundation, Opportunity International, Unitus, and Women's World Banking, all leading players in global microfinance, put out a common statement in September 2010 stating that "microfinance is particularly able to empower women, giving them access to the material, human and social resources necessary to make strategic choices in their lives: establishing or strengthening financial independence; transforming power relationships; improving stability and family prospects by directing more income towards families; and, particularly, engendering dignity and pride."[2]

---

[1] Interview with Ishaan Tharoor, "Paving the Way out of Poverty," *Time*, October 13, 2006, available at www.time.com/time/world/article/0,8599,1546100,00.html.

[2] "Measuring the Impact of Microfinance: Our Perspective," available on each of their websites, for example at http://www.accion.org/Document.Doc?id=794.

While less certain of itself today, the hype promoting microfinance is still present: on January 27, 2011, the Microcredit Summit Campaign issued a press release beginning: "Nearly 2 million Bangladeshi households involved in microfinance—including almost 10 million family members, net—rose above the US$1.25 a day threshold between 1990 and 2008." The report does go on to say that there is no proof of causality here, but the bold linking of the numbers moving out of poverty with the numbers receiving microfinance is evidently intended to be suggestive, just as it was for Yunus in the quote above. And even the otherwise level-headed latest *Banana Skins* report on the industry by the Centre for the Study of Financial Inclusion,[3] while fully acknowledging how much microfinance has changed, states in its preface, without offering any evidence at all, that the microfinance movement "remains one of the few developmental initiatives that has clearly been on balance positive."[4]

Chapter 8 challenges microfinance's macro impact as a development initiative. This chapter examines the evidence for individual poverty alleviation. In the first section, the problem of what is to count as evidence is examined: until relatively recently, there had been no randomized control trials (RCTs) of microfinance, and there are problems of methodological weaknesses in the anecdotal, before-and-after and "impact" studies that we had, most especially their lack of measuring dropouts from microfinance programs. We do now have a number of RCTs, however, and these will be examined in the second section—and the absence of evidence that microfinance does in fact lift its borrowers out of poverty observed. It is, sadly, just not the case that microfinance has, on balance, clearly been a positive for its borrowers.

The third section considers the evidence of empowerment in depth. This is even harder to measure than the impact on poverty alleviation: but the evidence we have is again sifted, and found mixed at best.

In the process of examining all this evidence, and establishing what we do know about the net overall impact of microfinance, we also learn how little we know about the distribution of returns from microfinance to its borrowers. Concluding that there is net zero impact, after all, is not at all the same as concluding that there is no impact: we still need to know how many are made worse off (and by how much) and how many are made better off (and by how much). For every one that does escape from poverty, how many (if any) fall back into a more extreme form of it? There is some evidence that the very poorest do the worst from microfinance and that some of the industry's well-meaning attempts to extend it to them are badly misplaced and backfire. The philosophical stance one takes toward questions of distribution of benefits and harms—whether all count equally, whether some form of priority should apply, whether large harms can be justified by offsetting even larger gains—will thus affect whether one thus sees microfinance as

[3] Lascelles, Mendelson, and Rozas, *Microfinance Banana Skins 2014*.

[4] Andrew Hilton, preface to Lascelles, Mendelson, and Rozas, *Microfinance Banana Skins 2014*, 1.

"working" or not. The ethical problems surrounding this are discussed in Part III, particularly chapter 6.

1. What Counts as Evidence

Over the past thirty years, there have been many studies by microfinanciers and academics to demonstrate the positive impact of microfinance: but the vast majority have been beset with methodological flaws that have rendered their findings of little applicability to the question of the overall impact of microfinance. In a recent systematic review of publications on the impact of microfinance,[5] Duvendack and coauthors surveyed 2,643 publications, but found only 58 worth studying in depth, observing, "Our report shows that almost all impact evaluations of microfinance suffer from weak methodologies and inadequate data . . . thus the reliability of impact estimates are [] adversely affected."

Beyond the fundraising and marketing storytelling, where an MFI selects a borrower with a particularly moving story to tell of how access to credit has transformed her life (with no counterfactuals or suggestion of representativeness), the early studies of microfinance were "before-and-after" studies, which compared a group of borrowers on various measures of health, children's education, and income at the onset of taking out a microloan, with the group a year or some years later. The problem with these studies is that although they can give rich details of a borrower's life, there is no counterfactual—there is no control group of similarly placed nonborrowers against which to judge whether any improvements were simply due to growth in the local economy or changed governmental welfare distribution policies, rather than the microloan.

Worst of all, "dropouts," those who leave their borrowing group, are seldom included in these studies. Thus Helen Todd's yearlong 1992 study of Grameen borrowers[6] studies only borrowers of some ten years' standing and does not look at how life fared for those who took loans, ceased repayment, and left the group. Todd's insights into group dynamics remain telling, but as an assessment of net positive impact of credit on borrowers (which she observes) the study tells us nothing, as any negative impact on those ceasing borrowing is not measured. With regard to how far the loan can be measured as the cause of any impact, in a recent study using data from a microfinance program in Nepal, Rajbanski, Huang, and Wydick find that "just over two thirds (68.3%) of the significant apparent impact observed by practitioners based on before-and-after observations of microfinance borrowers is illusory."[7]

---

[5] Duvendack et al., "What Is the Evidence."

[6] Todd, *Women at the Center.*

[7] Ram Rajbanski, Meng Huang, and Bruce Wydick, "Measuring Microfinance: Cognitive and Experimental Bias—with New Evidence from Nepal," working paper, 2012.

It is not surprising, perhaps, that not measuring impacts on dropouts seriously skews results; after all, if it is largely unsuccessful clients who drop out, not measuring them amounts to simply not measuring one's failures and only measuring one's successes. Alexander-Tedeschi and Karlan also found that failing to include dropouts biases estimates of impact.[8] Criticizing the Assessing the Impact of Microenterprise Services (AIMS) methodology used by USAID to assess impact (which recommends excluding program dropouts in calculations), they find that including dropouts changes the measures of impact dramatically: "Where the AIMS cross-sectional methodology showed an increase of US $1200 in annual microenterprise profit, including dropouts caused the estimate to fall to a decrease of about $170."

Most of the 2,643 studies Duvendack and coauthors discount are more sophisticated than before-and-after studies; they are "impact studies" that do use a control group to attempt to measure the counterfactual, although many still have a problem with not tracing dropouts from the target group. There have been other problems associated with these studies, as Mosley lays out.[9] The main biases that can enter impact studies using control groups are sample selection bias, misspecification of underlying causal relationships, and motivational problems. Sample selection bias is perhaps the most major of these.

Mosley notes that there is a significant risk that the comparison between the control group and the target group may become contaminated by factors that prevent the control group from effectively simulating the without-project situation. The target group—the borrowers—may possess qualities the control group does not have, such as an entrepreneurial ability that drives them to become borrowers in the first place: but it is then impossible to say if any subsequent success is due to the loan or their more driven approach. Mosley also notes Roethlisberger and Dickson's observation of "Hawthorne effects,"[10] where factory workers who knew themselves to be the subject of an experiment simply become more productive than those workers not singled out as such. Sample bias can also occur because, being fungible, a loan is not used for the purpose intended: Goetz and Gupta showed that the proceeds of some loans awarded to women were passed through and used by men who were not necessarily in the target group against whom impact was being measured, meaning that here, potential impact—positive or negative—of a loan was simply not being recorded.[11] Sample bias can also enter by the control group becoming contaminated by outside events—unless the MFI extending loans

---

[8] Gwendolyn Alexander-Tedeschi and Dean Karlan, "Microfinance Impact: Bias from Drop-Outs," Financial Access Initiative and Innovations for Poverty Action (2006), available at www.financialaccess.org.

[9] Paul Mosley, "The Use of Control Groups in Impact Assessments for Microfinance," Working Paper No. 19, International Labour Office, Geneva, 1998.

[10] Fritz Roethlisberger and William Dickson, *Management and the Worker* (Cambridge, MA: Harvard University Press, 1939).

[11] Anne Marie Goetz and Rina Sen Gupta, "Who Takes the Credit? Gender, Power and Control over Loan Use in Rural Credit Programs in Bangladesh," *World Development* 24 (1996): 45–63.

to the target group is and remains the only MFI in the area, members of the control group may over the course of the study get loans from elsewhere, thus invalidating the impact of a microloan study.

As Armendáriz and Morduch observe, "This is not an esoteric concern that practitioners and policymakers can safely ignore. It is not just a difference between obtaining 'very good' estimates of impacts versus 'perfect' estimates—the biases can be large."[12] Armendáriz and Morduch quote McKernan's study of Grameen Bank, which "finds that not controlling for selection bias can lead to overestimation of the effect of participation on profits by as much as 100 per cent. In other cases discussed later, controlling for biases reverses conclusions about impacts entirely."[13]

Careful construction of target and control groups can reduce some of these issues. Where an MFI is starting up, has no competitors in town, and is rolling out its program, it can use as a control group for new borrowers those identified as borrowers-in-waiting (those who want to borrow, perhaps in a year's time when funds to the MFI became available). Hidden factors such as entrepreneurial ability can also be controlled for. The number of studies reaching this criterion is of course much fewer than the whole: and among these, the problem of tracing and measuring impact on those who drop out of the program remains a large issue. Graham Wright found dropout rates as high as 25%–60% per year in East Africa,[14] and Hulme and Mosley found dropout rates of 15% in Bangladesh.[15]

In 1998 Pitt and Khandker published a study that promised to get beyond the problems of before-and-after studies and impact studies using control groups by taking a quasi-experimental approach.[16] This became the most influential study of microcredit's impact until the more recent development of randomized control trials. It studied nearly two thousand households and focused on the difference in outcomes for those who qualified for a microloan and those who did not, the eligibility criteria being owning less than half an acre of land. The idea was that there was actually little difference in the poverty level of those just below and just above the half-acre cutoff point, so this could be used to measure the difference between those in poverty receiving a microloan, and those in similar poverty who did not. Pitt and Khandker's principle finding was that one hundred taka lent to a female borrower increased household consumption by eighteen taka (increases in household consumption when the loan was made to a male were lower). However, this

[12] Armendáriz and Morduch, *The Economics of Microfinance*, 201.

[13] Signe-Mary McKernan, "The Impact of Microcredit programs on Self-Employment Profits: Do Non-credit Program Aspects Matter?" *Review of Economics and Statistics* 84, no. 1 (2002): 93–115.

[14] Graham Wright "Dropouts and Graduates: Lessons from Bangladesh," *Microbanking Bulletin* 6 (2001): 14–16.

[15] David Hulme and Paul Mosley, Finance against Poverty, vol. 1, Effective Institutions for Lending to Small Farmers and Microenterprises in Developing Countries (London: Routledge, 1996).

[16] Mark Pitt and Shahidur Khandker, "The Impact of Group-Based Credit Programs on Poor Households in Bangladesh: Does the Gender of Participants Matter?" *Journal of Political Economy* 106, no. 5 (1998): 958–996.

study's soundness was challenged by Morduch,[17] who argued that the eligibility rule did not seem to have been followed consistently, and later also Roodman and Morduch.[18]

Roodman and Morduch sought to replicate the Pitt and Khandker study, which had been drawn on heavily by promoters of microfinance, and particularly by Yunus to back his claim that 5% of Grameen Bank's clients were helped to get out of poverty every year. Roodman and Morduch found that they could not. After considerable academic argument, Pitt made his own computer code available to Roodman and Morduch: their running of this did cancel the fact that they had found a negative result instead of Pitt and Khandker's positive one, but still could not replicate a positive result, and left Roodman summarizing: "The bottom line is the same: these studies can show correlations but cannot credibly prove causation."[19] Morduch concluded: "We need to look elsewhere for reliable evidence."[20]

We can see, then, that the vast majority of the very many studies carried out on the impact of microfinance historically have suffered from methodological flaws. When we see that selection bias can overestimate profits by 100% (McKernan) or that two-thirds of positive impact implied in before-and-after studies can be illusory (Rajbanski, Huang, and Wydick), we need something better. In the last few years, a number of genuine randomized control studies, the recognized gold standard for studies in medicine, have been carried out in microfinance. The next section examines them. It is, admittedly, a small number of studies on which to draw conclusions: but it is perhaps better to rely on a methodologically sound few, and the outcome of the systemic reviews, than the methodologically flawed many.[21]

2. Randomized Control Trials: Evidence for the Micro Impact of Microcredit on Borrowers

We now have around half a dozen RCTs that examine the impact of microfinance, and a few more that examine the impact of microsavings. RCTs are widely used in medical trials (especially drug trials) because, unlike qualitative studies and quantitative quasi

[17] Jonathan Morduch, "The Role of Subsidies in Microfinance: Evidence from Grameen Bank," *Journal of Development Economics* 60, no. 1 (1999): 229–248.

[18] Roodman and Morduch, "Impact of Microcredit."

[19] Roodman, *Due Diligence*, 165.

[20] Morduch and Armendáriz, *The Economics of Microfinance*, 290.

[21] In this, I follow the argument made by Roodman in *Due Diligence* (but am fortunate to now have more RCTs on which to draw than were available to him in that book). This argument—that we can really rely only on RCTs, not flawed impact studies, for judging the overall impact of microfinance on poverty levels (impact studies may have roles at a finer-grained level)—is criticized for setting the methodological barrier too high. Indeed, Roodman asks himself, how can 150 million women asking for microcredit all be wrong? But easy as it is to become emotive in the face of borrowers demanding loans, 150 million requests for a loan may say much about the need for financial services, even on the terms at which microcredit is offered, but says nothing about whether at the end of the day the loans alleviate, do nothing for, or exacerbate poverty.

experiments such as that of Pitt and Khandker discussed above, they can prove causality. Of course, they have their weaknesses too: they may only provide a limited understanding of context. And depending on the method of randomization, they may or may not capture the effects of microfinance on others in the community who do not take it up. But for the question at issue here—the impact of the provision of microcredit on levels of poverty—they are largely what we do want. All the studies are important, but the largest and most resonant is the "Spandata" study, which was carried out in the heart of Indian microcredit, Hyderabad in Andhra Pradesh.

The Spandata study was the first randomized evaluation of the impact of introducing microcredit in a new market.[22] Spandata, a fast-growing MFI, was expanding into Hyderabad and chose 104 poor neighborhoods of the city as it planned new target markets. It then randomly chose 52 of these to begin lending into in 2006 and 2007. All 104 districts (some 6,850 households) were then surveyed fifteen to eighteen months after lending had begun. In the areas Spandata had targeted, 26.7% of households took a microloan, two-thirds from Spandata: in the control areas this was 18.3%. The difference in usage of microcredit overall between the two groups was the basis for assessing the impact of microcredit. The fact that both groups were so large should mean that any biases arising would be present in both control and target groups in equal measure: all shared the same slum background, and an approximate US$3 a day to live on.

Banerjee and coauthors summarized their initial results as follows: "Fifteen to eighteen months after lending began in treated areas, there was no effect of access to microcredit on average monthly expenditure per capita, but expenditure on durable goods increased in treated areas and the number of new businesses increased by one third."[23] No impact on average consumption was found, then: or, for that matter, on empowerment issues: "We find no impact on measures of health, education or women's decision-making."[24] What they did find was an increase in the purchase of durables, especially business durables. The loans seem to have been used largely for capital investment in existing small-scale businesses. This did not, in the time frame measured, feed through either positively or negatively to the poverty levels of those who received the loans.

The findings of the initial study, then, were simply that where there was an existing business, loans were used to expand it: where there was not a pre-existing business, loans were used to increase nondurable consumption (food or, possibly, paying down more expensive debt). Overall, on the substantial evidence it gathered then, the study found no clear impact of the provision of microcredit on poverty. Given the size and methodological solidity of this study, and the fact that it was aimed at the profile of borrower who many have most sought to help, this was a sadly disappointing outcome for the proponents of microcredit.

---

[22] Duflo et al., "The Miracle of Microfinance?"NOTE – should this not be 'Banerjee et al.', not 'Duflo et al.'?

[23] Duflo et al., "The Miracle of Microfinance?" 1.

[24] Duflo et al., "The Miracle of Microfinance?" 1.

Two years after the end of the first endline survey, the team interviewed the same households again. This enabled them to assess the longer-term impacts of microfinance on households and businesses. The vast majority (around 90%) of those first surveyed (both treatment and control group) participated again and answered exactly the same questions. By the time of the second survey, roughly the same proportion of households from both groups were borrowing from microfinance groups (around one third), but those in the treatment group had generally been borrowing longer.[25]

The team found, again, that for the vast majority, access to microfinance was not increasing the profitability of their businesses. For the very top fifth percentile—the largest (though still small) 5% of businesses—it *did* make a positive difference; but for no one else.

Microfinance did not enable households to consume more (the main measure of poverty alleviation) though it did enable the purchase of consumer durables like a color TV set, which was repaid both through reducing spending on so-called temptation goods—tobacco, alcohol, minor festivals—and through doing an extra amount of the usual business by increasing labor hours, presumably of the woman borrower, possibly of her children.

In areas where microfinance was introduced afresh by Spandata, the new businesses created were typically smaller than in the non-treatment area—petty trading, low capital intensive businesses compared to the more capital intensive businesses such as rickshaw driving in the non-treatment area, and the smaller businesses in the treatment area were much less likely to employ anyone. The team's assessment was that borrowing here was probably largely used to pay for a durable good, and then some small part of it used to buy inputs to do some additional work to contribute towards the loan repayment. They concluded that microfinance can indeed be associated with some business creation, especially by women, but that "these marginal businesses are even smaller and less profitable than the average business in the area, the vast majority of which are already small and unprofitable. Microfinance does also lead to greater investment in existing businesses, and an improvement in the profits for the most profitable of those businesses. For everyone else, business profits do not increase, and, on average, microfinance does not help the business to grow in any significant way. Even after three years, there is no increase in the number of employees of businesses that existed before Spandata started its operation."[26] In other words, they conclude, and excepting the top 5%, microfinance is associated with creating even more unprofitable businesses than had already existed.

The picture was, if anything, even worse when it came to measuring empowerment. No effect was found on health outcomes, sanitation, children's education, food expenditure

[25] Banerjee et al., "The Miracle of Microfinance?" 3–4.

[26] Abhijit Banerjee, Esther Duflo, Rachel Glennerster, Cynthia Kinnan, "The Miracle of Microfinance? Evidence from a Randomized Evaluation," *American Economic Journal: Applied Economics* 7, no.1 (2015): 45.

or food share. The result was a very little better for the top quantile (the top 5% who had increased business profits), but not for the other 95%.

Banerjee and coauthors' conclusion, after the three-year follow up, as to the impact of microfinance, is quietly devastating. Drawing confidence from five other RCTs that have since echoed their results in different contexts and settings, they sum up: "In short, microcredit is not for every household, or even for most households, and it does not lead to the miraculous social transformation some proponents have claimed."[27] Delicately easing their way over their disembowelment of microfinance's raison d'être, they summarize: "The only mistake that the microfinance enthusiasts may have made is to overestimate the potential of businesses for the poor, both as a source of revenue and as a means of empowerment for their female owners."[28]

The additional RCT studies referred to by Banerjee and coauthors as producing findings echoing their Indian study were carried out in Morocco,[29] Mongolia,[30] Bosnia,[31] Ethiopia,[32] and Mexico.[33] Banerjee, Karlan, and Zinman summarize these in the *American Economic Journal: Applied Economics* in January 2015.[34] The additional RCTs varied in whether they studied rural or urban settings and in the precise method of randomization used. But overall, conclusions were consistent. Where there was an existing business, the loan was used to put more money into it, and business activity increased. But after two years there was little or no effect on total household income, on average consumption, on health or education, or indeed on female empowerment where this was measured. The Mongolian study saw a small, positive increase in the proportion of borrowers' children going to school: but the opposite effect was found in Bosnia, where teenage (aged sixteen to nineteen years) children of borrowers were 19% less likely to attend school than those in the control group.

---

[27] Banerjee et al. "The Miracle of Microfinance?" 25.

[28] Banerjee et al., "The Miracle of Microfinance?" 52.

[29] Bruno Crépon, Florencia Devoto, Esther Duflo, and William Parienté, "Estimating the Impact of Microcredit on Those Who Take It Up: Evidence from a Randomized Evaluation in Morocco," *American Economic Journal: Applied Economics* 7, no. 1 (2015): 123–150.

[30] Orazio Attanasio, Britta Augsburg, Ralph de Haas, Emla Fitzsimons, and Heike Harmgart, "The Impacts of Microfinance: Evidence from Joint-Liability Lending in Mongolia," *American Economic Journal: Applied Economics* 7, no. 1 (2015): 90–122.

[31] Britta Augsburg, Ralph de Haas, Heike Harmgart, and Costas Meghir, "The Impacts of Microcredit: Evidence from Bosnia and Herzegovina," *American Economic Journal: Applied Economics* 7, no. 1 (2015): 183–203.

[32] Alessandro Tarozzi, Jaikishan Desai, and Kristin Johnson, "The Impacts of Microcredit: Evidence from Ethiopia," *American Economic Journal: Applied Economics* 7, no. 1 (2015): 54–89.

[33] Manuela Angelucci, Dean Karlan, and Jonathan Zinman, "Microcredit Impacts: Evidence from a Randomized Microcredit Program Placement Experiment by Compartamos Banco," *American Economic Journal: Applied Economics* 7, no. 1 (2015): 151–182.

[34] Abhijit Banerjee, Dean Karlan, and Jonathan Zinman, "Six Randomized Evaluations of Microcredit," *American Economic Journal: Applied Economics* 7, no. 1 (2015): 1–21. They are reassured that their conclusions here also echo Banerjee's survey using other studies, "Microcredit under the Microscope: What Have We Learnt in the Last Two Decades, What Do We Need to Know?" *Annual Review of Economics* 5 (2013): 487–519.

The conclusions that Banerjee, Karlan, and Zinman derive from this survey are in line with Banerjee's 2013 survey of other studies.[35] Microfinance is not transformative. It facilitates an increase in business investment and activity: but not necessarily a profitable one, nor one that has an impact in reducing borrowers' poverty. It increases choice, but there is nothing to suggest that it will be a good choice to make. There was little support for strong claims of impact, positive or negative, on the *average* borrower, but some support—albeit more analysis needs to be done—for the idea that microfinance benefits a very few by a significant amount and that the losers from it are generally the poorest of borrowers. This last point – that the losers from microcredit generally are found amongst those who, being the poorest, start out with the most to lose, was also found by Paul Mosley and David Hulme back in 1998.[36] The ethical question of whether one significant winner is really a sufficient offset for one significant loser, or whether worsening the poverty of those least able to bear it counts for more than helping alleviate the poverty of the better off among the poor, is taken up in chapter 6.

The Moroccan and Indian studies found that much of the total profit made was made by just a very few of the borrowers, who had larger businesses: the Moroccan study found that for a substantial minority—25%—the impact of introducing microcredit was negative on business profits. In other words, the average impact of zero for microcredit looks to be masking a positive impact for a very few least-poor clients and a negative impact for the poorest, presumably least able to bear it.

It may be that the publication of these six studies, and Banerjee and coauthors' summary of them in the *American Economic Journal: Applied Economics*, will come to be seen as marking a watershed for the sector. The industry's response to previous critiques of its results has been to tell more micro stories that do not address the macro critique given. Muhammad Yunus was happy to respond to Duflo's critique that microfinance was not the miracle previously presented by saying that if a family moves from one meal a day to two, that is development enough.[37] The point of Duflo's work, and that of all the RCTs, of course, is that, on average, not even that much can be said for microfinance.

These studies have been produced by heavyweight academic researchers committed to reporting what they find, but who are certainly not predisposed *against* microfinance. Brushing aside six serious studies in six different countries across four different continents is simply no longer an option for the sector. Instead, the true implications of this work need to be taken to heart.

---

[35] Banerjee "Microcredit under the Microscope."

[36] Paul Mosley and David Hulme, 'Microenterprise Finance: Is there a Conflict Between Growth and Poverty Alleviation?' *World Development* 26: 783–790

[37] Muhammad Yunus in (public) conversation with Caroline Daniel at an *intelligence*^{2} debate, Mermaid Theatre, London, April 3, 2015.

There have now also been three studies published that look at the impact of providing microsavings, as opposed to microcredit.[38]

The results of these have been rather more positive than those for microcredit. Savers seem to be able to use microsavings to smooth income, and as self-insurance, and see higher incomes down the line. There is an absence of potential negative effects, but exactly how these accounts help is perhaps not yet fully understood. To the extent these accounts help female savers resist demands from friends and family for cash that males have little difficulty resisting, they may empower: but at what cost to those relationships, and whether that is ultimately positive or negative across the community, is not known.

Because this book is concerned with the ethics of the making of small loans to the poor, the savings studies will not be examined in more depth. This book has no argument with the offer of savings facilities to the poor as such: it is the much more dominant offer of loans to the poor that concerns us.

On the best evidence we have, then, that of randomized control studies, there is no clear, direct evidence of positive impact of microcredit on reducing poverty levels. There is some evidence of positive indirect impact through enabling borrowers to manage unexpected demands on income that might otherwise hurt their ability to retain employment in the formal sector:[39] but that is of little relevance to the target client typically aimed at by MFIs, the small-scale entrepreneur in the informal sector. The evidence from the RCTs on offering microsavings is more positive. Without suggesting dramatic impact in reducing poverty, it does suggest a positive smoothing effect, a protection against shocks and as a result an improvement in income. As an industry, however, compared to microcredit, microsavings independent of a credit offering is still embryonic.

In 2010 the United Kingdom's Department for International Development funded two systematic reviews of microcredit: that of Duvendack and coauthors,[40] quoted earlier, which whittled 2,643 studies of microcredit globally down to 58 considered sufficiently free of methodological flaws to study in depth; and that of Stewart and coauthors,[41] which searched three specialist systematic review libraries, eighteen electronic online databases, twenty-four MFI websites, and an online directory of books to identify thirty-five studies of the impact of microcredit or savings in sub-Saharan Africa, of which twenty were excluded because of poor reporting or methodology or both, and fifteen

[38] Pascaline Dupas and Jonathan Robinson, "Saving Constraints and Microenterprise Development: Evidence from a Field Experiment in Kenya," Working Paper No. 14693, 2009; Lasee Brune, Xavier Gine, Jessica Goldberg, and Dean Yang "Commitments to Save: A Field Experiment in Malawi," Impact Evaluation Series 50, Policy Research Working Paper No. 5748, 2011, World Bank Development Research Group; Ronald Abraham, Felipe Kast, and Dina Pomeranz, "Insurance through Savings Accounts: Evidence from a Randomized Field Experiment among Low-Income Micro-entrepreneurs in Chile," unpublished paper, 2011.

[39] Karlan and Zinman, "Expanding Credit Access."

[40] Duvendack et al., "What Is the Evidence."

[41] Ruth Stewart, Carina van Rooyen, Kelly Dickson, Mabolaeng Majoro, and Thea de Wet, "What Is the Impact of Microfinance on Poor People? A Systematic Review of the Evidence from Sub-Saharan Africa," technical report, EPPI-Centre, Social Science Research Unit, University of London, 2010.

were then studied in depth. Stewart and coauthors concluded that "microcredit and micro-savings have mixed impacts on the poor in sub-Saharan Africa, with both positive and negative impacts on their wealth and their livelihoods . . . micro-savings appears to be the more successful intervention, both in theory and practice."[42]

Duvendack and coauthors' conclusions, as noted earlier, are, if anything, even bleaker: "Our report shows that almost all impact evaluations of microfinance suffer from weak methodologies and inadequate data . . . thus the reliability of impact estimates are adversely affected. This can lead to misconceptions about the actual effects of microfinance programmes, thereby diverting attention from the search for perhaps more pro-poor interventions."[43] This causes them to question whether there might not have been better interventions that did better benefit poor people / empower women over the past decade or so. They note: "There are many other candidate sectors for development activity which may have been relatively disadvantaged by ill-founded enthusiasm for microfinance."[44] Duvendack and coauthors' call is then for more and better research, to obtain "a clearer picture on the impacts of microfinance, on whom, where, and when (e.g. under what circumstances), and the mechanisms which account for these effects."

Both the RCTs, then, and the systemic reviews of all the studies of microfinance carried out, conclude that there is a grave lack of evidence for microcredit's claims to raise borrowers out of poverty. Given equal prominence in microfinance's early claims, however, was the claim it empowered women. The RCTs that have been examined in this section found no positive impact on issues of empowerment either. What, then, of any other evidence of microfinance empowering—or indeed disempowering—its borrowers?

3. Evidence of Empowerment

The World Bank defines empowerment as "the process of increasing the assets and capabilities of individuals or groups to make purposive choices and to transform those choices into desired actions and outcomes. . . . Empowered people have freedom of choice and action. This in turn enables them to better influence the course of their lives and the decisions which affect them." Acknowledging that perceptions of being empowered vary across time, culture, and domains of a person's life, the World Bank summarizes: "In essence empowerment speaks to self-determined change."[45] In defining empowerment in this way, the World Bank draws on the academic literature, where, classically, empowering a woman is defined by Kabeer as the process by which those who were denied the

---

[42] Stewart et al., "What Is the Impact," 6.

[43] Duvendack et al., "What Is the Evidence," 4.

[44] Duvendack et al., "What Is the Evidence," 75.

[45] "What Is Empowerment?" World Bank, 2011, available at http://go.worldbank.org/V45HD4P100.

ability to make strategic life choices acquire this ability; empowerment is the ability to make choices, and it entails a process of social change.[46]

The focus here is on social empowerment. The microfinance industry embraces two different conceptions of empowerment. The "financial inclusion" model focuses on how access to credit can open up possibilities for a borrower of control over her own financial life. It refers simply to economic empowerment: a borrower is empowered simply by generating wealth, which increases her choices in life and her independence. Since, as we have seen, there is no clear evidence that, on average, credit does in fact generate net wealth, this form of empowerment *overall* is not to be found, although of course some individuals, especially those in the few per cent who do appear to benefit from credit, may enjoy it. Equally, the poorest, who appear to do worst from credit, may become even more disempowered.

The second, and original, use of empowerment, used by the developers of microfinance in Bangladesh, encompassed this economic version of empowerment in their definition of empowerment, but also saw a much more radical impact on the social structure within which the borrowers lived. They saw microfinance, through its group-lending structure, empowering women to challenge the social norms of their society itself. Roy calls this the "Bangladeshi" model.[47] In a society generally accepted as being repressive to women, Bangladesh microfinance firms wanted to use the group-lending model (hierarchical as it itself was) to challenge and indeed change some of these norms: the intention was to create a sense of solidarity through the groups that would allow other services to be delivered, including a commitment to political participation.

Empirical studies measuring overall empowerment are even thinner on the ground than those measuring poverty. A notable study by Hashemi, Schuler, and Riley in Bangladesh tried to measure empowerment,[48] using eight different indicators.[49] Measuring these before and after credit was extended, they did find an empowering effect; but unfortunately there was no control group of potential, would-be borrowers, so we do not know whether or not it was women who were already more empowered who signed up for microfinance in the first place, a potential selection bias the authors acknowledge.

A lot of early research studies claimed that microcredit increased mobility and strengthened networks among women who were previously confined to their homes.[50]

---

[46] Naila Kabeer, "Resources, Agency, Achievements: Reflections on the Measurement of Women's Empowerment," *Development and Change* 30, no. 3 (1999): 435–464.

[47] Roy, *Poverty Capital*, 104–112.

[48] Syed Hashemi, Sidney Ruth Schuler, and Ann Riley, "Rural Credit Programs and Women's Empowerment in Bangladesh," *World Development* 24, no. 4 (1996): 635–653.

[49] These are mobility, economic security, ability to make small purchases, ability to make larger purchases, involvement in major household decisions, relative freedom from domination within the family, political and legal awareness, and involvement in political campaigning and protests.

[50] E.g., Hulme and Mosley, *Finance against Poverty*; Muhammad Abdul Latif, "Programme Impact on Current Conception in Bangladesh," *Bangladesh Development Studies* 22, no. 1 (1994): 27–61; Sidney Ruth Schuler and Syed Hashemi, "Credit Programmes, Women's Empowerment and Contraceptive Use in Rural Bangladesh," *Studies on Family Planning* 25, no. 2 (1994): 65–76.

But the position is complex. In Asia at least, it is not uncommon for women to hand over control of the loan to their spouse or invest it in a family enterprise.[51] Goetz and Sen Gupta argue that what is really happening is that "the household is internalizing the high transaction costs of lending to men. . . . These costs are primarily those of monitoring men's loan use and enforcing regular repayment. Women in effect offset these costs by using intrahousehold gender relations of obligation or persuasion to recover weekly loan repayments."[52] Women can fulfill this role of internalizing the costs of lending to men within the household because they "are easy to locate, being much less able than men to leave a locality temporarily to evade field workers, and they are easier to intimidate into repayment than men, who can always threaten violence."[53]

It was perhaps always unlikely that access for women to credit by itself would overturn entrenched patriarchal systems of control where these existed. In societies where women's secondary status has many causes—lack of access to financial services being only one among many, such as lack of property rights, lack of power over divorce procedures and settlements, lack of control over custody of children in the event of divorce—just tweaking one of these issues may not be enough to change the overall social norm.

Matters are complicated further by the fact that for some women, empowerment came when they had enough extra income to restrict mobility and choices by opting for some form of purdah,[54] which could not be observed if one was working in the field all day. Kabeer notes, "If empowerment entails the extended capacity for making choices then . . . the paradox is that in many cases, this leads women to opt for some form of purdah if they can afford to, both to signal their social standing within the community and to differentiate themselves from those women who do not have this choice."[55]

These women, in an impact study measuring mobility, one of Hashemi, Schuler, and Riley's criteria, would count as less empowered. But to the extent that they are exercising their own autonomous choice, albeit to limit their own freedoms, this is not clear.

A recent study has shown the picture to be even more complex than this presentation of it has been so far. A study of two villages in Bangladesh repeated the finding that the husbands usually took control of the loan, but went further: men used their patriarchal authority to compel women (wives, mothers, sisters) to get the loan as the NGOs (BRAC and Grameen) would not lend to men.[56] Intimidation was used if the woman refused. There usually was a temporary improvement after taking the loan in the family's economic position, and this was then used by the men to buy their wives burkas

---

[51] Goetz and Sen Gupta, "Who Takes the Credit?"

[52] Goetz and Sen Gupta, "Who Takes the Credit?"

[53] Goetz and Sen Gupta, "Who Takes the Credit?"

[54] I.e., the concealment of a woman's form and restrictions on contact with males from outside the kinship group.

[55] Naila Kabeer, "Conflicts over Credit: Re-evaluating the Empowerment Potential of Loans to Women in Rural Bangladesh," *World Development* 29, no. 1 (2001): 63–84.

[56] Aminul Faraizi, Taskinur Rahman, and Jim McAllister, *Microcredit and Women's Empowerment: A Case Study of Bangladesh* (London: Routledge, 2011).

or hijabs to wear as a symbol of their newfound wealth and prestige. It was entirely unclear that the women in this study themselves wanted to adopt this dress. The authors reflected that "we could not find any hard evidence to support the view that microcredit empowers women or promotes their liberation. . . . The microcredit programme does not directly challenge any official views that subjugate women."[57] Where they did find economic empowerment—they cite a case of a woman who successfully set up a hand-rolled cigarette business, unfortunately using cheap child labor as the only way of making it profitable—they did not find social empowerment followed. The profits were used by this woman to pay increased dowry for her daughter.

An interesting (and also somewhat paradoxical) example of the original, positive use of the group-lending mechanism to deliver empowerment is reported by Maddocks in his discussion of a study of the Small Enterprise Foundation's (SEF) efforts to increase awareness of HIV/AIDS among its staff and clients in Limpopo province.[58] Here 24% of all deaths were as a result of AIDS, and 28% among women. SEF linked its microfinance operation to the health education work of the Rural AIDS and Development Action Research program (RADAR). SEF loan group members were met with every two weeks to discuss gender inequality, partner violence, and how AIDS was typically spread. SEF director John DeWit commented: "What we found was during the first four sessions of SFL training, people really hated it; they really strongly opposed it because of the sensitive issues it was raising, such as 'Do you have a son who is a migrant worker who has a girlfriend in Joburg who, when he comes home, might be infected.'" Members were compelled to stay, however, to get their loans, and over time came to value the training and even pass it on: client retention rates among those who had received the training rose. The study looked at the impact of microfinance on poverty and empowerment by taking one group that had received the training and one that had not, as well as a control group, and showed that only those who had had the training demonstrated increased empowerment. (This study did include dropouts as well.)

Specifically, it found

> participation . . . was associated with increased "power within" measured by greater self-confidence, financial confidence, as well as more progressive attitudes to gender norms. Women with an intimate partner reported an increase in "power to" measured by higher levels of autonomy in decision making, greater valuation of their household contribution by their partners, improved household communication and better relationships with partners. . . . Over a two-year period, levels of intimate partner violence were reduced by 55% in women in the intervention group relative to those in the comparison group.[59]

---

[57] Faraizi, Rahman, and McAllister, *Microcredit and Women's Empowerment*, 118.

[58] William Maddocks, "How Can Microfinance Programs Help the Struggle against Social Problems Such as Begging, Child Labor, Prostitution, Violence against Women, Criminality, Gangs, and Drug Addiction?" commissioned paper for the Global Microcredit Summit, Valladolid, 2011.

[59] Maddocks, "How Can Microfinance Help," 7.

These are powerful results: the irony is, of course, that the increase in empowerment observed in the treatment group to talk more freely about sexual and violent matters had to be coerced through refusing to continue with microfinance lending unless participants had the initially hated training. Note, though, that this is only partially a victory for the concept of microfinance as empowerment. It is the knowledge these women gained that empowered them: microfinance was merely the mechanism for forcing them to acquire it.

A recent study from India provided another example of a microcredit program being used to empower women in fields beyond simply finance.[60] Chakravarty and Chaudhuri show how nongovernmental activists were able to encourage microcredit groups to look beyond their pure credit function and mobilize against domestic abuse, alcoholism, and the practice of witch hunts, which were not uncommon in the area studied (the tea plantations of Jalpaiguri). Tribal workers' belief in the existence of witches and willingness to kill the "witch" (often blamed for diseases in villages with no doctors or medical facilities), especially when fueled by alcohol, were easier to counter when the microcredit group banded together to resist the tradition.

The problem with the group-lending model being used to coercively empower its members, to their benefit in cases where the program bolted onto the offer of credit was designed to empower, is that, of course, that same group-lending model can also be coercively used to disempower.

Where a borrower has fallen behind on payments, loan collection methods used by an MFI may be coercive and shaming, as will be seen in chapter 4. Arunachalum[61] quotes the extreme case of an eight-year-old girl kidnapped by a moneylender[62] operating as an agent for an Indian MFI; she was held as collateral until her parents made the due payment on a debt (he notes that the local microfinance bank then, and still months later, listed women's rights and "empowering the girl child" as its key priorities). But, because the group liability model requires a struggling borrower's peers to cover her payments and they are often around the poverty line themselves, the group peers' methods of loan collection may be even worse than the MFI's. Karim and Rahman both describe cases of ostracization, housebreaking, violence, and asset removal being used by peers to make good some of their loss.[63] The female empowerment narrative runs that in the group-lending model, borrowers support each other and willingly help each other out in time of need. And of course perfectly genuine examples of this are true. But when times are tough—and we are discussing the poorest here, so these times are not rare—powerful incentives work the other way.

---

[60] Anuradha Chakravarty and Soma Chaudhuri, "Strategic Framing Work(s): How Microcredit Loans Facilitate Anti-Witch-Hunt Movements," *Mobilization* 17, no. 2 (2012): 175–194.

[61] Arunachalum, *Journey of Indian Microfinance*, 18–19.

[62] Named as Mrs. Lalitha, awaiting trial when Arunachalam's book was published.

[63] Karim, *Microfinance and Its Discontents*; Rahman, *Women and Microcredit*.

Conceptually, it is perhaps not surprising that there is so much ambiguity over whether microcredit empowers, overall, or not. The offer of credit can empower a poor woman by enabling her to start an activity that generates income for herself and over which she has control (although it can of course also overindebt her, and she may not in fact have control over the income produced). But even on the best case, assuming the offer of microcredit itself empowers, the form through which it is (mostly) offered, group lending, is inherently disempowering. Even where there is individual lending rather than group liability, the fact that it is still (largely) done in groups places heavy burdens on the borrower. It may start off by empowering borrowers against poverty and indeed culture, by challenging social norms, but end up reinforcing patriarchal norms to ensure repayment. Repayment has to be ensured somehow or the MFI will not be able to continue without fresh external subsidy: coercive peer and loan officer pressure replaces collateral. The traditional setup, of a group of poor women gathering weekly to have their loan repayments paid over to a (usually male) loan officer who may enforce sanctions such as not allowing anyone to go home until the last payment is made and, most of all, to take on personal liability for the repayments of others in their group, is inherently disempowering. As a USAID consultant reflected to Roy: "Do you and I, as women borrowing from a bank, have to do this when we take out a loan from the Bank of America? . . . Why do poor women? . . . And how can this pass as women's empowerment? True empowerment is to have a choice; to be able to purchase a service without all these conditions and rituals."[64]

Mayoux, Margaret, and Cerqueira summarize the two sides of this debate as follows:

> Many programmes are group based. Group formation can reinforce the development contribution of microfinance through providing an organisational base for non-financial services and information in areas like enterprise development, health, literacy and gender equality. Likewise, the groups can provide a base for collective community action, networking and advocacy, and strengthening of civil society and democracy. Examples exist of microfinance programmes which have made all of these potential contributions to development. However an increasing body of evidence shows that badly designed microfinance programmes may increase rather than reduce poverty through creating a downward spiral of debt. Thus, female-targeted microfinance may disempower women through shifting on to them the full burden of family savings and debt. Women may not control their own incomes and men may divert more of their incomes to their own personal expenditure.[65]

It is of course possible to advocate microfinance without the group-lending model. But we have largely yet to get beyond it as a way for MFIs to secure repayment. As Mayoux

---

[64] Roy, *Poverty Capital*, 49.

[65] Linda Mayoux, Margaret Jiri, and Marinela Cerqueira, *Microfinance for Urban Poverty Reduction: Sustainable Livelihoods Project, Angola* (London: One World Action, 2002).

puts it, "Unless micro-finance programmes move beyond complacent assumptions about automatic contributions of group formations to women's empowerment, they risk becoming little more than another cynical self-help means of shifting the costs of development onto poor women."[66]

Attempting to sum up a net, overall, level of empowerment or otherwise is difficult, in part because we do not have adequate data, and in part because each study that has been done is so locally economically and socially specific, generalizations seem to make little sense. The Banerjee and coauthors study, because it followed the impact of a microfinance firm, Spandata, that clearly followed the Grameen Bank model that has been replicated worldwide, may be one of the more generalizable—but found no significant impact of female empowerment across sixteen measures. A recent study by Kabeer, Mahmood, and Tasheen returns to the widespread study of the impact of work, including that financed by microfinance, on the empowerment of thousands of Bangladeshi women.[67]

Kabeer, Mahmood, and Tasheen interviewed a sample of 5,198 women aged over fifteen from locations spread over eight districts in Bangladesh, chosen to represent different socioeconomic conditions. They were then divided by primary occupation into those who did paid work outside the home (13%), subdivided into work in the formal (4%) and informal economy (9%), paid work within the home (46%), unpaid subsistence production (15%), and economic inactivity (22%). Within these groupings, it should be noted, informal work outside the home would be largely represented by those working through microfinance loans: many of those working informally inside the home would also be taking microfinance loans (to rear cows, for example).

Each group was then measured for control over income, mobility in the public domain, participation in public life, and attitudes and perceptions.

With regard to control of income, most women across all groups retained some income for their own use, but there was a significant difference between those in paid, formal work and the rest. Almost all of this group retained income, and a much higher proportion of this group (90%) could choose their own clothes and had a savings or insurance account (24%) against around 80% and 8% for those working in the informal sector and 42% and 10% for those in subsistence production. In terms of control over income, then, there was a significant (positive) difference in empowerment for women in the informal sector dominated by microfinance borrowers, but a more significant difference again between them and those in the paid formal sector.

These results were repeated with regard to mobility in the public domain—a woman going unaccompanied to a health clinic or the market or being able to visit her natal family (women in Bangladesh typically leave their own family for that of their husband

---

66 Linda Mayoux, "Tackling the Downside: Social Capital, Women's Empowerment and Micro-finance in Cameroon," *Development and Change* 32 (2001): 462.

67 Naila Kabeer, Simeen Mahmood, and Sakiba Tasheen, "Does Paid Work Provide a Pathway to Women's Empowerment? Empirical Findings from Bangladesh," IDS Working Paper No. 375, 2011.

on marriage, who is not usually from the same village, so the woman is classically cut off from her own birth family's support).

With regard to participation in public life, measured by knowledge of labor laws, consultation by others, voting and own decision in voting, attendance at rural committee meetings unaccompanied, and even participating in protests, there was a similar gulf between those in the formal sector and the others: 48% of those in paid labor knew labor laws, but only 11%–14% of the other economically active groups. Similarly, 52% of formal workers might be consulted by others, but only 27%–33% of the economically active remainder.

Kabeer, Mahmood, and Tasheen conclude that "it is the nature of the women's paid work, rather than the simple fact of earning money, that has the potential to bring about shifts in gender relations in terms of how women view themselves and how they are viewed by others, as well as in their capacity for voice and agency." It would seem that if a microfinance loan finances a business that is carried on outside the home, there is an empowering effect relative to a business carried on from inside the home: but real empowerment lies in getting a job in the formal sector.

Education was what in fact had the highest correlation with empowerment, especially at secondary and higher levels. One surprising correlation not usually measured in the academic literature was the effect of watching TV (often done collectively) in broadening women's horizons.

Kabeer, Mahmood, and Tasheen noted that NGO membership did seem to increase mobility in the public domain, and observed that other studies[68] suggest that the purer the focus on microcredit by an NGO (as opposed to other social aspects), the more impact was limited to purely economic impact and was not otherwise empowering. A subsequent study by Kabeer, Mahmud, and Castro has followed this up.[69] Studying a range of NGOs in Bangladesh that covered a spread from microcredit only (ASA) to social mobilization and awareness training only, with BRAC and Grameen in the middle, it was found that the pure offer of microcredit led to no increase in empowerment: offering social programs only added the most, and mixed programs hovered between the two. Access to credit, then, did not empower: NGOs' specialized training on a broad range of social issues did.

Kabeer and coauthors' work suggests that formal paid work has empowering effects on women beyond just the increased income: but this was much less clear of those working in the informal sector. There were some empowering effects on those working outside the home, far fewer on those using their microfinance loans to work inside the home. For both formal and informal workers, it was the nature of the work done (whether it was

---

[68] Nabila Kabeer, "Between Affiliation and Autonomy: Navigating Pathways of Women's Empowerment and Gender Justice in Bangladesh," *Development and Change* 42, no. 2 (2011): 499–528.

[69] Nabila Kabeer, Simeon Mahmud, and Jairo Guillermo Isaza Castro, "Strategies and the Challenge of Development and Democracy in Bangladesh," IDS Working Paper, 2010, 343.

outside the home, its status in society) that correlated to empowerment, not the extension of credit as such (which was not correlated to empowerment).

The empowerment MFIs believe comes to women borrowers, then, would seem to come from the extent to which the MFI has worked with its borrowers outside the field of pure credit—to educate, to train, to provide solidarity, as with the sexual health education in South Africa and the fight against witch hunts in India. Women's solidarity and interest groups empower. Credit per se does not. Credit can disempower if it becomes a debt spiral, so whether microcredit overall empowers will never have a clear answer: it will depend in how and to whom and with what solidarity-building it is offered.

Kabeer sums it up as follows:

> It is clear that while access to financial services can and does make important contributions to the economic productivity and social well-being of poor women and their households, it does not "automatically" empower women—any more than do education, political quotas, access to waged work or any other interventions that feature in the literature on women's empowerment. There are no magic bullets, no panaceas, no blueprints, no readymade formulas which bring about the radical structural transformation that the empowerment of the poor, and of poor women, implies. These various interventions are simply different entry points into this larger project, each with the potential for social transformation, but each contingent on context, commitment and capacity if this potential is to be realised.[70]

We saw in the previous section, however, that there is some evidence that access to savings, as opposed to credit, can raise income and indeed empower. The work of Rutherford and more recently Collins and coauthors has used financial diary keeping[71] with the impoverished in a number of different countries to get at, first, just how complex the financial life of the poor is, and how this can be alleviated not (or not only) with the simple, blunt instrument of a loan, but with access to a suite of financial services—savings, insurance, loans from kin, flexible loans (moneylenders may be much more flexible with regard to repayment than MFIs).[72] The central observation of *Portfolios of the Poor* is that the poor do not live on $2 a day: they live on $3 one day, 50 cents the next, nothing for a while, and so on: income comes from a variety of sources, is not reliable, and is barely able to cope with emergencies when they come along. With little

---

[70] Naila Kabeer, "Is Microfinance a 'Magic Bullet' for Women's Empowerment? Analysis of Findings from South Asia," in *Microfinance and Women's Empowerment: A Critical Assessment*, ed. S. Rajagopalan (Hyderabad, India: Icfai University Press, 2009), 80.

[71] Where households keep daily records of all their financial transactions, however minute, which are then shared weekly with researchers to build up a picture of the complex juggling of different sources of income and borrowing that is widespread.

[72] Stuart Rutherford, *The Poor and Their Money* (Oxford: Oxford University Press, 2001); Collins et al., *Portfolios of the Poor*.

access to secure savings accounts, a small surplus one month may simply be spent, leaving nothing to fall back on when a large lump-sum need arises, such as health costs or funeral expenses. A microloan may be taken out to pay for these (probably with another, "business" purpose for the loan fabricated for the MFI) and then the cycle of indebtedness can begin. The idea in propounding the virtues of access to a range of financial services is that the poor can manage their uncertain income streams so as to avoid the large-item expense disasters that seem to freshly impoverish just when a household begins to claw its way out of extreme poverty.

Of course, the fact that it makes a lot of economic theoretical sense to think that providing financial access would enable poor households to smooth consumption and manage unanticipated disasters does not mean that we have empirical evidence that this is so. We no more have a randomized control trial to show that access to a suite of financial services leaves the poorest better off than those without, than we have proof of empowerment. It will be recalled that the RCTs that have looked for evidence of empowerment as well as poverty alleviation were unable to establish it. The case for financial access is an argument in logic rather than empirical fact thus far. Still, it is a good logic with limited downside: if the issue of security of savings can be resolved, access to a mix of savings, insurance, and credit threatens to do much less harm than the sole use of credit to attempt to meet each of these needs.

Whether, at the macroeconomic level, providing access to a range of financial services is the best use of the development dollar is a quite different question. It might indeed be a good thing for the poor to have access to financial services, especially savings facilities that are not contingent on taking out a loan: it might be an even better thing for them to have access to free healthcare, clean water, or a quality free education. No attempt is made here to judge the relative merits of each of these.

If the claim that access to financial services works, even if microcredit alone fails to turns out to be true, then there may be a role for microcredit as a part of that suite, even if a more modest one than its adherents had claimed for it. Its role may be made the greater if it is the part of that suite that is helping to pay for the rest: if it is hard to profitably/sustainably serve the poor with credit even when high levels of interest are being charged, it is still harder with products such as insurance or savings. Here the immediate return on the product to the provider is much lower and greater volume (and a much longer timescales and higher client retention levels) would be necessary for the product to be profitably or sustainably offered.

Even if microcredit could be justified, to some extent, as the bill payer for a wider, more useful range of financial services (and that is still supposition as yet), even if this does end up on the "plus" column for microcredit, we still need to weigh up, as far as we can, all the other pros and cons. It may be that even if microcredit did facilitate the provision of a broader suite of financial services, and even if other elements of that suite were somewhat effective in alleviating poverty and ameliorating the worst downsides from the poor's lives, the costs of microcredit are still too high. This is the equation to which Part II now turns.

II Microethics

THE PRACTICES OF MICROFINANCE

It is not fair. They say that the interest rate is 4 per cent, but every week I have to pay interest based on all the money I have borrowed. . . . Additionally I have to give a 10 per cent deposit at the beginning (which is not deducted from the loan and also charged with an interest rate) and each meeting I have to make some additional payments: a fee for being late, a collection for the trip of the women from the group who will go to the city to deposit the weekly payment, savings.[1]

3 From Empowerment to Exploitation

MFIs AND THEIR BORROWERS

FOR THE VAST majority of its borrowers there is no evidence that microfinance either enriches or empowers.* If there were, these goods might be thought of sufficient weight that we need not have looked below the surface of microfinance to the nitty-gritty of its practices. But here in Parts II and III we will now do that and look at the ethical implications of the way in which microfinance is practiced.

The ethics of microfinance can be examined at two levels. At the "micro" level, the examination is of the relationship between the microfinance institution and the borrower. Central concerns are whether MFIs wrongfully exploit or coerce borrowers. Seldom discussed is whether the MFI fails to exercise a duty of care to the borrower, but I will argue that this is so, and arguably the most serious of the charges: for if MFIs exercised that duty, they would run much lower risks of either exploitation or coercion. These "micro" issues fill chapters 3 to 5.

The second level at which the ethics of microfinance can be examined is the "macro" level of the consequences of its practices across the society in which it is practiced. Is

* This chapter elaborates on a previously published chapter: L R Sherratt 'Is exploitation permissible in microcredit?' in eds. Tom Sorrell and Luis Cabrera *Microfinance, Rights and Global Justice* (Cambridge University Press, 2015).

[1] Interview with a Mexican microcredit client, Doña Eva, quoted by Agatha Hummel in "The Commercialization of Microcredit and Local Consumerism: Examples of Over-indebtedness from Indigenous Mexico," in *Microfinance, Debt and Over-indebtedness: Juggling with Money*, ed. Isabelle Guérin, Solène Morvant-Roux, and Magdalena Villarreal (London: Routledge, 2014), 258.

the distribution of benefits and burdens of microfinance acceptable? Does its practice encourage and support illegality? What is its overall impact on the economy of a country in which it is practiced, on borrowers and nonborrowers alike? These questions are discussed in chapters 6 to 8.

In this chapter, I begin with arguably the most emotive issue: does microfinance wrongfully exploit its borrowers?

The most obvious way in which lenders might be thought to exploit borrowers is through the level of interest rate charged. Other ways are also possible, such as the imposition of onerous terms and conditions of the loan, and these will also be discussed, but it is on interest rates that I shall concentrate. The first section of this chapter lays out the factual background, then, of what interest rates are charged in microfinance. The second section lays out some alternative theories of exploitation—it is, philosophically, a contested topic. The third section applies these alternative theories of exploitation to MFI rates and practices to see whether any, or indeed all, of them would find microfinance wrongfully exploitative.

Although these theories vary in their nuances, there is considerable shared ground between them, which does indeed find microfinance, on the terms on which it is frequently offered, wrongfully exploitative. I will consider the argument from MFIs that these are the only terms on which they can sustainably offer credit, and suggest that, if the only terms on which they can offer microfinance are wrongfully exploitative, and that wrongful exploitation cannot be compensated for by, for example, producing poverty alleviation and empowerment, then in those circumstances, microfinance might be better not offered.

1. What Interest Rates Are

Setting out what interest rates are charged around the world ought to be straightforward: unfortunately, it is not. The interest rates that MFIs state that they lend to borrowers at frequently understate the actual percentage rate paid. An MFI might state that it charges 5% per month for a twelve-month loan, and that that equates to 60% per annum, but omit to mention that this is on a "flat" rather than a "declining" basis or that it does not include the impact of "compulsory savings" or fees. A flat rate of interest charges interest on the whole of the capital sum originally lent each month for the whole loan period, despite the fact that part of this capital is repaid each month. A declining basis, the usual basis in formal finance, only charges the interest rate on the capital sum still outstanding each month. The effect of this is to push that 60% rate up to over 100% on the average loan balance that the borrower actually receives.

"Compulsory savings" is the practice of many MFIs of holding back 10% or 20% of the loan amount as "savings," effectively collateral, so that the borrower only receives 80% or 90% of the loan amount, but still pays interest on 100% of it. This means that the loan that appears to be at 60% per annum, but is over 100% on a declining balance basis, may be half as expensive again, depending on whether compulsory savings have been taken at 10% or 20%.

The most comprehensive provider of information on what MFIs charge is the Microfinance Information Exchange (MIX). MIX is a database of some twenty-one hundred MFIs accounting for fifty-eight million borrowers in ninety-eight countries. Not all MFIs report to MIX, but it is a reasonable sample. It calculates a "portfolio yield" for each MFI, which is used widely in the industry as representing the price of loans, and is the best proxy available for MFIs' interest rates. This is the actual interest and fee income received over a year by an MFI divided by its average outstanding loan book over the same period. This is indeed a much more accurate reflection of what is charged than the MFI's stated interest rates, but in some cases will still substantially understate. This is because MFIs do not have to disclose to MIX whether or not they enforce "compulsory savings," so for those that do, true rates paid by borrowers are much higher than MIX suggests.[2]

An alternative source of data on microfinance interest rates has until recently been MicroFinance Transparency (MFT), an organization dedicated to bringing some transparency to microcredit interest rates[3]. It analyzes interest rates charged by country on an annual percentage rate (APR) basis. This is clearly superior to the MIX database's "portfolio yield," but unfortunately the range of MFT's database is much more limited. As an indication of how big the difference between the two ways of estimating microfinance interest rates can be, an internal MIX analysis in 2011 compared MIX data to MFT country-equivalent data, and found that the MIX interest yield underestimated the MFT APR by, on average, 6%. However, the sample was considered too small to generalize from.[4]

Taking MIX Market data, then, for its comprehensiveness, but also MFT country data for its higher quality where it is available (also giving a sense of how much the MIX Market data may be understating by), table 3.1 compares microfinance rates at a regional level with MIX data, and at the country level using MFT data, to commercial bank prime rates. The commercial prime rate is included for context, so that it can be seen if all interest rates in any given country are absolutely high, perhaps as a result of inflation, or just those of microcredit.

---

[2] Using the portfolio yield will also understate what actual borrowers pay because it nets off defaults, so that if some borrowers have failed to make interest repayments, that will lower the portfolio yield. Those who have repaid, then, will have paid a higher rate than the portfolio yield shown. If the portfolio yield is shown as, say, 25%, based on (for example) total interest income received being $250,000 from $1 million lent, but in fact $100,000 of loans are not being repaid, then that $250,000 is actually coming from the $900,000 of loans that are paying, making the interest rate for borrowers of *those* loans 27.8%, not 25%.

[3] Unfortunately, it closed in March 2015, although its website remains online.

[4] Quoted by Richard Rosenberg, Scott Gaul, William Ford, and Olga Tomilova, "Microcredit Interest Rates and Their Determinants: 2004–2011," in *Microfinance 3.0: Reconciling Sustainability with Social Outreach and Responsible Delivery*, ed. Doris Kohn (Heidelberg: Springer, 2013), 74.

TABLE 3.1

COMPARISON OF MICROCREDIT INTEREST RATES TO COMMERCIAL PRIME RATES

	Microcredit rates				**Commercial bank prime lending rate**[a]
	Small loans average	Small loans range	Larger loans average	Larger loans range	
South East Asia & Pacific					
MF Transparency					
India	29.5%	22%–45%	28.9%	23%–35%	10.3%
Pakistan	36.8%	16%–59%	33.2%	5%–57%	11.5%
Cambodia	33.7%	14%–51%	27.1%	22%–36%	13%
Philippines	91.3%	17%–250%	76%	24%–140%	5.8%
MIX Market S. Asia	27.4%				
MIX Market E. Asia Pacific	29.5%				
Latin America & Caribbean					
MF Transparency					
Bolivia	34.5%	8%–96%	23.1%	7%–35%	11.4%
Ecuador	25.9%	12%–42%	23%	14%–38%	8.7%
MIX Market LAC	26.5%				
Eastern Europe & Central Asia					
MIX Market ECA	26.6%				
Middle East & North Africa					
MIX Market MENA	29.1%				

Africa					
MF Transparency:					
Ethiopia	31.1%	10%–77%	26.2%	10%–50%	12%
Ghana	101.5%	0%–420%	97.2%	36%–195%	27%
Kenya	61.5%	17%–233%	52.3%	17%–80%	17.1%
Malawi	125.2%	11%–308%	102.2%	26%–234%	29.5%
Mozambique	75.9%	27%–197%	76.8%	30%–118%	15.6%
Rwanda	56%	16%–124%	43.5%	15%–119%	16.3%
Tanzania	98.7%	26%–336%	88.1%	39%–243%	13.6%
Uganda	72%	11%–157%	53.1%	20%–100%	23.7%
Zambia	152%	30%–388%	120.4%	30%–259%	10.4%
MIX Market Africa	43.3%				

Source: All individual country data are from MF Transparency.org Pricing Transparency Indices, accessed April 15, 2014. All regional data are from MIX Market Cross Market Analysis, median yield on gross loan portfolio 2013 (nominal), http://reports.mixmarket.org/crossmarket. The commercial bank prime lending rate is from the CIA World Factbook at https://www.cia.gov/library/publications/the-world-factbook/index.html.

[a]December 31, 2013 (est.).

I have also included in this table further data from MFT that splits the rates charged between the rates charged on smaller loans and those on larger ones and the *range* of rates charged that each of these averages represents.[5] It is necessary to do this because just using the average hides the huge range that exists in many countries. The ranges show, again, that not only does the average small loan cost more than the average larger one, but also that the most extreme rates at the top end of the ranges apply again to the smallest loans—in the case of Ghana, Malawi, Tanzania, and Zambia being over 300%.

Given that loan size is widely taken as indicative of the poverty of a client (the poorer the client, the smaller loan size she can both make use of and be allowed by the MFI on risk grounds), it seems that the poorer a client, the higher the interest rate she is charged. When considering whether microfinance is wrongfully exploitative or not, then, in section 3, we need to be aware not only of the rates paid on average by borrowers, but of the fact that in the very wide-ranging spread that makes up that average, it is the poorest who pay the most.

Some of the numbers on this table are eye-catching, such as the range for small loans in Zambia of 30%—388%, with an average of around 150%. A general pattern emerges of microcredit rates being lowest in Asia, higher in Latin America and highest in Africa. Many factors could drive that: the important point to note here, however, is that in all cases, microcredit rates are two to four times the rates of the formal sector, with the most extreme cases of ten times arising in Africa.

The main reasons given by MFIs for high rates, with reason, are loan size and costs. Cull, Demirgu-Kent, and Morduch,[6] quoting Gonzales,[7] lay the emphasis on loan size. Clearly lenders need to reach a critical mass of clients, and Gonzales found that scale economies disappear after about two thousand customers (others are higher). After that, margins are increased by larger loan sizes and cross-selling other services. The larger loans made by banks, and additional products they cross-sell to clients, translate into lower costs per dollar lent for the bank as opposed to the MFI. The median bank spends 12 cents per dollar lent on operating costs, the median NGO 26 cents.

This is so despite the average operating cost per borrower being $156 for the median NGO and $299 for the median bank. The NGOs keep costs down by spending less on staff, premises, and so on—but it is not enough to compensate for the diseconomies of transacting small loans. Mordoch shows that it is operating costs, rather than capital costs or loan loss provisions, that drive the differences in total costs between different kinds of MFIs.

---

[5] The larger loans are usually around twice the size of the smallest for each country.

[6] Robert Cull, Asli Demirüç-Kunt, and Jonathan Mordoch, "Microfinance Meets the Market," *Journal of Economic Perspectives* 23, no. 1 (2009): 167–192.

[7] Adrian Gonzalez, "Efficiency Drivers of Microfinance Institutions (MFIs): The Case of Operating Costs," *Microbanking Bulletin* 15 (2007): 34–42.

An MFI's interest rate reflects four major components: its own costs of funds, its loan loss expenses, any profits it makes, and operating expenses.[8] Of these, operating expenses are the largest component: expressed as a percentage of the loan portfolio, they are 30% in sub-Saharan Africa,[9] 17% in South Asia,[10] and 19% in Latin America and the Caribbean.[11] Operating expenses are personnel and administrative costs such as salaries, depreciation, and transport for loan officers.

Personnel costs vary widely. In sub-Saharan Africa they represent 14% of the loan portfolio,[12] in South Asia 6%,[13] and in Latin America and the Caribbean 11%.[14] The number of borrowers each loan officer serves tend to be fairly constant: the difference comes in the salary of loan officers. In sub-Saharan Africa the average salary of employees of MFIs expressed as a percentage of gross national income is 918%,[15] in South Asia 280%,[16] and in Latin America and the Caribbean 270%.[17] A likely difference for the relatively expensive salaries in Africa is the lack of a large enough educated pool in the population from which to draw, leading to the salaries of those who have completed formal education being bid up. The percentage of the population educated to secondary school level for the three areas above is, respectively, 41%, 63%, and 88%.[18]

Barring outliers such as Compartamos, it does not seem to be the case that profits are the main driver of the level of interest rates. Rosenberg, Gonzalez, and Narain have calculated that if the median MFI foreswore all profits, it would reduce the interest rate by only about one-sixth.[19] The profiteering of a few is not representative of the whole. This does not, of itself, determine the question of wrongful exploitation—to begin with, operations may be unnecessarily inefficient—but it is worth noting, as Rosenberg, Gonzalez, and Narain put it, "For the median MFI, the extreme and unrealistic scenario of complete elimination of all profit would cause its interest rate to drop by only about

---

[8] Operating expenses are all expenses related to operations i.e., personnel expense, depreciation, amortization, and administration expense.

[9] Sub-Saharan Africa Microfinance Analysis and Benchmarking Report 2010, MIX Market, Microfinance Information Exchange, Inc.

[10] Asia Microfinance Analysis and Benchmark Report, 2009, MIX Market, Microfinance Information Exchange Inc.

[11] Latin America and Caribbean Benchmark Report 2009, MIX Market, Microfinance Information Exchange, Inc.

[12] Sub-Saharan Africa Microfinance Analysis and Benchmarking Report 2010.

[13] Asia Microfinance Analysis and Benchmark Report, 2009.

[14] North America and Caribbean Benchmarks, table 2009.

[15] Sub-Saharan Africa Microfinance Analysis and Benchmarking Report 2010.

[16] Asia Microfinance Analysis and Benchmark Report, 2009.

[17] Latin America and Caribbean Benchmark Report 2009.

[18] Gross enrolment ratio as a percentage of the relevant age group educated to secondary level, for sub-Saharan Africa, South Asia, Latin America, and Caribbean, respectively, World Bank World Development Indicators, table 2.11, available at www://wdi.worldbank.org/table/2.11.

[19] Richard Rosenberg, Adrian Gonzalez, and Sushma Narain, "The New Moneylenders: Are the Poor Being Exploited by High Microcredit Interest Rates?" CGAP Occasional Paper No. 15, 2009.

one-sixth. Such an interest reduction would not be insignificant, but it would still leave microcredit rates at levels that might look abusive to politicians and the public, neither of whom usually understand the high costs that tiny lending inevitably entails."[20]

Unfortunately, it is very hard to tell from the level of top-down statistics whether MFIs are reasonably efficient or their operating expenses include avoidable "fat". Operating costs are affected by loan size primarily, but also client location and density, transport infrastructure, salary levels, and the type of loan provided. We have seen that on average MFIs have to pay much higher relative amounts to employ loan officers in Africa than Asia; and they also face much higher transportation costs there, where the population density is 36 people per km^2 compared to 331 in South Asia. Thus for an African loan officer to service roughly the same number of clients as a South Asian loan officer, he really does need the expensive motorbike as opposed to a pedal bike to get around to client meetings (at least until new technologies reduce the need for as many loan officers, as lending through mobile phones is doing in Kenya).

A very high administration expense ratio here could therefore simply reflect the problems outlined in Morduch above, that reaching the very poorest goes hand in hand with small loan size and sometimes very high transport costs. But it could also just be reflective of a bloated administration base, of Western-style executive salaries being taken by senior executives even within a developing country-based NGO. We will consider in section 3 whether this matters in the assessment of wrongful exploitation.

Most of this chapter focuses on whether, and to what extent, the interest rates charged by MFIs to their borrowers are exploitative. Before moving there, we should also just note that it is not only the interest rate microfinance offers that may wrongfully exploit borrowers. So may the accompanying terms and conditions of the loan. There are two principal such terms and conditions. The first is the imposition of group liability on borrowers. This is the condition that loans are extended to borrowers in groups, and that if one in the group defaults on an interest payment or the capital, others in the group must make good the payment for her. Such a condition would be regarded as extraordinary in the developed world or, for that matter, in the formal sector of developing countries. In the next chapter, we shall see that the practice of group liability goes beyond what may be deemed mere wrongful exploitation and can be seen to lead to coercion. But it is still worth noting that its imposition is potentially wrongfully exploitative. Surveys of borrowers' attitudes suggest that while they sometimes see merit in group lending, in loans being extended to groups in villages who may provide support to each other, none have shown support for group liability, the guaranteeing of each other's loans.[21] This is resented, but accepted as the only way to achieve access to the loan.

[20] Rosenberg, Gonzalez, and Narain, "The New Moneylenders," 21.

[21] See, for example, Malcolm Harper, "What's Wrong with Groups?" in *What's Wrong with Microfinance?* ed. Thomas Dichter and Malcolm Harper (Rugby: Practical Action Publishing, 2007), 35–49.

The second condition that is potentially wrongfully exploitative is the enforcement of "compulsory savings," discussed earlier, the use of which makes the interest rate very much less than transparent and leads to the borrower paying a very much higher rate of interest than she may be aware of. Again, the borrower has no choice but to accept this condition as a term of her loan, and her need for credit means that she accepts it.

Before concluding that any of these terms of a microloan (an interest rate a multiple of the formal sector, group liability, compulsory savings) are exploitative or not, however, we first need a clear grasp of what exploitation actually is, and whether is is always wrong to exploit. The next section explores this.

2. What Exploitation Is

The standard dictionary definition of the word "exploit" is "use or develop for one's own ends; take advantage of (esp. a person)."[22]

In the broadest sense, exploitation is the making use of, or turning to your advantage, someone, a set of circumstances, or even another's attributes, for your own purposes. In this broadest sense, it is not prejudicial. Exploitation is always done by a person: someone exploits something or someone when he takes advantage of it or him in some way: we exploit natural resources, wind power, and our own particular skill sets and attributes (brains, beauty, sports ability, etc.). As Feinberg puts it: "To exploit something, in this most general sense, is simply to put it to one's use, not to waste it, and there are no limits on the sorts of things that can be exploited. Even in this general nonpejorative sense, the exploiter is always a person; diseases, landslides and tropical storms have never exploited anything."[23]

Exploiting something in this morally neutral sense is distinguished from merely "making use" of something by the fact that the exploiter manipulates or controls the object of exploitation in some way. A rambler who picks wild blackberries as he walks simply makes use of what is there; a horticulturist who plants blackberry bushes in his carefully enriched plot exploits the soil.

A benefit is often derived from the exploitation by the exploiter—that is usually why he exploits—but it is not strictly necessary for this broad, morally neutral account of exploitation. If the horticulturist, having harvested his blackberries, then loses money on his enterprise because the price of blackberries has collapsed that year, he has still exploited the plot, simply not ended up benefiting from it. But when it comes to exploiting people (and when exploitation is wrongful), it seems that actual derivation of a benefit is required: or, at any rate, it seems necessary that the exploiter *believes* that he

---

[22] *Little Oxford Dictionary*, 7th ed. (Oxford: Clarendon Press, 1994).

[23] Joel Feinberg, "Noncoercive Exploitation," in *Paternalism*, ed. Rolf Sartorius (Minneapolis: University of Minnesota Press, 1984), 201–235.

is deriving a benefit from his exploitation (he may, of course, be mistaken). However much one person or agency may manipulate or control another—such as advocates of "nudge" theorists who try to manipulate people into eating more healthily by making the salads more easily accessible than the chips—we do not usually regard this as exploitation unless the advocate derives or thinks he derives a personal benefit from it. The benefit usually accrues to the exploiter, but it is possible to wrongfully exploit on behalf of a third party. A set of ruthless parents who deny doting grandparents access to their child unless the grandparents put all their wealth in trust for that particular grandchild to inherit in twenty-five years, wrongfully exploit the grandparents' dependence on them for access, though they derive no personal benefit.

Attributes or circumstances of people can be exploited while remaining within the neutral sense of exploitation. We can take advantage of our own talents and skills, train our voices or athletic ability to benefit from a singing or athletic career, without doing anything wrong. We can also exploit the attributes of other people without necessarily doing anything wrong: Alex Ferguson did nothing wrong in exploiting David Beckham's speed to maximize the efficiency of the Manchester United attack.

Much exploitation, defined by taking advantage of someone or something, involving the manipulation of him or it and deriving a benefit in the process of doing so, raises no moral issues. I exploit the services of a taxi driver when I ask him to take me somewhere; he exploits me and all those like me by making his living out of people who sometimes want to shorten their journeys or avoid the rain. The term is used neutrally here because the taxi driver and I are free to reach any price for that journey, and both have options (other fares, other taxis) if we cannot reach agreement. Neither of us is a monopolist or monopsonist. Not only in this transaction do we have freedom of action and hence valid consent, but there is nothing in the background conditions or social structure in which we make our deal that either of us do, or could reasonably, object to. In the different accounts of morally wrongful exploitation that follow, all agree as to the innocence of this type of exploitation, whether because where there is such freedom of maneuver there is no unfairness or because the copious number of taxis and other potential passengers means that neither of us is vulnerable to the other.

Some forms of exploitation, then, are harmless or at least morally neutral. Other forms of it are wrong and impermissible, and others wrong but permissible, all things considered. Exploitation is wrong but permissible when the total benefits derived from allowing a wrongfully exploitative transaction to continue are thought to exceed the costs of the wrongful exploitation.

To consider whether exploitation is ever permissible in microcredit, then, we need to distinguish what makes some exploitation morally neutral and some morally wrong. We can then ask, if microcredit does indeed exploit, whether it does so wrongly; and if it does, whether it could still be permissible, taking everything into account—for example, if it really did enrich and empower its clients. We should begin, then, with clarifying what it is that makes some person-to-person exploitation morally wrong, and some not.

DISTINGUISHING WRONGFUL EXPLOITATION FROM MORALLY NEUTRAL EXPLOITATION

There are two principal lines of thought concerning the wrong in wrongful person-to-person exploitation. The first, propounded by Alan Wertheimer, centers on the idea that wrongful exploitation must take advantage of a person in some *unfair* way.[24] The second, developed by Robert Goodin and Allen Wood,[25] is that the wrongful exploitation takes advantage of a *vulnerability* in a person and that it is taking advantage of a vulnerability that is wrong. Of course, if unfairness always consisted of taking advantage of another's vulnerabilities, then the difference between this "unfair usage" account and the second, "vulnerability," account, would disappear. I shall indeed argue that Wertheimer does not produce a single common feature of unfairness other than vulnerability. He successfully dismisses other candidates, but his attempt to dismiss vulnerability itself fails. Vulnerability accounts of exploitation then have to answer whether the taking advantage of *any* vulnerability amounts to wrongful exploitation, or whether only some vulnerabilities "count," and, if so, which these are.

Those less interested in the philosophical intricacies of this exposition can cut to the chase by going directly to the start of section 3 (p. 64), which summarizes this section and section 1.

The Unfair Usage Account of Exploitation

Wertheimer defines exploitation, at its most general level, as "A exploits B when A takes unfair advantage of B."[26] But he immediately concedes the point that such a broad account means that there will "be as many competing accounts of exploitation as theories of what persons owe to each other by way of fair treatment."[27] So Wertheimer needs to narrow down where the unfairness lies: he states that this could be either in the outcome of the transaction or in the process.

With regard to the outcome, he deems a benefit necessary to A, but this alone is not enough as it covers morally innocent transactions as well as morally wrongful ones. With regard to harm to B, he concludes that it is not necessary, because exploited parties can benefit more from an exploitative transaction than exploiters do. "It is precisely because A generally stands to gain less utility than B from what might appear to be a fair transaction that A can drive what appears to be a hard bargain."[28] This is indeed so. The poorly

---

[24] Alan Wertheimer, *Exploitation* (Princeton, NJ: Princeton University Press, 1996).

[25] Robert Goodin, "Exploiting a Situation and Exploiting a Person," in *Modern Theories of Exploitation*, ed. Andrew Reeve (London: Sage, 1987), 166–200 Wood, "Exploitation."

[26] Alan Wertheimer, "Exploitation," in *The Stanford Encyclopedia of Philosophy*, ed. Edward N. Zalta, Fall 2008, http://plato.stanford.edu/archives/fall2008/entries/exploitation.

[27] The point being made by Richard Arneson in "Exploitation" in *Encyclopedia of Ethics*, ed. Lawrence C. Becker (New York: Garland, 1992), 350–352.

[28] Wertheimer, *Exploitation*, 223.

paid sweatshop worker nonetheless prefers that job to subsistence farming, and he both consents to the exploitation and has a higher marginal utility than if he did not take the job, so it is hard to say that he is harmed by it. Similarly, the microfinance borrower may indeed prefer borrowing from the MFI to borrowing from the moneylender, even if she would prefer the lower rates of the formal sector to either.

Wertheimer recognizes that distinguishing what makes a mutually beneficial transaction unfair is difficult "because there is no non-problematic account of unfair transactions."[29] It would not seem to be because the transaction is in an "incommensurable" good because it is not clear which goods are incommensurable, nor why exchanging incommensurable goods is necessarily unfair. And as we saw above, it seems not to be necessary that the distribution of the gain is unfair, that A gains more than B because "if we measure the parties' gain in terms of marginal utility from the no-transaction baseline, the exploitee often gains more than the exploiter."[30]

To locate where the unfairness of an exploitative transaction lies, Wertheimer considers what outcome of a transaction might have been achieved in a competitively benchmarked situation. The problem here is that some of the exploitation issues that worry us most come about precisely where the market has failed or simply does not exist. High microfinance rates are possible just because there is a lack of any access to capital. Wertheimer does consider what parties "ought to gain" as perhaps being a "hypothetical competitive market," but this baseline is too poorly defined to be useful. Is the hypothetical microfinance rate what commercial banks would charge if they supported a branch network in the areas in which the very poor live, or what rates commercial banks would be prepared to make very small loans at, or perhaps both? Competitive markets can be defined by quite different sets of rules; so Wertheimer's benchmark for unfairness is indeterminate.

Leaving aside the problem of defining a competitive benchmark, it is doubtful that using such a benchmark is always appropriate in the first place. As Wolff argues, it is not obvious that the arbitrary factors of any given level of supply and demand can tell us what is normatively fair as opposed to "market price-determined" fair.[31] He challenges David Miller's claim that "it is generally speaking a necessary condition of A's exploiting B that, in exchange between them, A does better and B does worse than each would under equilibrium prices."[32] All market prices do is reflect the preferences of economic agents. There simply is nothing normative about that. Preferences are just preferences, and there is no reason to suppose that the market-clearing price they set is fair in any morally meaningful sense. If this is so, Wertheimer's attempts to use a competitive market equilibrium

---

[29] Wertheimer, "Exploitation."

[30] Wertheimer, "Exploitation."

[31] Jonathan Wolff, "The Ethics of Competition," in *The Legal and Moral Aspects of International Trade*, ed. Geraint Parry, Asif Quershi, and Hillel Steiner (London: Routledge, 1998), 82–96.

[32] David Miller, "Exploitation in the Market," in Reeve, *Modern Theories of Exploitation*, 162.

benchmark to measure exploitation cannot work. We are back to something else being required to tell us when a transaction is "fair," or not.

It could be that unfairness resides in taking advantage of a vulnerability of B's, as the "vulnerability" accounts of exploitation suggest, but Wertheimer rejects the idea. According to him, it is not enough that B is vulnerable to A, because we can imagine examples where B is vulnerable to A but is not treated unfairly. An example would be B falling ill and finding a doctor. The doctor could charge B an extortionate amount for a life-saving operation, but instead just charges the going rate. B is vulnerable to doctor A, but A does not act unfairly. This only demonstrates, however, that vulnerability is not sufficient for exploitation, not that it is not necessary for it. It could be necessary, with further features being required for sufficiency.

Wertheimer does also consider if the unfairness in the transaction could be in its process, that is, there is some defect in the process by which an exploitative transaction comes about. The major candidate for a defect in the process is that it is less than fully consensual on B's part: B is perhaps coerced or manipulated or defrauded in some way. But Wertheimer does not permit himself this route either, stating: "By contrast with cases of coercion and fraud, there are at least some cases of alleged exploitation in which *B*'s consent is not defective in either of these ways. In many cases of alleged exploitation, *A* gets *B* to agree to a mutually advantageous transaction to which *B* would not have agreed under better or perhaps more just background conditions, where *A* played no direct casual role in creating those circumstances, where *A* has no special obligation to repair those conditions, and where B is fully informed as to the consequences of various choices. Although B might prefer to have a different range of options available to him, she can make a perfectly rational choice amongst the various options."[33] Wertheimer leaves us hanging, then, as to where the unfairness lies. Other accounts site it in the taking advantage of a vulnerability.

Vulnerability Accounts of Exploitation

Robert Goodin's account of exploitation was the first to locate the moral wrongness of exploitation in the taking advantage of vulnerability. He argues:

> Using people is . . . a necessary condition of exploiting them. But this is not a sufficient condition. What more is required in order to make it sufficient is not the presence of harm, or the absence of consent, or the presence of coercion, or the absence of reciprocity, or some specification of the ways in which people are being used. . . . The analysis of exploitation thus reduces to an analysis of why, and in what respect, it is wrong (unfair, exploitative) to use certain attributes of people and their situations in certain ways.[34]

---

[33] Wertheimer, "Exploitation."

[34] Goodin, "Exploiting a Situation," 180–181.

Force or coercion is not enough to establish wrongful exploitation because, although compelling in economic circumstances, they operate weakly elsewhere. "When exploiting friends or lovers, we are not forcing them to do anything whatsoever."[35] The disparity of value, the notion of "unequal exchange" is also strong in the economic sphere, but not outside it (and is also subject to all the problems discussed above in any event). Manipulation is also dismissed, because although deception, as an element of manipulation, is often present in exploitation, this need not be so—as Goodin observes, OPEC tried to deceive nobody when openly using their near oligopoly on the supply of oil to achieve a high price for it in the 1970s.

Morally neutral exploitation, for Goodin, is the taking advantage of something or some circumstance distinguished from merely making use of by taking advantage of it in unusual circumstances or in a very particular way. Exploiting a person is a special case of exploiting a situation, and occurs where one person is in a strong position of power relative to another, making the exploitee vulnerable to the exploiter. It is that power/vulnerability relationship that defines what counts as exploitation of a person, and it is exactly the same feature that makes all person-to-person exploitation morally wrongful for Goodin, because it breaches what he regards as the moral norm of a duty to protect the vulnerable. He argues that what marks out one person's wrongfully exploiting another (as opposed to merely making use of him) is the vulnerability of one to the other: and he holds that it is always morally wrong to take advantage of that.

So for Goodin, what makes exploitation wrongful, when it is, is just the same as why it is wrongful. He notes: "Occasions for exploitation arise when one party is in an especially strong position vis-à-vis another. These same circumstances impose upon the stronger party a heavy moral duty to protect the weaker . . . just as the analysis of the notion of adultery is parasitic upon an analysis of the duty of marital fidelity, so too is the analysis of exploitation parasitic upon an analysis of this duty to protect the vulnerable."[36]

Goodin argues, then, that exploiting people's vulnerabilities is wrong because it breaks what he regards as the moral norm to protect the vulnerable, including from ourselves. It is a two-part duty: a negative duty not to press your advantage against those vulnerable to you, and a positive duty to take measures to assist those who are vulnerable to you. A failure to meet the second, positive duty is deemed a failure in one's obligations, but falls short of exploitation. For that, breaching both positive and negative duties to protect those vulnerable to oneself is required.

Goodin would allow that there may be countervailing considerations that would mean that while taking advantage of another's vulnerability for one's own gain remains, of itself, a wrong, it would not always be wrong to do. It might even be desirable if it prevented a greater evil occurring, such as when a spy exploits enemy officers' susceptibility to her charms to garner secrets needed to save lives and win a (just) war. But even

[35] Goodin, "Exploiting a Situation," 174.

[36] Goodin, "Exploiting a Situation," 167.

outside of such exceptions, establishing a positive duty on the strong to help or protect those vulnerable to them, as opposed to the negative duty not to harm, is problematic. If the vulnerability of the weak to the strong were all that mattered, a patient awaiting a life-saving kidney transplant operation would have the right to demand a kidney from the rare match, whoever that match was, for the patient is certainly vulnerable to the few that possess it.

Allen Wood argues that rooting an account of wrongful exploitation in a duty of the strong to the weak, or a duty to help, is difficult when the extent of positive duties of the strong to the weak is controversial. He adds, however, that it is also not necessary for a vulnerability account of wrongful exploitation to do so. We should root a vulnerability account of what is wrong with exploitation (when it is wrong) elsewhere: in cases where taking advantage of a vulnerability also degrades. For Wood, "Proper respect for others is violated when we treat their vulnerabilities as opportunities to advance our own interests or projects. It is degrading to have your weaknesses taken advantage of, and dishonourable to use the weaknesses of others for your ends."[37] Wood, then, needs to show us what vulnerabilities "count," if only some do, and what amounts to "degradation" if that is a critical distinguishing factor.

Unfortunately, Wood leaves degradation undefined, but we need to know more of what it is for one party to degrade another if it is to be a yardstick by which we can measure whether or not microcredit wrongfully exploits. Is it feeling degraded, or being degraded, that matters?

There are several relationships at play. A can treat B in a degrading manner; B may or may not feel degraded: and whether he does or not, B may or may not actually be degraded. What we are interested in is the last aspect: but this highlights that the principle that we must respect people and not degrade them does not of itself tell us what actions count as degradation. Consider the degradation relationships that run like poison through the veins of Emily Brontë's *Wuthering Heights*: Hindley degrades Heathcliff by treating him as a servant rather than a family member; Catherine disastrously believes that as a result marrying Heathcliff would degrade her; Heathcliff takes his revenge by degrading Hareton, Hindley's son through depriving him of education, and so on. Some of these characters feel degraded when the reader might say that in fact they are not: others become actually degraded through their actions. Feeling degraded will reflect a person's psychological makeup and culture, as well as the society and time in which he or she lives.

Wood argues that exploitation is wrongful when it takes advantage of a vulnerability in an agent in a way that degrades that agent. So chess players do not suffer wrongful exploitation, even though they take advantage of each other's vulnerabilities, because they do not degrade each other. But, it is not clear that this is the factor that determines

---

[37] Wood, "Exploitation," 15.

when it is wrong to take advantage of a vulnerability. Is the sweatshop worker *degraded* by working in a sweatshop? It would seem possible to take advantage of a vulnerability without degrading, as when many people take up an offer that takes advantage of a commonly shared vulnerability, with the result that there is no obvious loss of relative social status between them. When a borrower borrows at an equivalent annual rate of 195% to set up some small business,[38] there will be many who feel that she must be wrongfully exploited, but without any suggestion that she is *degraded* by taking out the loan, setting up the business, and attempting to repay.

It seems that degradation is not quite what we are looking for in distinguishing wrongful exploitation of a vulnerability from simply exploiting a vulnerability as a chess player might do. Rather, I suggest that taking advantage of another's vulnerability amounts to wrongful exploitation when it takes advantage of a low degree of autonomy on the part of the exploitee. Taking advantage of a person's vanity or greed or characteristics that rational, autonomous agents can control does not count as wrongful exploitation. But taking advantage of vulnerabilities that result from a low level of autonomy, is a distinguishing characteristic of wrongful exploitation.

This is so because our agency is central to our concept of ourselves as moral beings. When advantage is taken of some reduced element of our autonomy, it offends against the idea that we are each of equal moral worth. Taking advantage of a vulnerability that comes from an impaired autonomy actively fails to treat others as equals. What makes us moral beings is our ability to use our rationality to make choices, to plan our lives, to exercise our autonomy for better or for worse, rather than, for example, always being driven by instinct. It can be debated whether our equal moral worth imposes a duty to promote the autonomy of others or a negative duty to refrain from reducing it in others, but the argument here is for a much weaker duty: to refrain from the taking advantage of a vulnerability in another when that vulnerability stems from a low degree of autonomy.

Using autonomy rather than degradation can also remove the need to try to distinguish vulnerabilities that count via an imbalance of power. The needs and desires that "count" as vulnerabilities the taking advantage of which would constitute wrongful exploitation, are those that are necessary for the exercise of my autonomy. Hence a ticket scalper does not wrongfully exploit me because of the vulnerability I have to him, created by the strength of my desire to watch the Wimbledon final: the vulnerability is not a fundamental one that threatens my rational agency. But any advantage taken that is based on a deception—such as misleading a borrower as to the true rate of interest payable—is always wrongful, because carrying out a deception always threatens an agent's exercise of his rational agency.

We began by searching for the distinguishing factor that made taking advantage of vulnerability morally wrongful rather than innocent. I argue that the vulnerabilities that

---

[38] See Roodman, "Does Compartamos Charge 195%?."

"count" are those that arise from a low degree of autonomy. Of course, the degree of the wrongful exploitation will vary with how low the level of the autonomy is. Being exploited is all or nothing—one is exploited or one is not—but the degree of wrongfulness is less determinate. There can be minor cases of wrongful exploitation as well as much more major.

It may be asked how wrongful exploitation could be explained in terms of autonomy when A making B an offer only increases B's options, which will typically be thought to increase her autonomy, assuming here that B is in fact in a position to make use of the offered option. But we can see that A can indeed make B an offer and still exploit her, where the offer itself is not the cause of B's low degree of autonomy, and where although it increases B's options, it does not raise B's autonomy to a level where she has real choice to exercise. In the case of developing country sweatshop workers, autonomy is low because of the workers' lack of external freedom, their lack of choices of employment. The offer of sweatshop work that B now receives does not make that worse, but neither does it sufficiently improve her situation to the extent that she is not still exploited when she accepts the offer.

A person's level of autonomy can be considered at either a local or global level. At a local level, it is this agent's ability to participate freely and rationally in this particular transaction: does she understand the terms offered, are there local competitors she could take this service from instead? At a macro or global level, the level of her autonomy will vary according to the circumstances into which she is born. To be fully autonomous, an agent needs not just freedom from constraints, but opportunities to choose from: genuine alternative ways to earn an income, or find a partner, or gain an education. Clearly, many born into poverty may have all the rationality required to be autonomous, but lack the positive liberties with which to make autonomous choice.

This account looks at the details of microcredit at the micro level, at the level of the details of the interaction between the microfinance institution (MFI) and microcredit borrower. It by no means precludes an account of structural, macro-level exploitation also being true, but the focus here is this: is the borrower vulnerable to the MFI; does that vulnerability arise from a low degree of autonomy on the part of the borrower; and does the MFI take advantage of that vulnerability in its offer of credit, thereby wrongfully exploiting the borrower?

To reiterate the start of this chapter, there are several ways in which MFIs might be thought to exploit their borrowers: by taking advantage of borrowers' vulnerability to them to charge high interest rates and to impose onerous terms and conditions when making the loan, notably "compulsory savings," inflexible loan repayment terms, and group liability. It is the borrower's exclusion from formal financial services that makes her vulnerable to the MFI, for it will often be her only source of capital other than a moneylender. This enables the MFI to impose the loan terms it chooses as a cost of getting the loan, and to charge rates up to, or indeed beyond, those of the moneylender. The fact that MFIs are, in practice, well positioned to wrongfully exploit their borrowers does not mean, of course, that they do. If they do not take advantage of the borrower's vulnerability by charging rates much in excess of those in the formal sector, then they do not exploit. We can now bring this theoretical section together with the practices described in the first section to determine if microcredit does, in general, wrongfully exploit its borrowers.

3. So Is Microcredit Wrongfully Exploitative?

We saw in section 2 that although there are different accounts of exploitation, they share some common ground. One party *wrongfully* exploits another when he (*a*) takes advantage of and manipulates the other in some way; (*b*) either derives (or believes that he derives) a benefit from the interaction or directs where that benefit should go; (*c*) is in a position of relative power in the particular circumstances of the interchange and, crucially, (*d*) takes advantage in some *unfair* way.

Accounts then diverged as to what constituted unfairness, Wertheimer's by trying to compare the terms of the interaction to a hypothetical competitive benchmark, "vulnerability" accounts by siting the unfairness in the taking advantage of a vulnerability of one party to the other. It was suggested that Wertheimer's argument that vulnerability was not sufficient for wrongful exploitation did not demonstrate that it was not necessary. In the absence of a hypothetical competitive market that could determine "fair" terms of exchange, the unfairness in wrongful exploitation does indeed lie in the taking advantage of a vulnerability, whichever further specifications are required for sufficiency.

Vulnerability accounts then break down with regard to what further conditions are required for wrongful exploitation. It can be held that the taking advantage of *any* vulnerability in another party to oneself is wrongful exploitation (Goodin); or that wrongful exploitation occurs when the taking advantage of a vulnerability degrades the exploitee (Wood); or that it is the taking advantage of vulnerabilities that stem from a low degree of local or global autonomy that marks some exploitation as wrongful (my own account). Accounts can also be split another way, into those that look for the fairness or unfairness at a micro or macro level,[39] that is, those that include issues of structural justice in their account of fairness (macro accounts) and those that do not (micro accounts).

[39] See, for example, Jeremy Snyder, "Exploitation and Sweatshop Labor: Perspectives and Issues," *Business Ethics Quarterly* 20, no. 2 (2010): 187–213. I do not discuss here what Snyder categorizes as "mere use" accounts. These are accounts of exploitation as commoditization: arguments that certain goods are of a nature that makes their trade morally repugnant or even incoherent, as Sandel argues of friendship. I prefer to call these arguments commoditization debates, but the word "exploitation" is sometimes used to cover both these and "taking advantage of" accounts. To the extent that these commoditization debates are considered exploitation, this account does not attempt to cover them at all: my account might indeed also find that a father selling a kidney to pay for his son's education was wrongfully exploited, but it would be for a coincident reason—that his low level of global autonomy gave him no other way of raising the money—rather than because it was an intrinsic wrong to make use of his body in this way.

We saw in section 1 the terms and conditions of loans MFIs in fact charge and impose, and the major reasons why interest rates are as absolutely high as they are in some places. To sum up the position of most MFIs and the rates they charge: typically, the average rate an MFI charges lies between rates in the formal banking sector and those of moneylenders, but they are multiples of the formal rates, not just an additional margin on top of them. Rates are at their lowest in Asia, where high population densities and a large pool of educated from which to draw loan officers keep operating costs down. Interest rates as stated by MIX Market, the best we have available, understate what is truly charged, possibly by a considerable degree. The average rates themselves hide a dispersion where the highest rates are very high indeed and are being paid by the poorest clients. The main driver of these high rates, however, is not profit, but the cost of transacting in very small units—essentially because it costs as much to administer and monitor a $50 loan as it does a $500 loan.

In *some* cases, the profit motive will be part of what is driving high interest rates, and in *some* cases it may be excessive salary and administration costs: but in many cases, it will also be true that the high interest rates that are charged do simply reflect the very high relative cost of making small loans.

The fact that the main drivers of high interest rates in microfinance are the small loan size and high personnel costs, rather than profit, does not of course answer the question as to whether or not these rates are exploitative or abusive. It is not incoherent to think that, for much of the industry, the only rates at which microfinance can be offered (at least sustainably) are in fact exploitative. This could be so, and such exploitation could conceivably also be justified—if microfinance did raise its borrowers from poverty or if there were another convincing reason for thinking that an exploitative interaction might still be better for the exploitee than no interaction at all.

So on the basis of these theoretical accounts of exploitation, and microfinance's actual practices, does microfinance wrongfully exploit its borrowers?

Wertheimer's account of exploitation is the classic micro fairness account: appeals to background justice or macro reasons why one party may be disadvantaged relative to the transacting partner are strictly circumscribed. What is fair is simply what a hypothetical fair market would produce. Taking advantage of a structural injustice the stronger party had done nothing to create would not count as exploitative. In the case of microfinance, because it is very unclear what a hypothetical competitive market price would be, it is not obvious whether Wertheimer would deem microfinance wrongfully exploitative or not. The global constraints on the borrower would be treated as irrelevant. But suppose that a "fair" rate *were* decided upon, and that microfinance rates typically exceed it. In that event, Wertheimer then discriminates between cases where the exploitation is harmful and those where it is not, that is, where both parties benefit from the interaction (however unequally)—cases of what he calls mutually beneficial exploitation.

If microfinance is considered to be beneficial to the borrower, it would count as mutually beneficial exploitation for Wertheimer and thus not be subject to condemnation or outside interference.[40] To the extent, though, that the microfinance borrower does *not* benefit from the MFI's loan or wrongly believes she will benefit because she is misled as to the true rate of interest she will pay and therefore the margin on her enterprise she must achieve to pay it, Wertheimer's account would find microfinance wrongfully exploitative.

Each of the "vulnerability" accounts of exploitation I explored in section 2 would also find microfinance, as practiced, wrongfully exploitative, even if the reason given would be grounded slightly differently. All would see MFIs as taking advantage of the borrower's vulnerability that has been created by her exclusion from formal financial services. Goodin would presumably argue that it is wrong to take advantage of that vulnerability because there is a duty on all of us to protect the interests of those who are vulnerable to us: and the MFI fails to do that. Wood would (also presumably) find microfinance wrongfully exploitative because he holds that exploitation is wrongful when it degrades the exploitee, and as it is always degrading to have one's weaknesses taken advantage of, which microfinance certainly does, then it must wrongfully exploit.

My own account holds that exploitation is wrongful when it takes advantage of a vulnerability arising from a low level of autonomy. In microfinance, the borrower is vulnerable to the microcredit lender because of her lack of choice. If she is lucky, she may have a choice between two equally high-charging microcredit firms, but she has no access to the lower rates in the formal sector. Her choice is also constrained in another way: living in rural poverty, she may have no options for raising herself from poverty other than borrowing capital to start a microenterprise. There may simply be no employment sector from which she can seek work. She is more than capable of autonomous choice from the point of view of meeting the minimum thresholds of rationality and self-consciousness, but her global, external autonomy is constrained by a lack of options resulting from the poverty into which she is born. When that borrower's vulnerability, arising from her exclusion from formal financial services limiting her options, is taken advantage of to charge her a multiple of the rates available in the formal sector (rates that can be in the hundreds of per cent in Latin America and Africa, from for profits and not for profit MFIs alike), she is wrongfully exploited.

This account of exploitation can operate at either the micro or macro level, as the concept of a low degree of autonomy can operate at either level. Daniel Butt argues for an account of exploitation that focuses solely on the macro: of microfinance taking advantage of structural injustice.[41] He argues that exploitation is wrongful when it takes advantage of victims of injustice, regardless of whether there is a duty to protect the interests of

[40] To use Wertheimer's classic example, MFIs would be like snow shovel sellers who charge twice the usual rate for their shovels in a snowstorm, but from whom the stuck driver buys a shovel anyway because the benefit of releasing his car is still deemed by him worth the excessive price; and his consent to pay it, while constrained by lack of choice in the circumstances of the storm, is still rational and genuine.

[41] Daniel Butt, "Microfinance, Non-ideal Theory, and Global Distributive Justice," in *Microfinance, Rights and Global Justice*, ed. Tom Sorrell and Luis Cabrera, Cambridge University Press, 2015, 63–83.

those who are vulnerable to us or whether or not that injustice is held to degrade them. For Butt, it is wrong to take advantage of a victim of injustice for the reason that moral agents have a duty to uphold and not undermine justice through their actions. Microfinance borrowers are the victims of the injustice of being excluded from formal financial services, so MFIs, when they take advantage of that vulnerability to charge high rates, not only exploit the poor, but exploit the wronged.

Despite their nuances, then, all these "vulnerability" and "macro" accounts of exploitation in practice would or do find microfinance wrongfully exploitative. One important line of objection not-for-profit MFIs might make in response to this is that they do not exploit borrowers where their aims are wholly altruistic, for they do not derive a benefit from the transaction. Clearly, commercialized, for-profit MFIs extract a benefit in the form of their profit, so this particular line of defense is not open to them. But what of not-for-profit MFIs?

There are various ways in which even not-for-profit MFIs can receive a benefit from the microfinance transaction. The first possibility of a benefit is through the salaries and employment created for its staff. A second might be the prestige and respect senior executives believe they enjoy among their social circle and peers from running an apparently altruistic, poverty-relieving charity. A third might be if participating in the extensive, and expensive, conference circuit of the microfinance sector were deemed a benefit. But the main issue is around employment and salaries. The not-for-profit MFI cannot make an offer of microfinance to borrowers if it has no staff. On the other hand, if it were giving local staff salaries and benefits that compared well with what they might earn elsewhere, and the head office staff are awarding themselves higher salaries and pension benefits on the basis of the number and geographical spread of the people in their employ, all paid for by the interest rate charged to the borrower, then we might be tempted to think that the MFI's employees are deriving at least *some* benefit from the interaction. Benefit can be derived from the terms and conditions of employment, especially where these go beyond what a similarly skilled employee might earn elsewhere, as well as through profits.

The not-for-profit MFI exists, of course, to fulfill a charitable purpose. It is the employees who are deriving the benefit here, rather than the MFI as an institution. But note that the MFI is directing the benefit derived from the borrowers to its employees, and just as with our parents exploiting grandparents' affection to benefit their child, that can be just as wrongfully exploitative as benefiting directly. The MFI's directors have a duty to ensure that they are fulfilling the trust deed, and not overseeing mission creep whereby the de facto focus of directors and staff has become using the interest payments received for the expansion and enhancement of numbers and terms for staff, rather than, for example, paying the bare minimum necessary and reducing the interest rate charged.

A difficulty with the not-for-profit MFI is that the source of its benefit, in terms of salary and employment, shifts over the life cycle of the MFI if or when it grows. When the not-for-profit MFI starts up, its funding is usually provided by governments or aid agencies, private donation, and founder capital. Before it starts charging interest to vulnerable borrowers, the bulk of the benefit of employment and salary is paid for by its donors/funders. In this start-up phase, the not-for-profit MFI is similar to a doctor working for the National Health Service in Britain. The *ultimate* point of interaction of both is with the vulnerable—poor borrowers, the sick—but at the point of service provision, all that is being exploited by the doctor or MFI employee is the desire of the organization to provide a service to potentially vulnerable people. This is the innocent, neutral use of exploitation discussed earlier. If in fact the doctor and MFI are benefiting from excessive salaries at this stage, the party being exploited is the government/taxpayer or the MFI's donors, rather than the sick and borrowers.

However, the position of the start-up not-for-profit MFI begins to change from the moment the not-for-profit MFI starts charging interest to its vulnerable borrowers. At that point, *some* part (initially, a tiny part) of the benefit in employment derived from the offer of credit comes from the vulnerable people served. When the initial, external, source of funding has been used up, even the not-for-profit MFI becomes wrongfully exploitative when it takes advantage of borrowers' vulnerability to charge rates that are multiples of the formal sector.

The MFI's position contrasts to that of the UK government when in 1861 Gladstone, as chancellor, set up the Post Office Savings Bank to provide basic savings facilities to the then financially excluded working-class poor of the United Kingdom. At a time when fifteen counties and a number of large towns had no savings banks and those that did exist were not open hours when the working classes could visit them,[42] Gladstone utilized the country's two to three thousand post offices to reach the working classes with a simple savings account. The point is that the government paid the extra sums for these savings accounts to be provided to the working classes, not the savers themselves. If there was any "fat" in the subsequent provision of these services, it was the government that was exploited, not the working class.

A troubling way in which an MFI might also be thought to exploit borrowers is where it uses the profits generated in one country to fund expansion in another. When an MFI becomes sustainable in an area, that does not mean that it has hit a point of perpetual break-even; it means that it has now reached a degree of scale where its operations are no longer loss-making but have turned profitable. It then has the option of reducing its interest rates to stay at break-even as further scale in its now operationally efficient area is added, or letting profits build up to fund expansion elsewhere. At this point, through its use of profits generated in Country A to fund expansion in Country B, the MFI is exploiting Country A borrowers to benefit Country B borrowers. Or it might be argued that the MFI is allowing itself to be the vehicle through which Country B borrowers exploit Country A borrowers. At any rate, the MFI cannot claim that it is not exploiting Country A borrowers because it derives no benefit from them. It does. The benefit may

[42] Hansard HC Debate, February 8, 1861, vol. 161, cols. 262–267.

be for third parties (Country B), but that is not of relevance to Country A borrowers unless they have explicitly signed up to help Country B themselves.

With regard to exploitation, then, the not-for-profit MFI is to some extent in the same boat as the commercial MFI. A benefit to both MFIs is derived from the offer of microfinance, and although the assumption will be that that is going to be greater for the commercial MFI than the not-for-profit, it need not necessarily be, if the commercial MFI is especially efficient in its operations and takes only a small profit, and the not-for-profit carries an especially fat expense base.[43]

With regard to the terms and conditions of loans, we saw that as well as very high effective interest rates, the imposition of group liability and compulsory savings had the potential to be wrongfully exploitative. All accounts would find that indeed they are.

The imposition of group liability wrongfully exploits because the MFI takes advantage of the borrower's vulnerability, her need for credit and lack of alternatives in terms of either price or terms and conditions, to impose this unwanted condition, the benefit to the MFI being of course the greater ease of collection and security of repayment it now has.

Compulsory savings exploit the same vulnerabilities and in addition wrongfully exploit because the effects compulsory savings have on the effective interest rate paid by the borrower are not spelled out to her, and working them out without some financial literacy training and a calculator is far from easy. The MFI benefits of course through achieving a higher effective interest rate on the loan than the declared "flat" rate. Neither group liability nor compulsory savings are of course practiced in the formal sector.

To conclude this section, then, all "vulnerability" and "macro" accounts of exploitation, and even arguably the "unfair usage" account (once it is acknowledged that microfinance is not mutually beneficial exploitation as overall it does not appear to benefit borrowers), would seem to find microfinance wrongfully exploitative. The fact that many MFIs are not for profit, and are driven by genuine altruistic concern, is not a defense to this where they have derived a benefit from it.

Does this mean, in practice, it is then almost impossible to offer microfinance ethically? If existing cost structures and profitability/sustainability requirements are taken as given, the answer is probably yes. However, the fact that a practice is, in itself, unethical, does not *necessarily* mean that it should not be permitted to continue. It does not follow from a transaction being wrongfully exploitative that it should automatically be restricted or banned: other issues may be at play that outweigh the wrong.

---

[43] It may be worth reminding ourselves that the sums behind this discussion of benefit are now very large indeed. Phil Mader has taken the portfolio yield declared by MFIs to MIX Market and applied it to the total size of the loan book of those MFIs to calculate the total amount of interest paid by MFI borrowers to MFIs in 2012. This came to $21.6 billion. That, of course, is not a profit figure, but it is an indication of the annual net transfer from borrowers, some living on a few dollars a day, to their MFIs. (See Mader's blog "Financialising Poverty," April 22, 2014, on the *Month of Microfinance* website, available at www.monthofmicrofinance.org/engage/blog/financialising-poverty.

If microfinance enriched and empowered, it should not necessarily be restricted just because it also exploits. These would be substantial goods possibly deemed well worth the price. The problem for microfinance is that, overall, it does not achieve these things. And most problematically, it does possibly help some, but while making life worse for others (see chapter 6).

In chapter 9 I shall consider what a nonexploitative interest rate would be, when considering how (if at all) microfinance can be practiced ethically. But it was noted above that high and opaque interest rates are only one form of exploitation in microfinance; the imposition of group liability could be equally important. We should not forget that all of those in the borrowing group are in poverty. When a fellow borrower gets into repayment difficulties, the sacrifice required of other members of her group to cover for her may be high, and strongly resented. Where this is so, imposing group liability can go beyond wrongful exploitation and lead to coercion. It is to this we now turn.

Client J: A client said that: "once at the time of weekly repayment, there was a death in the neighbour's house who was also a member and the collections agents told the bereaved family that unless she paid the last two overdue instalments, they would not allow the body to be lifted or rites to be performed."

Client I: A client remarked that in the case of defaulting members, if the defaulter did not repay the loan over dues, the group leaders and MFI centre leader simply took over the defaulter's assets into their possession and then, they repaid the loan amount by liquidating it.

Client E's Husband: Some collection agents were really rude—after my wife committed suicide. They came and said: "If you cannot find means to repay, then you should send out your two beautiful daughters and get them to earn money by other means (prostitution . . .) and then repay to us." One of them even said, "If you cannot do that, send them to me and I will use them and pay off your instalments. They are very beautiful and would be able to earn a lot." I wept as I heard this.[1]

4 From Solidarity to Coercion

THE DYNAMICS OF GROUP LIABILITY

I HAVE ARGUED in chapter 2 that microfinance often wrongfully exploits its borrowers and, overall, cannot offset that exploitation with the claim that it is mutually beneficial exploitation and raises borrowers from their poverty even while exploiting them. This chapter examines whether the ethical status of microfinance's practices is worse than that and goes beyond exploiting borrowers by operating as a coercive force as well. I shall argue that coercion does indeed operate in the practice of microcredit and that, ironically, the main mechanism by which it does so is through the structure originally introduced with the intent of enhancing solidarity between borrowers, the group-lending and liability model.

This chapter proceeds by laying out what might be thought to be coercive practices in microfinance and then steps back to be clear as to what should count as coercion and when it can be justified. That theory is then applied to the apparent coercion found in microfinance, and it will be seen that some—but *only* some—of those instances are justified. Most are not, and some are especially ethically complex, for it is not just MFIs, their loan officers, and agents who coerce, but borrowers themselves who can be very effective

[1] Quotes taken from *Candid Unheard Voice of Indian Microfinance: What Is Coercion in Repayment; a Client Perspective from Indian Micro-Finance*, a blogsite by Ramesh S. Arunachalam, a rural finance practitioner, November 12, 2010, stored on http://microfinance-in-india.blogspot.co.uk.

at coercing their fellow borrowers. Where they are, it is then a further question as to how far the MFI is complicit in their coercion of others. The chapter concludes by examining where the moral responsibility for coercion lies or should be split when a borrower exercises unjustified coercion over another borrower, having herself first been (sometimes justifiably) coerced by the MFI. I also argue that the simplest way to eliminate unjustified coercion in microfinance would be to abandon the group liability model.

1. Coercion in Microfinance

As explained in chapter 1, although the use of individual lending is growing, most microcredit is delivered through group-lending, where borrowers form into groups to receive and repay loans and, with group liability, where each borrower commits to repay the missed interest and capital repayments of any one borrower in her group who defaults on her loan. This has its roots in how microfinance groups were first set up by NGOs such as BRAC and Grameen, with the borrowers' groups intended to be mutually supportive, helping each other out in difficult times and indeed potentially coming together to be a force for positive change for women's role in society. It was through the idea of lending in groups, which could form the basis for education, training, and mutual exchange of views, as well as providing an efficient mechanism for loan distribution, that empowerment was supposed to be achieved.

Originally, group-*lending* was not synonymous with group *liability*. Groups could be a useful form of credit distribution without one member of a group having to be liable for another. But as microfinance grew, the two did indeed become synonymous. Very high repayment rates were a key driver for microfinance's expansion, because they spoke to the speed with which an MFI could achieve sustainability, and to donors that, if donations could be recycled many times over as loans, giving to an MFI to on-lend, really was the gift that would keep on giving. Group liability was perceived as key to high repayment rates.

The economic theory behind this was that with uncollateralized loans, borrowers might lack incentives to repay their loans. Lenders also lacked information on which borrowers were most *likely* to repay loans: it was not as if microfinance borrowers came with long credit histories. Group liability offered a solution to both issues. Distant MFIs might not know which borrowers were the best credit risks, but a woman's neighbors possibly did, so having women choose and be liable for their own lending groups circumvented this problem of "information asymmetry." Making them liable for each other's loans also meant that social and peer pressure, types of pressure an MFI might find hard to exert itself, would now be much more likely to be exerted by the borrowing groups themselves.

But, of course, once members of the lending group became liable for each other's interest and capital payments, the lending group itself became the first place for an MFI's loan officer to seek repayment from, rather than the individual borrower. Chasing down individuals behind on payments who might skip repayment meetings, refuse to answer if at home, and generally seek to avoid the loan officer if possible would be extremely time-consuming and not necessarily productive. Being able to exert pressure for repayment on a group, to find whoever had the funds to make a covering payment on any given week, with the group ready gathered for the purpose of repayment and fresh lending, was both far more efficient and far more likely to achieve success.

The evolution of group liability alongside group-lending also profoundly changed the relationship between MFI and borrowers. If the members of the lending group become responsible for individual borrowers' repayments, having to either persuade a defaulting borrower to pay or cover the sum themselves, then to a certain extent the members become part-time loan collection officers for the MFI. Given their own poverty and lack of ability to absorb any extra costs themselves, it would be no surprise if lending groups' own loan collection practices were more severe than those of the MFI.

MFI practices of debt collection are seldom discussed—it would be a rare MFI that boasted in its marketing materials of what coercion goes into achieving a 97% repayment rate!—but do emerge when periodic large-scale repayment crises hit. A survey of 130 borrowers in the Krishna district of Andhra Pradesh, conducted after the repayment crisis there in 2006, found that allegedly coercive collection practices led borrowers to "abscond," migrate out of the village or even commit suicide.[2] The principal reasons for flight or even suicide given to the survey were, in order of importance: (1) joint liability, (2) compulsory attendance at meetings, (3) fines, and (4) keeping all members waiting until repayments are made.

Crisis in Andhra Pradesh re-emerged in 2010,[3] where the extension of microcredit had exploded from 40 billion rupees to eight million borrowers in 2007 to 225 billion rupees to twenty-five million borrowers in 2010. The rush to lend led to a loss of credit discipline from lenders and clients talking on multiple loans and becoming overindebted. Fresh reports of suicides among those unable to service their debt prompted Andhra Pradesh's government to pass an emergency ordinance to protect borrowers from 'harassment' by MFI loan officers and agents. This latest crisis in Indian microfinance prompted one rural practitioner, Ramesh Arunachalam, to begin blogging on what clients were reporting to him in Andhra Pradesh, Tamil Nadu, Karnataka, Orissa, and West Bengal. Arunachalam

---

[2] Prabhu Ghate, "Learning from the Andhra Pradesh Crisis," in Dichter and Harper, *What's Wrong with Microfinance?* 169. It has to be noted, though, that while suicides certainly occurred, there is no concrete evidence that suicides among microfinance borrowers were any higher than the 14 per 100,000 in the population as a whole.

[3] See Abhijit Banerjee, Pranab Bardhanm, Esther Duflo, Erica Field, Dean Karlan, Asim Khwaja, Dilip Mookherjee, Rohini Pande, and Raghuram Rajan, "Help Microfinance, Don't Kill It," *Indian Express*, November 26, 2010, online at http://www.indianexpress.com/story-print/716105, or "Andhra Pradesh 2010: Global Implications of the Crisis in Indian Microfinance," CGAP Focus Note 67, Washington, DC, 2010.

reported the following strategies as being used by some (not all) MFIs to achieve loan repayment when clients were struggling:

> Strategy # 1—Life/Work Obstruction: Field workers, agents, centre leaders and/or group leaders may hinder and obstruct the normal life and work of clients and/or their families and thereby, force them to repay, using several means (borrowing from moneylenders, take over assets etc) that may not necessarily be in the clients' interest and one which could cause undue hardship to them.
>
> Strategy # 2—Threats: Collection agents/field workers could threaten the clients that they would resort to violence and/or physical abuse if money is not repaid; they may also carry the threat out, if money is not forthcoming from clients.
>
> Strategy # 3—Verbal Abuse: Field workers/agents may (verbally) insult, abuse and/or intimidate the borrowers and their family members and get the repayment.
>
> Strategy # 4—Following the Client and Pestering: Field workers/agents could continually follow the borrowers and their family members from place to place and pester them for repayment and keep on embarrassing them, until the money is paid.
>
> Strategy # 5—Repossession and Sale of Property: Sometimes, the centre leaders and/or group leaders/other members may even take over property owned or used by clients and sell that and take the repayment.
>
> Strategy # 6—Satyagraha Outside Client's House/Place of Work: Field workers/collection agents could sit outside the house or places of work (like fields/shops) for hours and hours and keep on harassing for payment and leave only after they get it.
>
> Strategy # 7—Embarrassment Strategy: Field workers/collection agents may sometimes even talk to business customers and/or guests of the clients and embarrass clients and thereby get them to repay.
>
> Strategy # 8—Physically Take Over Assets/Documentation as Collateral: The centre leaders, group leaders and/or members could forcibly remove assets/documents of the borrower (like ration card etc.,) and not return it until repayment is made by the client
>
> Strategy # 9—Physical Intimidation: Field workers/collection agents may physically intimidate the clients and get local toughs to rough them up once or twice, so that repayment is forthcoming thereafter.[4]

Part of what is striking in Arunachalam's depiction of loan collection practices is that it is not just the loan officer of the MFI owed the repayment who is involved. In many cases MFIs are hiring third-party agents to do their collection for them: although this is

[4] http://microfinance-in-india.blogspot.co.uk/search/label/Coercive%20Repayment.

just an extension of the MFI, it is hardly unheard of for third parties to be less scrupulous than the original lender in collecting loans, as they do not have a "brand" to defend in the lending marketplace.

Alongside the agents, however, are the loan group members themselves, collecting on behalf of the MFI in order to avoid having their own savings confiscated. These instances in Andhra Pradesh are not isolated. Extreme coercion was reported back in the late 1990s; one of BRAC's own research studies, quoted by Richard Montgomery,[5] reports a conversation with BRAC women in which "they told . . . with pride that they had pulled down a member's house because she did not pay back her housing loan."[6] Montgomery suggests that such violent action may not be common, but "examples of 'forced' acquisition of household utensils, small livestock, or other assets of defaulting members were mentioned."

Lamia Karim, an assistant professor of cultural anthropology at the University of Oregon–Eugene who spent eighteen months studying the microfinance industry in Bangladesh, argues that the fusion of the collective responsibility for loan repayments and the cultural norms of kin obligations in Bangladesh "are toxically synergistic, and coupled together they work to operate within an economy of shame."[7] She adds: "In analysing the reasons why rural men allowed their women to become NGO members even though it brought their women in contact with non-kin men, one noticed a deep level of complicity between NGOs and rural men. Despite rural codes of honor/shame that dictated that women should not come in contact with non-kin men (and most NGOs, especially Grameen Bank, have male officers), rural men found it useful to allow their women to join NGOs because they (rural men) work during the day. Poor men who lack physical collateral 'give' their women in membership to NGOs as economic reassurance. In reality, *the collateral that Grameen women and all other NGOs extract from the poor is the Bangladeshi rural woman's honor and shame*. The poor give their honor embodied in their women to the NGOs in exchange for loans."[8]

Yet even the issue of shame is complicated—it does not always result in the infliction of violence on women by men, though Rahmen records this.[9] The husband may also feel intense shame if his wife is humiliated in such ways and he is not able to protect her. After the 2010 Andhra Pradesh crisis, press reports focused on the reported suicides of women borrowers, which were certainly tragic enough, but there were also male suicides. Indeed,

---

[5] Richard Montgomery, "Disciplining or Protecting the Poor? Avoiding the Social Costs of Peer Pressure in Micro-credit Schemes," *Journal of International Development* 8, no. 2 (1996): 297.

[6] The report cited was N. Khan and E. Stewart, "Institution Building and Development in Three Women's Village Organisations: Participation, Ownership and Autonomy,", unpublished paper, BRAC Research and Evaluation Division, Dhaka.

[7] Lamia Karim, "Demystifying Micro-credit: The Grameen Bank, NGOs, and Neoliberalism in Bangladesh," *Cultural Dynamics* 20, no. 1 (2008): 15.

[8] Karim, "Demystifying Micro-credit," 16.

[9] Rahman, *Women and Microcredit*, esp. 120–124.

a recent report finds that while a rise in all suicides seems to accompany microfinance growth and penetration, this is especially so of male suicides.[10]

During her research, Karim observed routine credit related strife among members and their families. This ranged from scolding, removing a woman's gold nose-ring (a symbol of marital status, symbolically divorcing/widowing her), and taking a woman's family's food supply, leaving them with none. NGO officers did not participate, but oversaw, and threatened to withhold future loans unless the defaulted money was recovered. In the worst cases, where the default was large enough that everything already was repossessed, members

> would sell off the defaulting member's house. This is known as house-breaking (*ghar bhanga*) and has a long history in rural society. It is considered the ultimate shame of dishonour in rural society. In other words, serious defaults led to homelessness of the families concerned. In my research area, house-breaking occurred several (six to seven) times, whereas smaller forms of public shaming occurred every week. There were several instances of suicide committed by men who had been shamed by their inability to protect the honor of their families. But those instances were rare, and were often the result of multiple causes, such as flooding in low-lying areas. What is important to note though is how the pre-existing coercive norms, of house-breaking for example, have become institutionalized as part of the NGO technologies of loan recovery.[11]

Karim reports that the NGOs also use the apparatus of the state, the police, to have defaulting women arrested until a loan is repaid. She met a number of women who had then been divorced by their husbands because they had "disgraced" their family by going to jail.[12] She reports the NGOs as fully aware of the consequences on borrowers of their, or the fellow borrowers', efforts to achieve loan repayment. But the perception is strong among MFIs that default rates would be higher on individual loans than group loans, and certainly the costs of collection would be very much higher for the MFI, since the lending group are essentially acting as its loan collection officers, unpaid.

---

[10] Arvind Ashta, Saleh Khan, and Philipp Otto, "Does Microfinance Cause or Reduce Suicides? Policy Recommendations for Reducing Borrower Stress", March 3, 2011, available at SSRN: http://ssrn.com/abstract=1,715,442 or http://dx.doi.org/10.2139/ssrn.1715442.

[11] Karim, "Demystifying Micro-credit," 15.

[12] David Hulme reported a similar instance in 1997. For a woman to leave home without familial male company breaks the rules of purdah, and where she is arrested for failure to repay debt (not that the police are entitled to do so on an uncollateralized debt) and held overnight at the police station, she faces divorce on her return home. These issues are rarely reported: the case Hulme reports on came to light only because a police vehicle carrying such debtors crashed, and all were killed. Quoted in "Is Microdebt Good for Poor People?" in Dichter and Harper, *What's Wrong with Microfinance?* 20.

Last, in her tale of Jahanara Begum, Karim describes a practice on the ground of microfinance about as far removed from every public image of the microfinance industry as it is possible to get. Jahanara is a very successful microfinance client. She borrows from multiple MFIs and uses the money to lend on at higher interest rates; she runs a very successful classic moneylending business, funded by Grameen and other NGOs. (It seems especially ironic, Yunus having decried other lenders for becoming the new moneylenders, that Grameen should be one of the sources of capital for Jahanara Begum's moneylending business. The MFIs really have become the moneylenders here.) Karim accompanied Begum as she went in pursuit of a fellow Grameen borrower who was behind on her repayments.

On the way to Kashai Bou's house, Jahanara proudly told us that she had broken many houses when members could not pay. "We know when they cannot pay, so we take a carpenter with us to break the house." I asked Jahanara, "Why do you break the houses of kin?"

> Jahanara became indignant at first. Her comment was "Why should we not? They have breached their trust with us. If they cannot pay, then we will have to pay. Why should I pay for them?" Then she became quiet and said after a while added, "It is not good to break someone's house, but we are forced to do it. This is how we get loans from Grameen Bank and other NGOs. They put pressure on us to recover the money, then we all get together and force the defaulting member to give us money."[13]

I do not argue that the offer of microfinance is coercive. But the effect of making group liability a condition of that offer would seem to foreseeably create the circumstances where coercion is used for loan collection in practice. At the heart of the practices described from the field, it is the basic, central plank of microfinance, the group liability model itself, that creates the pressure that results in coercive loan practices being used. It is a requirement of a borrower taking a loan, that she guarantee the repayment of the others in her lending group as well. There is no choice in this: it is a condition of taking out the loan. Her position is already one of poverty: when a fellow borrower does get into trouble, then, her ability to cover that debt may be limited, and she may very well resent the sacrifice it will impose on her.

Furthermore, it is reasonably standard practice of MFIs that fresh loans are not extended to a group when they are due to rollover, until all in the group have repaid. This means that for those borrowers for whom the microcredit is the lifeline that keeps them and their business going, the MFI threatens to cut that off unless they either cover the repayment of the defaulting borrower or find a way to force her to repay it. Their behavior, as chronicled above, can then indeed become fiercely coercive. This is a far cry from the

---

[13] Karim, *Microfinance and Its Discontents*, 110–111.

idea of "self-help" that the group-lending model is supposed to generate in the microfinance literature.

Stepping back, then, there are a number of relationships in the practice of microcredit that can become coercive. Nonetheless, to describe an act as coercive is not necessarily to condemn it. Like exploitation, coercion does not have to be used in a moralized way; just as some exploitation is not wrongful, some coercion can be justified. No modern society exists without any legal acts of coercion.

So the question then becomes, are any of the practices described above instances of justified coercion?

2. What Is Coercion?

Before we can discuss whether any of the apparent examples of coercion above are justified or not, we need to be clear as to precisely what coercion is. Among philosophers, this is also contested, but happily rather less so than the complexities of exploitation.

There are two main strands of thinking on how we define coercion: moralized accounts and empirical accounts. Moralized accounts, of which the principal one is Alan Wertheimer's,[14] hold that the truth conditions of coercion claims rest on prior moral claims. We determine if Q has been coerced by P into doing act A by determining if P had a right to make his proposal to Q, and whether Q had any obligation to resist it. Empirical accounts of coercion—starting with Nozick's seminal "Coercion" article[15] and developed by Frankfurt, Gorr, Feinberg, and more recently Zimmerman and Anderson—hold that the truth conditions of coercion claims are empirical. If various conditions are met by P's proposal to Q, then it simply is coercive, although further questions then arise as to what coerced acts are then acceptable in a society.

Both prongs of Wertheimer's moralized account are open to objection. With regard to the first prong, the essence of coercion does not seem to be expressed by whether or not P has a right to threaten Q, but by the fact that he is threatening him in the first place. Certainly, not all threats coerce: but what distinguishes coercion from ordinary threatening may be better found in further, empirical, facts, than in what rights P and Q possess. Wertheimer's view commits him to finding a criminal gang's proposal to take away your car unless you pay over large sums of money coercive, but not the police impounding your car until you pay your road tax. Structurally, these are the same, with the latter simply being coercion that we regard as justified. Most of us are happy to think that we should pay our taxes, that taxes are justified, and yet allow that the collection of taxes is coercive (because we are threatened with jail if we don't pay them).

---

[14] Alan Wertheimer, *Coercion* (Princeton, NJ: Princeton University Press, 1987).

[15] Robert Nozick, "Coercion," in *Philosophy, Science, and Method: Essays in Honor of Ernest Nagel*, ed. Sidney Morgenbesser, Patrick Suppes, and Morton White (New York: St Martin's Press, 1969), 440–472.

With regard to the second prong of Wertheimer's account, it seems extraordinary to say, for example, as Wertheimer does, that Q is not coerced by P when P threatens to break his arm unless he kills C, because Q should refuse to kill C, even at the risk of having his arm broken. Rather, Q surely is coerced, but the coercion is not sufficient to relieve him of all his moral responsibility for his act, and certainly not sufficient to justify murder. As Arnold puts it: "To analyse coercion primarily in terms of rights and obligations (or other moral considerations such as utility maximization) does not adequately highlight the fact that coercion constrains individual freedom and undermines individual autonomy. For these reasons it is necessary to provide an empirical rather than a moralised account of coercion."[16]

Coercion may relieve an agent of some, sometimes all, responsibility for his act: but how much depends on the moral balance of the choice he had to make. A coerced choice retains some voluntariness: this apparent paradox will be developed below.

Arnold[17] distinguishes three types of activity that different accounts of coercion have sometimes included under that name:

1. Physical compulsion, that is, brute force, such as manacling, kidnapping, and imprisoning. These activities are what are, for Anderson, paradigmatically coercive.
2. Psychological compulsion. Here the psychological state induced in the victim by the proposal is so extreme he becomes incapable of rational choice at all, but wholly identifies with a desire to do what the coercer asks of him, for example, the overwhelming fear of the knife at the neck, of being pushed from a building, Winston's fear of rats in his face in Room 101.
3. Rational compulsion. Here you deliberate the highwayman's "your money or your life" proposal and decide, after more or less reflection, to prefer your life to your money.

Of course on some occasions these different types of coercion can run together. But it is worth distinguishing force and coercion from each other, for as Hayek notes, when one is coerced, one still acts. "It is not that the coerced does not choose at all; if that were the case, we would not speak of his 'acting'. . . . Although coerced, it is still I who decide which is the least evil in the circumstances."[18] Compulsion offers the victim no choice. If I stop you from jumping in front of a train, I have forced you, not coerced you. Under compulsion you have no alternatives to what those forcing you want: under coercion, you have alternatives, but the range of these has been fixed by the coercer. The point is also made by Nozick that not all infliction of force or violence constitutes coercion: rather, it is the future threat of it that does so. "If a drunken group comes upon a stranger and beats

[16] Denis Arnold, "Coercion and Moral Responsibility," *American Philosophical Quarterly* 38, no. 1 (2001): 53–67.

[17] Arnold, "Coercion and Moral Responsibility."

[18] Friedrich Hayek, *The Constitution of Liberty* (London: Routledge and Kegan Paul, 1960), 133.

him up or even kills him, this need not be coercion. For there need have been no implicit threat of further violence if the person doesn't comply with their wishes, and it would indeed be difficult for this to be the case if they just came upon him and killed him."[19]

Compulsion, then, removes autonomy altogether: one does not act at all but is acted upon. Coercion infringes autonomy by presenting a forced choice among options the coercer has limited: but some autonomy remains to the victim of coercion that his choice between options is still a choice. With exploitation, as we have seen, it is a vulnerability that stems from a low degree of autonomy that the exploiter takes advantage of: in coercion, the coercer first impairs the autonomy by limiting choice to his chosen set of alternatives for the coercee to choose among, and then hopes to exploit the coercee's choice.

The account of coercion that I wish to present focuses on the third category above, rational compulsion, and would not count either of the first two as coercion, but as different forms of pure compulsion.

Coercion as Constrained Choice

At the center of coercion is the constrained choice: an agent is obliged to make a decision from a set of alternatives that she has not chosen voluntarily. Her autonomy has been limited by the setting of two or more alternatives on her by another agent, but she does still retain enough autonomy to then make a voluntary choice between those imposed options. The coerced act is both free and unfree: the decision whether to choose your money or your life is made freely and autonomously; the setting of an agent's options to being only her money or her life (not both) is wholly involuntary. At the heart of coercion is what happens to an agent's freedom and autonomy. It is impaired through the limitation of choice to the coercer's set of options, but the choice between that set of options remains to be made.

If we accept this account of a coerced act as a forcibly constrained choice, we can see why in fact we do not absolve agents wholly from legal or moral responsibility for coerced acts. An act being coerced mitigates an agent's being responsible for it: it may be mitigated entirely, but not necessarily, depending on the scale of the threat and the penalty offered, what the agent had to choose between.

The empirical account of coercion that I am putting forward is in the Nozick tradition,[20] but emphasizes the importance of the constrained choice that the coercee makes.

---

[19] Nozick, "Coercion," 444.

[20] Or, at any rate, the empirical tradition of Nozick's "Coercion" article cited above. In *Anarchy, State and Utopia* Nozick gives a different account of coercion, where if an agent has a choice between working and starving, his choice is coerced only if all the other individuals who have taken better jobs prior to this agent did not act within their rights in doing so. If they did act within their rights, then this agent's choice was not coerced. This is open to the same objections as have been made to Wertheimer's account: it is not the rights of others whom we may not even be able to track that determine if this agent is coerced or not, but facts about the limits on his freedom and autonomy.

The emphasis is less on the unattractiveness of the options that P presents to Q, than on the fact that P has forced this, and only this, set of options on Q.

The account can be put in Nozickean terms as follows:

P coerces Q where

(1) P imposes on Q a choice of a or b (or a to n) and makes the pre ante status quo impossible: in particular, Q can no longer have a and b.
(2) Each of the options made in the proposal to Q is significantly less attractive than his preproposal position.
(3) P intends that Q choose one of the options he offers.
(4) Q accepts one of the choices.
(5) Q would not have chosen the course of action he does if he had not been obliged by P to make a choice between these particular options.

In (3), there is a case for saying, as Nozick does, that P intend that Q choose his, P's, preferred option for Q: the highwayman wants Q's money, and he is not imagined to be indifferent between being made rich by Q or killing him—he wants to be made rich. But while it would seem natural to say this, it would mean saying that if Q chooses P's non-preferred option, then he is not coerced. And that would be odd. The tortured rebellion leader who chooses a slow, painful death over revealing the secrets of his revolutionary friends' whereabouts has still been coerced. He is coerced by being forced to make the choice between painful death or betrayal, not by what he chooses.

Some will say that the rebel leader was subjected to coercive pressure, but since he did not choose the torturer's option, he was not ultimately coerced. I do accept that coercion is a "success" word; the question is whether to measure success by P's obtaining the choice of Q's that he preferred or to measure it by Q having to make one of the limited set of choices imposed on him (so failure here would be the rebel leader escaping and neither dying nor betraying his colleagues).

If I hold that rebel leader is coerced here, even when he chooses death, then I will need to differentiate this type of case from seemingly trivial ones where P does impose a choice on Q, but a silly one. Imagine P threatens Q: "Give me a million pounds or I'll cry 'Boo!'" to which Q replies, "Well, cry 'Boo!' then!" Q has taken one of the alternatives offered to him, which would suggest that I would have to say that he is coerced here. The reason I need not hold that Q is coerced here is by appealing to clause (2) above. This requires that each and every of the options that P forces Q to choose among puts Q in a significantly worse position than he was preproposal. P crying "Boo!" is not less significantly attractive than Q's preproposal situation of before P came along and annoyed him, because Q may be assumed to be pretty indifferent as to whether P goes around crying "Boo!" or not. (If Q suffers from some sort of extraordinary boo-phobia, perhaps this would be different.) To put it generally, trivial threats do not coerce because the trivial threat option does not significantly worsen the potential coercee from preproposal to proposal situation.

A different type of modestly threatening proposal that needs distinguishing from coercion is the simple one of such everyday practices as a shopkeeper raising his prices. The shopkeeper does indeed say, "An increased price must be paid or you can't buy from me," but he can do nothing to stop the purchaser just rejecting his set of options and walking out of his shop. He does not coerce because while he offers the purchaser a limited set of options, he cannot prevent the purchaser from just rejecting the whole set. As O'Neill puts it, what marks out coercion is that there is no "no deal" option available to the coercee. He has to take one of the alternatives. The mark of coercion is the unrefusable "offer," not the unrefusable "option."[21]

The focus in this account of coercion, then, moves from the nastiness or otherwise of the options offered, to the enforcing of a constrained choice on an agent.

The "forced offer" account I give of coercion here, then, will typically find it wrongful because it always constrains an agent's autonomy.[22] The reasons for placing a high value on autonomy were given when discussing exploitation. But it is possible to justify coercion (as with some state coercion) and thus coercion is not wrongful by definition. More importantly for microfinance, coercion can also be justified when the agent herself has sanctioned it.

The drug addict who voluntarily goes into rehab knowing he will be coercively prevented from gaining his usual access to drugs while there has, by his earlier consent, justified the coercion that is then imposed on him. Of course, much will depend on the quality of the consent that is given, how truly voluntary it is, but it is certainly possible that valid consent can be given to future coercion.

So which of the practices described in section 1 were coercive, and were any of them cases of justified coercion?

3. Justified and Unjustified Coercion in Microfinance

The strategies Arunachalam describes MFIs, their loan officers, and agents using for loan collection in section 1 above—harassment, threats, abuse, embarrassment—are certainly coercive and, when it comes to breaking the house of a borrower, represent compulsion. The coercion is not justified. The borrower has not given collateral on the loan, she has not agreed in advance to these sanctions: they are an ugly side of microcredit and are not justified.

---

[21] Onora O'Neill, "What Are the Offers *You* Can't Refuse?" in *Violence, Terrorism and Justice* ed. R. G. Frey and Christopher Morris (Cambridge: Cambridge University Press 1991), 182.

[22] A utilitarian will find the "forced offer" account of coercion prima facie wrongful because it frustrates the desire of the agent to stay in the preproposal situation, and desire frustration is always prima facie wrong. A Kantian response would also find "forced offer" coercion wrong, because it fails to treat the coercee as an end in himself, rationally setting his own goals.

When the MFI coerces the group of borrowers, however, threatening to dip into their savings that it holds to make good the default on an interest payment by one member of the group, it is justified in doing so. This is the *only* sanction that has been consented to in advance, and the MFI is entitled to use it.

In practice, MFIs often prefer not to, at least at first, but rather prefer to threaten to withhold new loans to the group unless they ensure the repayment of the defaulting borrower. This is preferred because otherwise the MFIs stand to lose the good business of the rest of the group going forward. But this is *not* a sanction that has been agreed to in advance by the group—it is not a part of the terms and conditions of *their* loan that future loans to them are dependent on the repayment by others in the group. This form of coercion, then, is *not* justified.

There has to be one major caveat to even the one form of coercion that can be seen as justified, the MFI withholding the savings of group members to cover the default of one. The examples above show that though this coercion may be justified, it can lead to the group itself, driven by its own relative desperation, issuing and enforcing cruelly coercive threats to the defaulting member or indeed using straight compulsion to steal her remaining assets in compensation for the payments made for her.

The question becomes: in the case of Jahanara Begum above, when an MFIs acts with justified coercion in taking out of Begum's savings an amount to cover a defaulting member of her borrowing group, how is the moral responsibility split between MFI, Begum, and the defaulting borrower when Begum subsequently breaks the defaulting borrower's house to make good her loss?

It could be argued that if a defaulting borrower knew that group liability was a condition of the loan when she took it out and had perhaps heard about the poor experience of it from others, then she is deemed to have given valid consent to the coercive practices that then follow. But this line of thinking is a mistake. The borrower consents to the offer of microfinance and the group liability model that comes with it. But even though she may know that group liability often or sometimes results in fellow borrowers imposing coercion and compulsion on their defaulting sisters, that knowledge does not mean that she consents to the use of that coercion. She consents only to the imposition of group liability, that is, that she will cover others' debts if they default. The coercion itself remains illegitimate: the loan is, after all, not collateralized. The fellow borrowers have a contractual agreement to repay her loan for her if she cannot (and vice versa): the fact that some then use extreme methods to try to escape that liability does not legitimize their doing so, and how common or otherwise that is does not carry with it the signing up borrower's consent to the practice.

I would argue then that attempts to blame the defaulting borrower herself for the coercion (and possibly compulsion) from other members of her borrowing group that follows her default hold little traction. What of Begum's own justification of her action, that she was "forced to do it" in order to get loans from Grameen and the other NGOs?

Begum has been coerced herself here, with the loss of her savings. Because she had voluntarily agreed to group liability, that was a justified use of coercion. Whether justified or not, at the point of her own coercion, Begum has a choice: she can break the defaulting borrower's house and use the proceeds to pay the MFI the defaulting borrower's debt, or she can stand by and see her savings depleted to the extent of that debt. Her options may be unattractive, but she retains moral responsibility for her choice. At most, the fact that she is coerced to choose between two unattractive options might mitigate her choice: but that would carry more weight if the coercion imposed on her were unjustified. But here, it is justified: she gave her sanction to group liability in taking out her own loan. There may be some case for her if the only terms available to her were borrowing with group liability: and indeed where this is so, I have argued that the MFI taking advantage of her lack of choice to impose group liability wrongfully exploits her. But that is not sufficient to excuse her for all, or even much, of her responsibility for her actions here.

What then of the MFI? If its coercion of Begum is justified coercion, does it carry no responsibility for what subsequently happens to the defaulting borrower?

This would not be so. It would depend how far the MFI knew—or should be expected to know—that borrower-on-borrower coercive practices are not uncommon and are the likely consequence of imposing group liability on a category of borrowers whose poverty is already such that the prospect of a further loss is likely to provoke desperate action.

The MFI cannot stand back and claim that it does not carry out coercive loan collection practices itself, that only the women borrowers (unfortunately, sometimes) do. For the women only act to recover back some of their costs in covering the defaulter's debt because the MFI would refuse to extend their future loans if they did not cover this debt. When the MFI has insisted upon the use of group liability and knows from experience that as a result practices such as housebreaking occur, it cannot claim to be innocent of them when they do. It bears the indirect responsibility for actions that are, in legal terms, the "reasonably foreseeable" result of its threat to the borrowing group.

4. Group Liability and Coercion in Microfinance

What shall we conclude, then, of the relationship between microfinance and coercion?

The offer of microfinance, itself, is not coercive. In general, where one agent takes advantage of the extremely difficult circumstances, of the low level of global autonomy of another to make an offer on terms that would not be accepted in happier circumstances, they exploit rather than coerce. The offer of microfinance does not fall within the "forced offer" definition of a coercive offer, because the offer set (loan on these terms, or no loan) can be rejected—there are other life options available, and even other finance offers, however unattractive.

But a central plank of the offer of microfinance, the group liability model, which is a condition of taking the loan, does in some circumstances lead to coercive loan collection. It has been shown that coercion is not, in most instances, justified by the prior consent of the borrower to the sanction: where the coercion is from the MFI to the group, expropriating their savings to make good a default, it can be, but all the other forms—coercion of MFI/agent/group against the borrower—are not so justified by consent.

Can coercion be justified by the consequences of the use of microcredit being so beneficial, in raising borrowers out of poverty, that a bit of coercion along the way is offset? Given the extent of some of these coercive practices, that seems unlikely: and it seems even more unlikely that even if the consequences were positive overall, that they were, individually, for the borrower who has had her house broken and is now homeless.

What can be done to reduce coercion in loan collection? The Smart Campaign has adopted "appropriate collection practices" as one of its client protection principles, but even if MFIs try harder to control coercion from their loan officers, that does nothing to prevent the coercion among borrowers that the use of group liability generates.

Microfinance consultant (with a focus on social performance) Anton Simanowitz provides a striking example of how an MFI just having a code in place is little guide as to what may happen on the ground. He describes a visit to an MFI in Malawi:

> On a recent visit to an MFI in Malawi I visited two groups, one that seemed to be performing well and another that had experienced frequent repayment problems. I was keen to understand to what extent the groups supported clients who faced problems, how their responses in times of client crisis differed, and what this meant for the clients involved.
>
> The first group was the one identified by loan staff as struggling with repayments on a number of occasions. A client was missing from the meeting, and the client's payment was missing. Group leaders explained to me that they did not know the reason that the member had not paid, but they would pay for her and then go to the client's home, seize assets, and sell them to cover their additional repayments.
>
> The second group also had an absent member without payment. Having spoken to clients it became clear that there had likewise been some problems, but the group had found solutions among themselves and the issue had not escalated to the point where loan staff needed to be involved. In this case the leadership told me that the member was in hospital, and that they would pay for her; and after the meeting would also visit her house... but would offer support and find out how they could help the client to overcome her problems.[23]

These two very contrasting stories are of borrowing groups with the same MFI and the same code of conduct with regard to loan collection practices. In the second case,

[23] Anton Simanowitz, "Challenges to the Field and Solutions: Overindebtedness, Client Dropouts, Unethical Collection Practices, Exorbitant Interest Rates, Mission Drift, Poor Governance Structures, and More," in *New Pathways out of Poverty*, ed. Sam Daley-Harris and Anna Awimbo (Sterling, VA: Kumarian Press, 2011), 53–120.

the MFI is not aware of the loan repayment difficulties of a client and so is unaware of whether pressure is being brought to bear on her or not (here, reportedly, not); in the first case, it is aware of problems and is fully aware of the coercion the struggling borrower is now facing from others in the group, and is happy to turn a blind eye: group liability is working too well in their own interests for them to wish to interfere with the resulting coercion.

What is going unchallenged here is to what extent the group liability model is truly essential to the offer of microfinance. Practitioners certainly typically assume that without group liability, defaults would rise sharply and they would become either unprofitable or unsustainable and have to reduce or cease business. But this has not been evidenced, because historically, relatively few have tried extending microfinance on an individual lending model basis. One study, however, claiming to be "the first rigorous global study of the relation between MFI gender focus and repayment performance, using a data set spanning 350 MFIs in 70 countries over 11 years,"[24] found that (among other things) "when women are offered individual tailor-made loans, repayment is enhanced, compared to group-lending methods."[25]

Broadly, the study found that the loss to the MFIs of being able to call on others' savings to cover a default was more than compensated for by higher individual repayment rates once repayment terms were made suitable to the cash flows of the individuals' projects, rather than being the usual weekly set rate. Note also that while lending to individuals is generally more expensive for MFIs than the efficiencies group-lending makes possible, it is perfectly possible to disburse loans to individuals in groups who gather to present the same efficiencies for loan officers—it is group liability that is the coercive force here, not group lending as such.

If microfinance as an industry wants to clean itself of the coercive claims heard against it, abandoning the group liability model, despite it being a traditional (but not original) plank of its business, may be the necessary thing to do: and may not be as painful as MFIs suppose.

This book has a number of key conclusions, which are summarized in chapter 9. But this is one of them. Group liability may have come into microfinance's practices originally as an add-on to group-lending and have at first seemed like an innocent enhancement of group solidarity. But imposing financial penalty on those struggling on the edge of poverty can just as easily bring the worst out of a group as the best. MFIs can set higher client protection standards to try to stop their own loan officers from coercing: but the only way to stop coercion among borrowing groups themselves, responsibility for which the MFI shares because it has created the conditions for it by imposing group liability, is to cease using group liability itself.

---

[24] Bert D'Espallier, Isabelle Guérin, and Roy Mersland, "Women and Repayment in Microfinance: A Global Analysis," *World Development* 39, no. 5 (2011): 758–772.

[25] D'Espallier et al., "Women and Repayment," 768.

"'Is there any point to which you would wish to draw my attention?'

'To the curious incident of the dog in the night-time.'

'The dog did nothing in the night-time.'

'That was the curious incident,' remarked Sherlock Holmes.'"

—ARTHUR CONAN DOYLE, Silver Blaze, from The Memoirs of Sherlock Holmes

5 The Dog Not Barking

A DUTY OF CARE IN MICROFINANCE

THE LAST TWO chapters have focused on the ethics of the relationship between the microfinance institution and the borrower, and argued that the practices of microfinance do, not without exception but on a fairly widespread basis, wrongfully exploit and coerce borrowers. This chapter goes beyond considering what harms MFIs should avoid inflicting, and considers whether MFIs have positive duties to borrowers, and specifically, whether they owe them a duty of care. I shall lay out what I mean by a duty of care, and argue that this is indeed owed to borrowers, but is not currently fulfilled.

On the face of it, this may not seem a very controversial claim. Few MFIs would deny that they have some form of duty of care to their borrowers; they recognize that borrowers are vulnerable, and, as we have seen, many claim not only to protect borrowers but actually to empower them. But when it gets down to examining the practices MFIs would argue fulfill that duty of care, there is little that really meets this standard. The practices MFIs argue are there to protect borrowers at best represent a gentle and justifiable paternalism, but fulfilling a duty of care requires more than that. Others of these practices are not even justifiable paternalism, being for the benefit of the MFI rather than the borrower. At any rate, practices that meet the specification of a duty of care—which represent a limited paternalism that is not only justified, but *required*—are, like the dog not barking in Conan Doyle's tale, notable only by their absence. This chapter proceeds by laying out what is meant here by a duty of care and whether microfinance is the sort of practice that can be subject to a duty of care, before turning to whether the existing practices of MFIs to protect borrowers meet that standard, and what a meaningful specification of a duty of care for a microfinance institution would entail.

1. The Duty of Care

To begin, then, with what I mean by a duty of care, and who owes it to whom. It is well defined and understood in UK and US law, but has more recently been used in the context of a wider, more extensive set of obligations in medical, virtue, and care ethics. When I refer to a duty of care here, I refer to the established, legal duty of care that is the cornerstone of the law of tort in the UK and the US. This comes with fewer obligations than when the term is sometimes used in medical and virtue ethics but has the advantage of these obligations being better defined, clearer to ground in moral principle, and of wider application (to any profession or transaction, including finance).

The obligation that the legal duty of care imposes is that one party may not cause harm to another when providing a good or service to him where the supplier of the good or service can foresee, or can reasonably be expected to foresee, that the recipient cannot judge for himself whether or not the good or service is harmful to him. If the duty of care is breached, the party owing the duty of care becomes liable for paying damages to the party to whom the duty was owed. Raz sees this as two types of duty:[1] "Morally speaking we have two (kinds of) duties: a duty of care and a duty not to harm by negligent breach of duties of care. In other words, there is a moral duty whose point, and therefore whose content, is to protect people from negligent harm."

The phrase "duty of care," or sometimes "duty to care," in medical ethics is used of a doctor's duty to his or her patients, and goes well beyond a duty to do no reasonably foreseeable harm. It is closer to a fiduciary duty: the International Code of Medical Ethics[2] states that "a physician shall owe his patients complete loyalty," and the debates of the boundaries of a doctor's duty of care focus around how far he has a positive duty of beneficence, even at the cost of self-sacrifice, to serve his patients' best interests, rather than merely an essentially negative duty to do no harm.

In care ethics (and virtue ethics to the extent that care is seen as a virtue and subsumed within it), care (for ourselves, the environment, each other) becomes central, the basic feature of a moral theory. Indeed, as Tronto puts it, "the ethic of care is a practice, rather than a set of principles."[3] Again, this is a very different interpretation of a duty of care than the older, simple, and more restricted principle of doing no (foreseeable) harm that is used here. The way duty of

[1] Joseph Raz, *From Normativity to Responsibility* (Oxford: Oxford University Press, 2011), 262.

[2] World Medical Association, International Code of Medical Ethics, *World Medical Association Bulletin* 1, no. 3 (1949): 109, 111.

[3] Joan Tronto, *Moral Boundaries: A Political Argument for an Ethic of Care* (New York: Routledge, 1994). The four elements of care to be practiced are attentiveness, responsibility, competence, and responsiveness.

care is used here is also distinct from a more extensive duty of care in medical ethics, which has wider boundaries and has its moral grounding in trust and loyalty. But to be quite clear, the legal definition of when a duty of care applies is used here not because it derives ethical status from being part of the law per se, but because it best describes the narrower circle of circumstances in which a *requirement* (as opposed to a justification) for the limited form of paternalism that a duty of care represents could arise.

The legal position on who owes whom a duty of care was reshaped in English and Scots law in the case of *Donoghue v. Stevenson*, 1932. In his leading judgment (which allowed the appeal of Donoghue to claim for suffering caused to her by ingesting parts of a decomposing snail in a ginger beer bottle manufactured by Stevenson), Lord Atkin expounded his "neighbour" principle:

> The rule that you are to love your neighbour becomes in law you must not injure your neighbour; and the lawyer's question: Who is my neighbour? receives a restricted reply. You must take reasonable care to avoid acts or omissions which you can reasonably foresee would be likely to injure your neighbour. Who, then, in law, is my neighbour? The answer seems to be—persons who are so closely and directly affected by my act that I ought reasonably to have them in contemplation as being so affected when I am directing my mind to the acts or omissions that are called in question.... A man has a Duty of Care to conduct himself in such a way as to avoid harm to others, where a reasonable man would have seen that such harm would occur.[4]

The Lords found that when a manufacturer sells a bottle of beer in darkened glass, so that the ultimate consumer has no possibility of inspecting it before opening and drinking it, then the manufacturer has a duty of care to the consumer to ensure that it is fit to drink. This landmark decision opened up modern negligence law, such that a provider of services or goods has to ensure they are fit for the purpose intended, whoever ultimately uses them, regardless of whether there is a contract between the ultimate consumer and original provider or not.

The duties of the seller to the buyer appear to ratchet up in line with the state of the equality of power and autonomous agency between the two parties. Caveat emptor, let buyer beware, is less common today as a governing rule of transactions than it used to be, but is still regarded as appropriate where both buyer and seller are equally matched, understand what they are doing, and the product is not potentially harmful to the buyer.

A duty of care begins to apply where both parties are not equal with regard to a transaction; where the buyer of a good or service is in some respects the nonexpert to the selling expert; where the buyer's ability to act autonomously, with full information with regard to the purchase, is restricted by his relative ignorance; *and* the product is

---

[4] *Donogue v. Stevenson*, SC (HL) 31 (UKHL May 26, 1932).

potentially harmful. It was important in *Donoghue v. Stevenson* that the ginger beer was sold in darkened glass: Donoghue's ability to act to inspect it herself first before committing to opening it was impaired. Medicine, of course, is a common area where a duty of care is required, and indeed where that duty of care may sometimes only be exercised paternalistically.

Note, though, that while the duty of care can be used here in a medical context as on occasion not only justifying but requiring paternalism, the fuller duties sometimes held by medical ethicists to be part of a doctor's duty of care are not here being appealed to. This is not to deny that a doctor has the fuller obligation not only not to harm his patient, but to act in his best interest: but it may be better to think of this as part of a doctor's fiduciary duty to his patient, rather than extending the "no harm" duty of care principle to cover these fiduciary duties as well. The fiduciary duty to act in a patient's best interests may well encompass the "no harm" duty of care, but the no-harm duty of care does not encompass further fiduciary obligations. The legally scoped duty of care is narrower in scope, covering only a duty not to harm, but is wider in application, to transactions and professions well beyond those involving fiduciary obligations.

The reason for distinguishing the doctor's more positive duty to act in her patient's best interest (or a teacher's to her class, or a lawyer to his client, perhaps) is that these more fiduciary type of obligations are both more extensive than the (no-harm) duty of care, and more restricted in the number of transacting relationships (in principle, all) where a no-harm duty of care could apply. The risk of using the term "duty of care" in the wider, fiduciary sense might be that we then deny it applies to certain transactional relationships where in fact the more limited "no harm" duty of care still does apply and can still do useful work. A limited paternalism from the expert is demanded in many exchanges.[5] They do not have to be only occasions on which a wider fiduciary obligation also holds.

An act is paternalistic when it operates against another's preferences, in a way that undermines or infringes upon that person's autonomy, for her own good or for the prevention of harm to her. Some argue that, because they undermine or override autonomy, acts of paternalism are wrong. I would argue, however, that paternalism can be justified when the autonomy that is infringed upon is only partial, or limited in some way; or when the degree of infringement to a fully autonomous agent's autonomy is low, and the potential good achieved for the agent/harm avoided is very high. Many examples of justifiable paternalism come from medicine, but microfinance could also fall within the category of justifiable paternalism, for we have seen how the borrower's ability to make an autonomous borrowing choice is impaired by the complexity and lack of transparency in interest rates.

[5] See, for example, Onora O'Neill, *Autonomy and Trust in Bioethics* (Cambridge: Cambridge University Press, 2002).

Indeed it is not only in the practice of medicine that we expect a limited paternalism on the part of the expert seller to the nonexpert buyer. In developed countries (at least) financial transactions generally are regulated differently according to whether they are expert-expert or expert-nonexpert. In the former—transactions between qualified professionals essentially—caveat emptor (broadly) applies. Thus for qualified, authorized traders in securities markets, there is a much more lax set of protections for buyers than, for example, for the general public trading with professional stockbroking firms (although misrepresentation would not be allowed in either case).

It may seem that what generates the duty of care is the fact that the transaction is between expert and nonexpert, rather than because what is transacted is potentially harmful to the purchaser. This is probably not so. A nonexpert selling a potentially seriously harmful product to another nonexpert would still have this duty (though his sale would probably be illegal, as unregulated). And there are plenty of expert to nonexpert transactions where a duty of care is not taken to hold: it was not required of digital TV salesmen in the United Kingdom that they ensure the potential purchaser could actually receive the digital signal before making the sale. What rules apply to the transactional relationship between expert and nonexpert can simply be cultural, the place at which a particular society has chosen to draw its own lines, involving no duty of care. The Cambridge economist Ha-Joon Chang expresses his surprise on arriving in the UK in the 1980s that "one could demand a full refund for a product, even if it wasn't faulty. At the time, you just couldn't do that in Korea, except in the most exclusive department stores. In Britain, the consumer's right to change her mind was considered more important than the right of the seller to avoid the cost involved in returning unwanted (yet functional) products to the manufacturer."[6]

But what links all cases where a selling expert has a duty of care to a buying nonexpert is where the product can harm him: where the seller, in selling it, would either breach the principle of doing no harm to others or, perhaps, take a very serious risk of doing so. This applies as much to the stockbroker selling his client a product promising a certain yield and capital security when in fact its structure is such that it is likely to wipe out the client's life savings, as it does to the doctor and surgeon.

It might be asked here, if a duty of care exists in financial services as much as in medicine, at least in some transactions, how come so many leveraged, risky, complex derivative products were sold to uncomprehending European regional local authorities and banks by Wall Street in the run-up to the 2008 financial crisis: and especially, how come so much subprime mortgage money was lent to the overborrowed American consumer?

The answer to that is that the regional European banks and local authorities at least purported to be professional. They signed away rights to protection in their transactions with Wall Street firms on the grounds that they were qualified to do their own analysis

---

[6] Ha-Joon Chang, *23 Things They Didn't Tell You about Capitalism* (London: Allen Lane, 2011), 5.

and get the better size and price of transaction as a result of being allowed to do so. They held themselves out as experts in expert-expert transactions. Perhaps they deluded themselves, but this is not an exception to the duty-of-care principle applying when a potentially harmful product is sold, but an unfortunate case of the buyer deliberately opting out of protection that was available to nonexperts.

The case of subprime is an exception, and in many cases was a case of a breach of a duty of care from seller to buyer that the sellers simply did not choose to recognize. What was extraordinary was that the sale of mortgages by mortgage brokers should have been unregulated: in developed countries it is hard to think of any financial transaction that touches the consumer that is not regulated, and yet this exception became a trillion-dollar market.

In a transaction, then, a duty of care applies between one party and another when (*a*) the product the seller is supplying is potentially harmful and (*b*) the purchaser's ability to assess the appropriateness for herself is foreseeably impaired (whether through her relative ignorance or the product being sold in such a way as for her not to be able to do so). For these circumstances to hold, the parties to a transaction will often be unequal in their negotiating power, and one may hold all the expertise: but it is the potential harm of the product and the restriction on the purchaser's ability to ascertain its suitability for herself that are key.

Is microfinance a case where this duty of care applies? It certainly seems so.

The application of this to microfinance is as follows. A loan carrying an interest charge, especially a very high one, is a potentially dangerous product for the borrower. It may facilitate some profitable transaction whose profit margin more than covers the interest rate cost: but as we have seen in previous chapters, it may also lead the borrower into a downward spiral of debt from which she cannot extricate herself, which in the poverty-ridden world of microfinance may see her bullied, coerced, and even driven to suicide.

The product of debt is, clearly, potentially dangerous, as with Stevenson's snail-infested ginger beer. There is also the required limitation on the borrower's ability to assess if the product is suitable for her or not: the woeful lack of transparency as to the true interest rate on most microfinance loans operates like the darkened glass on the ginger beer. Without knowing the true rate, the borrower cannot properly assess if the product is suitable for her, if the true cost of the loan exceeds the margin she can make using the loan, or if her cash flow from other sources of income can make up the loan repayments. There will be occasions where the borrower demands the loan despite these problems, and exercising the duty of care then is paternalistic, but justifiably so.

A duty of care in lending has not, hitherto, been clearly established. That may partly have been because in the past, a financial institution may often have acted in the same way as it would have done had one been recognized, from its own self-interest in maximizing the chances of getting the loan repaid. In developed countries, analysis of a borrower's cash flow or business prospects for a business loan is standard practice before extending a loan: not from paternalistic motives of preventing overindebtedness in the borrower, but to protect the profitability of the financial institution, which would suffer severely if more than a few were unable to repay loans. A duty of care may always have existed but been subsumed from our notice by the institution's own self-interest in acting in the same way as if it had been. It has been the advance of securitization in developed markets, and the group liability model in microfinance, that have divorced the interest of the lending institution from that of the borrower with regard to repayment. In the US housing market, once the original, long-practiced "originate to hold" method of making housing loans (old-fashioned savings and loans and banks making mortgage loans directly to known clients of the institution and then holding them until repaid many years later) gave way to the "originate to distribute" methodology that securitization made possible in the 1990s, the commonality of repayment interest between borrower and lender ceased to hold, and the subprime mortgage crisis became possible. In the world of microfinance, as we have seen, the group liability model means that the lender does not require that any particular borrower be able to repay her loan, only that some or all of the group be capable of doing so on her behalf if she fails to.

So old-fashioned prudence in lending, which masked and made unnecessary an explicit duty of care to the poorest borrowers (who are more vulnerable to harm in the event of failure to repay), ceased to be applied. But that, of course, hardly means that the moral duty of care ceased to apply. Rather, that duty now needs enunciating since changes in financial practice have left its assumed absence exposed. But if we accept a duty of care in construction, in medicine—in, in fact, the manufacture and sale of all products—there is no reason not to accept it in lending as well just because we once had no apparent need to. It was always there: it was subsumed by good practice, and it now stands clear again in times of bad practice.[7]

What, then, does a duty require on those who have the duty? Does it imply a limited, but required, paternalism? In medicine we think so. Where the product is potentially harmful and the patient unable to assess its advantages and disadvantages to him, but believes he wants it, we expect the doctor to override the patient's autonomy and refuse to prescribe where he believes it will do more harm than good. Ditto financial services: the borrower may want a loan, but if considering his business prospects or overall cash flow, the lender perceives it to be more likely to harm than benefit him (even though not

[7] There are other reasons why a duty of care in finance is harder to establish legally (as opposed to morally). Peter Cane notes in his entry "Negligence in Civil Law" in *The New Oxford Companion to Law* (Oxford: Oxford University Press, 2008), 828, that "foreseeability is normally a sufficient condition of the existence of a duty to take care not to harm another's body or physical property (cars, houses, and so on); but it may not be sufficient in relation to mental harm or financial loss. This is partly because it is considered not as important for the law to protect people from mental harm and financial loss as from bodily injury and property damage." But of course, the fact that a duty of care is harder to establish in the case of financial loss than in the case of physical loss does not mean it cannot be established: especially where, as here in microfinance, the group liability structure for repayment means that it is foreseeable to the MFI that a financial loss may easily translate into physical loss (to person or property) as the group tries to recover what it can.

necessarily harm the lender where group liability exists), and there are grounds to believe that the borrower is unable to figure this out for herself (pressure of poverty or lack of transparent interest rates), then the lender has a duty to the borrower, paternalistically, not to make that loan.

Microfinance, then, has a duty of care not to extend loans to borrowers when the loan at the rate lent is likely to be harmful, and when through the lack of transparency on interest rates, the borrower cannot adequately assess this for herself. By and large, as an industry it is failing to deliver on this duty of care. Yet it is not as if many MFIs are indifferent to the poverty of their borrowers and their borrowers' vulnerability to having that poverty deepened by making poor borrowing choices: on the contrary, the benign intentions of many are not being questioned (only the outcome). MFIs might reply to this that some have a variety of practices in place already to protect the client, and that these in total fulfill their duty of care. And there are *some* practices in microfinance that MFIs could argue go *some* distance toward fulfilling their duty of care. I shall look at these now.

MFI Practices Claiming to Protect Borrowers

MFI practices that are claimed to exist to protect or generally be to the advantage of the borrower fall into two camps: those that actually do have that as their primary intent, and those that make that claim for the practice, but whose primary purpose is to work in the interest of the MFI. I shall take those that could be seen as in the interests of borrowers first.

MFI Rules in the Interests of Borrowers

Compulsory Setting of Social Goals for Borrowers

Most MFIs emphasize the importance of their social role as well as their financial one. Many stress how women can be empowered by group membership, and this for some is an important claim to make good on in order to attract donor funding. The validity of such claims was considered in chapter 2. Here I simply consider if the requirement by MFIs that clients adopt these social goals is aimed at borrowers' own interest, and thus might be paternalistic, but is arguably justifiably so.

Grameen, famously, requested all borrowers learn and practice in their daily lives the "Sixteen Decisions." (BRAC also has its "Seventeen Rules.") Grameen borrowers have to be able to recite the Decisions in order to obtain a loan, so the Decisions were certainly imposed upon them. The Sixteen Decisions are as follows:

1. The four principles of Grameen Bank—Discipline, Unity, Courage and Hard work—we shall follow in all walks of our lives.
2. Prosperity we shall bring to our families.
3. We shall not live in dilapidated houses. We shall repair our houses and work towards constructing new houses at the earliest.

4. We shall grow vegetables all the year round. We shall eat plenty of them and sell the surplus.
5. During the plantation seasons, we shall plant as many seedlings as possible.
6. We shall plan to keep our families small. We shall minimize our expenditures. We shall look after our health.
7. We shall educate our children and ensure that they can earn to pay for their education.
8. We shall always keep our children and the environment clean.
9. We shall build and use pit-latrines.
10. We shall drink water from tubewells. If it is not available, we shall boil water or use alum.
11. We shall not take any dowry at our sons' weddings, neither shall we give any dowry at our daughters' wedding. We shall keep our center free from the curse of dowry. We shall not practice child marriage.
12. We shall not inflict any injustice on anyone, neither shall we allow anyone to do so.
13. For higher income we shall collectively undertake bigger investments.
14. We shall always be ready to help each other. If anyone is in difficulty, we shall all help him.
15. If we come to know of any breach of discipline in any center, we shall all go there and help restore discipline.
16. We shall introduce physical exercise in all our centers. We shall take part in all social activities collectively.[8]

The Sixteen Decisions emphasize discipline, unity of the group, hygiene, and hard work. In a commitment not to give or take dowry, they are quite radical. Rahman[9] and Karim[10] both argue, however, that as Grameen has evolved and grown, the Sixteen Decisions have become rhetorical. The purpose of the group centers has become wholly one of loan repayment, with recitation of the Sixteen Decisions now only taking place if there are special visitors, rather than at every meeting as originally required. Rahman notes that while Grameen reported in 1994 that there were more than thirty thousand dowry-free marriages among Grameen borrowers, there was no evidence of any dowry-free marriages in the village he lived and studied in. On the contrary, "All Grameen borrowers reported giving dowries for their daughters, accepting them for their sons, or planning to follow the practice in the future."[11] Indeed, he observes loans that were clearly taken out for the

[8] Quoted as appendix B by Rahman, *Women and Microcredit*, 159.
[9] Rahman, *Women and Microcredit*, 93.
[10] Karim, *Microfinance and Its Discontents*, 131.
[11] Rahman, *Women and Microcredit*, 93.

very purpose of paying dowry, regardless of the technical business purpose that the loan was said to be required for.

The Sixteen Decisions were introduced by Grameen as a social development program, and they do work toward empowerment of borrowers, but they are far short of a women's rights charter. They are more, as Helen Todd describes them,[12] "a sort of Mrs Beecham's Better Housekeeping for rural Bangladesh." They cover health, discipline, and mutual support, but not (for example) domestic violence, arbitrary divorce, inheritance rights, or gender discrimination. Their general concern "is with the women's better functioning as mothers and household managers," and so the Decisions reinforce "the culture of maternal altruism which persuades women to sink their own interests in the good of the family."[13]

These social development goals would be paternalistic if they were imposed on borrowers. If, however, the borrowers happily sign up to them, there is no lack of voluntariness or infringement to autonomy and so there would be no paternalism. Todd's study draws a picture where the Sixteen Decisions are happily embraced by the borrowers, even if not actually practiced. Even with regard to dowry, her study showed that women did regard the practice as an evil, but saw no alternative but to actually practice it.

Todd's study, however, was carried out in 1992, after Grameen had been present in the village she studied for a decade, but before the use of microcredit had exploded very much further in Bangladesh. Even in the first flush of enthusiasm for a new program, if the borrowers did not agree with one of the Sixteen Decisions, they just ignored it. It was perhaps the case that if a potential borrower could not recite the Sixteen Decisions, she would have disbursement of her loan stopped until she had relearned them,[14] but there seems little evidence that loans were refused for noncompliance with the Decisions once extended, as the continued use of dowries and slow take-up of pit latrines showed.

Still, to the extent that forcing borrowers to learn the decisions by rote was paternalistic, an argument can be made that the early results of doing so may have justified this. Todd surveyed the weight and height gain of children of Grameen Bank borrowers compared to a control group of nonborrowers, and there was a measureable difference in favor of the Grameen children. Interestingly, as time went on, the health advantage of Grameen borrowers' children against nonborrowers diminished somewhat as good hygiene practices were copied in the village: essentially, if the wider community observed a social practice working, they were happy to follow it too when possible. But in fact even this is not true justified paternalism, for the beneficiaries, the children, are not those who were paternalized, the mothers.

The health and lifestyle items among the Sixteen Decisions, then, were either never paternalistic because accepted voluntarily and thus did not impose on autonomy, or did

[12] Todd, *Women at the Center*, 160.

[13] Todd, *Women at the Center*, 223.

[14] Todd, *Women at the Center*, 22.

impose on borrowers' autonomy but were not paternalistic because the benefits were for others or, in just a few cases, were examples of justified paternalism where the benefit really did go to the borrower herself. This is much less clear of the *financial* Decisions, 13 and 15. It is not obvious that these are in the interests of borrowers, and 15 in particular paved the way for the coercive loan collection practices enforced by fellow borrowers observed in the preceding chapter. These financial goals, as opposed to social goals, really fit in section "MFI Rules in the Interests of MFIs" below—rules that present a facade of justifiable paternalism, but are in fact more simply in the interests of the MFI itself.

Training

Many MFIs require that a borrower have some experience of running a business before a loan will be extended: and even when she has, that she complete training that will cover some basic accounting and management tools for her business. Where the woman is already very experienced, this training may seem paternalistic, but in the majority of cases it may be welcomed by the borrower. The insistence on training is of course just as much for the sake of the MFI as the borrower, in order to try to prevent business failure and loss. Few instances of training will represent pure unjustified paternalism: they will, rather, divide into cases where the training is genuinely wanted, so no compromise of autonomy is involved and no question of paternalism arises, and cases where it is not wanted, but imposed anyway. Where this is only for the sake of the borrower, it is paternalistic, though perhaps justifiably so where the MFI has experience in observing how much worse borrowers do who undertake businesses without this prior training compared to those who do take it. Where the training is for the sake of the MFI itself, to avoid its loss, it ceases to be paternalism as such and just becomes routine imposition on the borrower as a cost of getting the loan. Realistically, it is likely to be a policy with a mixed rationale: in the interests of both borrower and lender alike.

MFI Rules in the Interests of MFIs (Rules Masquerading as in the Interests of Borrowers)

Weekly and Fortnightly Meetings

In the original Grameen model and that of BRAC and their replicas, the group of borrowers met weekly: many, now, fortnightly. Sometimes, their doing so is presented by MFIs as empowerment: a rare chance (especially in Muslim countries) for women to travel outside the home compound, to meet other women, exchange tips, and gossip. In presenting the frequent group meetings as being required of the women, but for their empowerment, the MFIs suggest that the practice is one of justifiable paternalism. This rather patronizing view overlooks the time commitment that has to be made by the borrowers and the fact that, when asked, they generally would prefer to meet less frequently. The reason for the frequent meeting is, in reality, loan disbursement and interest repayment: and the reason the timescale is so frequent is to enable the MFI to stay closely in touch with the progress of borrowers and flag up default risk if a payment is missed. Weekly and biweekly meetings are not paternalistically run as a sort of debtors' Women's Institute: they are for the MFI's benefit of loan collection. The imposition on a woman's autonomy exists: she may judge it worth it in autonomously deciding to take out the loan, and her consent would then validate the practice, but it remains a cost to her of taking the loan and is not a case of justified paternalism.

It may of course have been the case for some of the older MFIs, and this would be true of Grameen, that when the practice of regular weekly meetings and other practices in this section were begun, the MFI's rationale for imposing them was mixed, and there was indeed an element of empowerment and protection for the borrower as well as the protection of the interest of the MFI. There may have been some justified paternalism initially perhaps. And there are of course still MFIs that use regular meetings to impart health education, where borrowers can derive benefit. But where the group liability and lending version of the microfinance model has been adopted globally *without* any actual empowerment elements—represented by the Sixteen Decisions or another collective activity raising social issues pertinent to the borrower, or where these practices have since been dropped, as with the Sixteen Decisions only now being recited when visitors come—then it is clear that the original beneficial intent is essentially no longer present and what remains is mainly the MFI's self-interest.

It might be asked why some MFIs keep up the language of these conditions of lending being for empowerment purposes, rather than for loan collection. The answer to that is that these claims are not necessarily made any longer to the borrower, but are necessary for the public perception of the MFI, with the impact that has on its fundraising. Hence these rules do in some instances masquerade as justified paternalism. No MFI wants to be perceived as just an institutionalized moneylender. Rules that impose quite heavily on a borrower's time and resources that are only for the purpose of loan collection could be seen in that way. Appearing paternalistic might not be ideal either, but would be preferred by many MFIs to the alternative.

Compulsory Savings and Insurance

Most MFIs insist on so-called compulsory savings and some also on the borrower taking out insurance against her death. Again, these are often presented as justified paternalism, encouraging the excellent habit of saving in borrowers for their own good, and encouraging prudence with regard to unexpected death.

In practice, both compulsory savings[15] and insurance are enforced to protect the MFI against the possibility of a borrower's default. We saw the way in which compulsory savings work in chapter 3; that the borrower must deposit a sum, 10% or 20% of the value

[15] Note I am writing here of the "savings" deducted from the loan amount, not genuine deposit accounts held separately with an MFI where this is permitted.

of the loan, with the MFI before the loan is disbursed. If she does not have this sum, it is deducted from the loan, so that she receives a loan of 80 instead of the requested 100—although she is still charged full interest on the 100 as if she had received it in full. She does not receive interest on her "savings" (rather, she pays interest on them), nor may she have access to them during the period of her loan. The "savings" are pooled with those of all the borrowers in a group and are held by the MFI, often not in a segregated and protected account, for use as collateral by the MFI in the event of borrower default.

It is not obvious what benefit the borrower derives from her "savings" here, so the claims by MFIs that they are justifiable paternalism helping the borrower develop good financial habits falls flat. The purpose of compulsory savings is to provide collateral for the MFI.

This can also be so in the case of compulsory insurance. Todd[16] reports that all Grameen members had to contribute five taka for every thousand taka received as payment into an emergency fund that pays out in the event of death or other extreme disaster. She reports that there was one such payment to a Grameen member during the year she spent with two villages in Bangladesh. "The husband of one of our GB members, who was himself a member of the male center in Ratnogram, died suddenly. There was a ceremony in which the branch manager handed a letter of condolence and a 5,000 Taka payment from the emergency fund to the widow. Immediately after the ceremony, the bank worker took back the 4,984 Taka that the husband still owed to the Bank, leaving the widow with the letter and 16 Taka."

The money is supposed to be a grant made to widows/widowers in the face of the death of a member (other uses were approved, but this was by far the most common). What this had become is a grant of sixteen taka and Grameen using the rest to recover its outstanding loan. Rahman[17] observed similar instances in his study of Grameen. Compulsory savings and insurance, then, as commonly defined by MFIs, are not the cases of justifiable paternalism presented, but are just additional ways for the MFI to achieve greater security on its loan.

Loan Use

Matters become more complex when we consider restrictions the MFI attempts to impose on what the loan is used for. A basic requirement of many MFIs is that the loans are used for productive purposes, not for consumption. Further, because interest payments become due on the loan almost immediately, the enterprise entered into needs to be immediately cash generative. Again, the MFI will claim that these are instances of justifiable paternalism.

---

[16] Todd, *Women at the Center*, 26–27.

[17] Rahman, *Women and Microcredit*, 127.

Like training, the insistence that the loan be used for productive, immediately income-generating purposes only—not for investments that produce a delayed or longer-term yield, such as agriculture or a child's education, let alone for consumption such as paying for healthcare or even just food—would be paternalistic if it were for the borrower's good. But as can be seen from what is not allowed, it is not for the borrower's good per se, but to ensure the MFI begins to be repaid straightaway. Investing in land or fertilizer or seed might very well produce a better long-term return (and the great prize of food security) than using the capital to set up a tomato-selling business. But a business model that buys wholesale then makes a quick turn by selling retail is strongly encouraged (and different models discouraged) because it is immediately cash generative, and the cash flow of this model matches the loan repayment requirements of the MFI.[18]

The MFI makes credit available, then, not for any business enterprise, but for enterprises that can repay high interest rates almost at once—the first repayment will be due just a week or two after the loan is disbursed. The borrower may well benefit more from investing in a higher return but poorer immediate cash flow business: the conditions of the loan seek to prevent this. This insistence on loan use for immediately productive purposes only, then, is not unjustifiably paternalistic, because it is not paternalistic at all—its aim is not the good of the borrower. Its aim is to maximize the MFI's chances of repayment.[19]

2. How the Duty of Care in Microfinance Should Be Met

Before discussing how the industry *could* meet its duty of care to borrowers, it is worth reminding ourselves of what else it does already to protect clients.

As discussed in chapter 1, the Smart Campaign was launched in 2009 to focus on issues of client protection. It is here, if anywhere, that we can start to find industry policies aimed at preventing overindebtedness and the charging of levels of interest rates (however defined) that will inevitably lead a client into a spiral of debt. The Smart Campaign does put forward seven client protection principles (CPPs) that, it is claimed, "address the mandate of all providers to treat clients fairly, with transparent and ethical standards that avoid harm."[20]

---

[18] I do not mean to suggest here that no MFIs make agricultural loans. Of course they do, but the standard approach is not to encourage borrowing for projects whose payoff is a year away and do not provide a means of servicing the interest in the meantime.

[19] In practice, of course, restrictions like this are very hard to enforce. Money being fungible, if a borrower engages in a mix of activities, it will be hard for the lender to ascertain exactly which (production or consumption, or among productive) his loan went to support. The lender's inability to fully enforce his policy, however, does not affect the point that the policy, presented as justifiable paternalism, is in fact simply in his own interest.

[20] See www.smartcampaign.org.

The seven client protection principles are the following:

1. Fair and respectful treatment of clients
2. Transparency
3. Prevention of overindebtedness
4. Responsible pricing
5. Appropriate product design and delivery
6. Privacy of client data
7. Mechanisms for complaint resolution

The problem with these is twofold. First, as discussed in chapter 1, they are not all fully specified. Originally, there was no guide as to what respectful treatment of clients meant in practice. And second, they are not enforced. Although there is now a certification program, there is no need to sign up to it.

With the launch of the certification program in 2013, Smart did increase the level of specification, but perhaps not by enough. To meet the indicator for fair and responsible pricing, the interest rate on the loan need only be around or just below market levels: so in a market where 100% rates are common, 90% counts as responsible.

Chapter 9 suggests a better way of determining what a nonexploitative interest rate would be. In all events, interest rates need to be transparent, not opaque, and the APR or EIR *always* made clear, even if other methods of demonstrating costs of repayment are used as well. And of course this rate needs to be at a level that does not take advantage of the borrower's vulnerability: it needs to be at prime plus a margin, not prime times a multiple.

Smart's client protection principles also seem to set a strange standard when looking at the standard for "appropriate debt collection practices."

The indicators for meeting that standard are laid out as follows:

> The FI [financial institution] clearly spells out in a Code of Conduct (i.e., in Code of Conduct, Code of Ethics, Book of Staff Rules) the specific standards of professional conduct that are expected of all staff involved in collection (including third party staff).
>
> The FI does not endorse a policy of zero tolerance for PAR [portfolio at risk].
>
> The FI's policy guarantees that clients receive a fair price for any confiscated assets; Has procedures to ensure that collateral seizing is respectful of clients' rights; Offers an explanation of the role of guarantors. In case collateral is kept in the financial institution premises, procedures are in place to ensure its security.[21]

[21] See Smart Campaign Client Protection Certification Standards, January 2013, available at http://centerforfinancialinclusionblog.files.wordpress.com/2013/08/certification-standards_english-1-22-mb.pdf.

It will be obvious where the problems lie with this. Having a code of conduct meets the standard: but the code of conduct can say anything at all, and there is no absolute guidance as to what constitutes ethical behavior. It is certainly good that the financial institution will not be certified if it endorses a zero tolerance for PAR (usually calculated as the number of loans where the interest has not been paid for thirty days, as a percentage of the whole loan portfolio), because a zero tolerance policy has been seen to encourage very aggressive loan collection by loan officers. But that does not stop there being a policy of almost zero tolerance, for instance a policy that will not tolerate even half a percent of loans being over thirty days past due. And while it is presumably comforting to clients to hear that they will receive a "fair price" for confiscated assets, how is fair defined? And these are loans that are supposed to be uncollateralized—if they are in fact collateralized, why is the interest rate charged on them so high? One of the justifications of the high rates was supposed to be the lack of collateral. And specifying that collateral taken from clients should be kept secure is doubtless correct: but it does tend to make the MFI sound like a pawnshop.

The biggest problem for the Smart Campaign and its specifications, however, is that it does nothing to tackle the problem inherent in the group-lending methodology. As we have seen, some of the worst problems for borrowers who struggle come only indirectly from the MFI, but are enforced by other members of the borrowing group. None of the CPPs address this, and none of the specifications of them will do so, according to Smart.[22] Thus, sadly, the certification program could exceed all its currently rather low expectations and set excellent standards that are followed and verified: and the problems of disempowerment of borrowers continue by proxy.

It seems reasonable to conclude, then, that neither the existing practices of most MFIs, nor the Smart Campaign's client protection principles to which some aspire, yet describe what a true duty of care to microfinance borrowers would be.

What would the practical requirements of such a duty of care look like, then?

The duty of care requires of MFIs that they safeguard their borrowers from the harm that can come to them from borrowing from the MFI. Essentially, MFIs should make every effort to only lend to those people who are, individually, likely to be able to repay them. Such a practice would include a clear demonstration by the MFI to the borrower of the true interest rate the borrower was going to pay over the life of the loan, and a realistic assessment of the margin and profit the business undertaken by the borrower will likely generate. Together, these would generate an awareness that, if things go to plan, the enterprise is actually capable of meeting the cash flow requirements of the debt. In other words, the MFI would keep records of the projected cash flow and profitability of the

[22] Q & A with Beth Rhyne, Smart Campaign, at a meeting of the UK Microfinance Gateway Club, November 27, 2012.

business and the true interest rate being charged on the loan and only extend the loan when the former exceeded the latter.[23]

Having such a policy in place could easily be paternalistic when it resulted in some loan applications being turned down for the good of the borrower, because she was deemed unlikely to be able to repay without having recourse to family, sale of assets, or other means that leave her worse off than she was to begin with. This would be an example of the MFI substituting its judgment for another's, the borrower's, to promote the borrower's benefit.

A strictly antipaternalistic approach would be unlikely to find this practice acceptable. One part of it might be—the clarification of the true interest rate the business is going to have to cover—because without this, the borrower will be acting in ignorance, substantially involuntarily, in reaching her decision that she can take on this rate. But beyond this the antipaternalist will be unable to go.

A broadly consequentialist approach will more easily justify the paternalism involved in declining to extend loans to those very unlikely to be able to repay, but who yet want them. The imposition on the ability to act autonomously by taking the loan is not insignificant, but the harm avoided in terms of the dangers of overindebtedness may justify this. At the least, a borrower who fails to repay and becomes subject to the coercive pressures of her group or who has to turn to a still higher rate moneylender to repay her loan may end up with less autonomy than she began with.

Some will be surprised that such fairly simple record-keeping as recording the true rate of interest on a loan, the proposed margin on the business of a borrower, and her cash flow, is not already carried out by MFIs in their own interest, to maximize the chances of being repaid, as would be the case if a small business loan were extended in developed countries. But this is to forget that, although the MFI may have been set up with the noble aim of alleviating poverty through the extension of credit, as we have seen earlier, the use of group liability creates perverse incentives for loan officers. Group liability, to recall, means that if one borrower in a group cannot make her repayments, others in the group have to do so for her. This means that the MFI is incentivized, not to ensure that every individual it lends to is capable of repaying her loan through generating a sufficient margin on the business she undertakes, but rather to ensure that there are enough (it need only be one or two) borrowers in the group who are doing so well that they can cover the payments of the struggling borrowers as well. Thus the MFI's purported interest in each individual borrower's ability to repay becomes subverted to an interest that just enough in the group can cover the repayments of all: which may leave some individuals seriously losing out from their microcredit experience, since as we have seen, those losses are not covered by other borrowers without cost to the original borrower.

---

[23] In fairness, the 2013 CPP standards do specify that the financial institution carry out good repayment capacity analysis. But, again, this is underspecified: there is no requirement here that anticipated margin exceed anticipated loan cost.

A practice, then, of MFIs keeping records demonstrating that, at least on the researched, projected business plan, the margin on the business at least exceeds the truly calculated interest rate charged—that is, the borrower looks likely to benefit from using microcredit, would be a good practice to implement, even if (justifiably) paternalistic. The risks to the borrower of not doing so are just too great: we are considering indebting the poorest, whose ability to withstand a failure is the least. If one stands back and imagines an MFI that made these calculations and understood which of its borrowers were most likely to fail—and then went ahead and lent to them anyway, because provided it gets repaid by the others in the group, it is in its financial interest to do so—we might more quickly see that what the MFI does here is wrong. If that is conceded, then a requirement not to make that loan when that information is available: and the prior requirement to garner that information, must follow.

Finally, while the duty of care on the MFI to its borrowers will be carried out by the MFI's executives (recording cash flow, income coverage of debt repayments, and so on.), a governance duty also falls upon the directors or trustees of the MFI. They are responsible for the oversight of the MFI's operations and should require as part of that oversight an audit trail of how the MFI's duty of care has been exercised. The fact that the clients are already so vulnerable is what gives particularly stringent director duties of oversight here.

The audit trail needs to include not just the measures listed above, of recording the true interest rate of the loan and the margins of the proposed business or cash flow of the borrower, but also what steps have been taken to ensure that the client is not, or is not about to become, overindebted. The trail should show how this particular loan fits in to the overall complexity of the borrower's financial affairs. An MFI's board needs to require its management to demonstrate that when a borrower takes out a new loan, it is affordable for her, or perhaps replaces a more expensive existing debt, but at the very least does not just add to an existing large burden of debt.

To summarize, we might normally seek to avoid being paternalistic, but paternalism can be justifiable where either autonomy is partial or the imposition on autonomy is trivial, and the benefit accruing to / harm avoided by the subject of the paternalism great. With regard to the practices of microcredit lenders, a case was found for viewing the paternalistic imposition of social goals and financial training on borrowers as justifiable: but the imposition of many standard practices often presented as justified paternalism—weekly meetings, compulsory savings and insurance, the use of loans for productive purposes only—were not found to be justifiable paternalism at all, as not even being paternalistic, but simply in the interest of the lender. Some practices of banning particular types of loan use were found not to be paternalistic, but justified by the prevention of harm to others.

Most challengingly, I have argued that there is a duty of care on microcredit lenders to their borrowers that, in some instances, not only justifies but *requires* paternalism in the form of refusing to extend loans to those demanding them who are very unlikely to be able to repay, and who may incur great harm when others covering their missed payment exert potentially severe coercive pressure on them. This application of a duty of care holds in microfinance as it does in other areas where a product is potentially harmful and the purchaser's ability to judge its suitability for himself is foreseeably impaired, but she yet still desires it. Of course, that duty of care may go beyond microcredit to the provision of financial services generally where the lending is to the poorest (and thus most vulnerable to harm if unable to repay) and where the rate lent at is equally obscure, be that subprime or payday lending. But the establishment of a duty of care in microfinance on the MFI to the borrower is all I seek to establish here.

III Macroethics

THE INDUSTRY OF MICROFINANCE

There is no doubt that we have caused grievous harm and even deaths to some families[1]

6 Silenced Stories

THE DISTRIBUTION OF BENEFITS & BURDENS WITHIN MICROFINANCE

THE EXAMINATION OF the effect of microfinance in chapter 2 was unable to demonstrate the clear positive impact on reducing poverty and empowering its borrowers that its proponents have claimed for it. But to conclude that it does not have net positive impact is not, of course, to conclude that it is not having any impact: it does, but the positives and negatives are netting out. The "success stories" are not false: on the contrary, we have seen that microfinance does enrich a few, some of the time. But we have also seen that it can have very negative impact when a borrower becomes overindebted, has a business failure, or otherwise finds herself unable to repay.

This chapter asks: what type of distribution of these benefits and burdens is acceptable? How many "winners" must we have in proportion to "losers" to make the offer of microcredit worthwhile? Does the extent of the gain/loss matter? If one in a hundred go from below to considerably above the poverty line as a result of their borrowing, is that worth two in a hundred who sink just a little deeper into poverty?

Of course we need to be able to quantify what the distribution of benefits and burdens that result from using microcredit actually is. And it must be conceded at once that the answer to this second question is going to be sketchy at best. Because, by and large, the industry does not count its dropouts or measure what happens to them when or after they do drop out, the information on which to judge the negative burden is hardly there. If microfinance were a medical intervention, such a lack of knowledge of impact

[1] Vijay Mahajan, founder of BASIX, interviewed by the BBC for 'Bankers and the Bottom Billion', broadcast on BBC Radio 4 FM at 8.00p.m., on May 17, 2011.

on the "losers" from the intervention would be wholly unacceptable. But in microfinance it is largely only the stories of success that get told. What we do know will be drawn upon here.

We need first to contemplate the type of distribution of benefits and burdens that we might find, theoretically, morally acceptable, and then consider, with the limited knowledge that we do have, whether we are likely to be within the range of that distribution in reality. From the weak evidence base we have, this chapter will suggest that as currently practiced, microcredit is likely to be generating too many "losers" in proportion to its few "winners" to be ethically acceptable. We could, however, improve the likely ethical impact of the industry by focusing on the principle "First, do no harm," by reducing lending to those with the highest risk of becoming worse off from having borrowed (the poorest), while still, hopefully, helping create some "winners."

1. Defining the Morally Acceptable Range for the Distribution of Benefits and Burdens in Microfinance

In 2012 David Roodman summarized his long inquiry into the industry of microfinance with the statement "on current evidence, the best estimate of the average impact of microcredit on poverty is zero."[2] One ethical stance that can be taken toward a distribution of benefits and burdens resulting in net zero impact overall, but which includes severe losses, even suicides at the worst end, is that it is straightforwardly unacceptable. Regardless of how the distribution falls between small-scale negatives and small-scale positives, with perhaps a few extreme winners, there should be no losses so bad that borrowers are driven to suicide. As Harper puts it, "It is surely unacceptable that an intervention that is intended to help the poor should injure any of them."[3] Since we know that there are at least a few who are injured by microcredit, anyone taking this position to its logical extreme would not find microcredit as an antipoverty intervention permissible. Perhaps the questions we need to answer are how to enforce sufficient client protection within microfinance that a harm beyond a certain extreme is never caused; and how to ensure that the total harms that are caused are in an acceptable proportion to the total gains – if indeed that is possible.

Here I argue for taking a consequentialist approach to weighing up the distribution of the benefits and burdens of microfinance, that is, that a distribution of benefits and burdens that involves negative burdens for some is acceptable if the totality of the positive consequences outweighs the totality of the negative consequences. That still leaves much

[2] David Roodman, "Due Diligence: An Impertinent Inquiry into Microfinance," Center for Global Development Brief, January 2012, 3.

[3] Malcolm Harper, "Some Final Thoughts," in Dichter and Harper, *What's Wong with Microfinance?* 259.

to consider within the consequentialist approach. We may care not just that total positive outcomes outweigh total negative, but who gets them—if they all accrue to a few winners who were among the least poor to begin with, and the totality of negative consequences is concentrated among some of the poorest, who slip into extreme poverty, we might not regard that as especially satisfactory.

The classic problem for a consequentialist approach is that, in theory, if the totality of consequences are all that matter, then the very small gains of the very many can outweigh severe sacrifices by just a few. (Note that this is in theory: it is not to suggest that this is the distribution of benefits and burdens in microfinance, which is discussed below).

There is a step some consequentialists take here to minimize the chances of endorsing the large sacrifice of a few for a small gain of the very many, and that is to build in a weighting that favors the worst off: the prioritarian view.[4] This version of consequentialism gives a higher moral value to the gain of a benefit (or avoidance of a loss), the lower the recipient's absolute level of benefits to begin with; so that, for example, the same ten-cent gain is given a higher value the poorer the starting position of the person who receives it.

By assigning an extra weight to losses taken by those below the poverty line, then, without altering the weighting given to the gains achieved by those who do gain from microfinance, the prioritarian consequentialist can argue that some distributions are unacceptable that the straight consequentialist would have to accept. In theory, this is not a complete answer. It remains the case that whatever distribution the prioritarian has rejected here that the straight consequentialist has to accept, there will always be another, more extreme distribution (achieved by changing the weightings given, or multiplying the number of very small winners) that he would have to accept.[5] Problematic as that is for pure theorists, back in the actual world of microcredit, it seems likely that once we calculate carefully for the difference made to actual utility, measured in welfare, for the gain or loss of a given amount of income for those around and below the poverty line, the straightforwardly calculating consequentialist may well achieve the same result as the prioritarian without the need for arbitrariness in weighting.

The level of poverty from which a person starts will greatly affect the utility of a gain or loss of a given sum to her. For a population hovering around and below the poverty line, the consequences of losing thirty cents a day are disproportionately higher than the positives of a

---

[4] See, e.g., Derek Parfit, "Equality and Priority," *Ratio* 10 no. 3 (1997): 202–222.

[5] We need some guide as to how to weight. The philosopher Derek Parfit gives an example of two hells in "Another Defence of the Priority View," *Utilitas* 24, Special Issue 3 (2012): 339–440. In Hell 1, fifteen people suffer one hundred years of agony, whereas in Hell 2 a billion people suffer one minute of agony. Total years of agony are higher in Hell 2 than Hell 1 (1,902 vs. 1,500), but Parfit is clear that Hell 1 is worse because each of the fifteen people suffers over fifty million times longer than those in Hell 2. So 15 × 50 million units of suffering is regarded as worse than 1 billion × 1 unit of suffering (even though in units it isn't) because we weight the fact that the fifteen are so very much worse off. But by how much? Is 15 × 30 million units of suffering still worse than 1 billion × 1 unit of suffering? This is now less than half the total suffering in Hell 2, but fifteen people are still getting 30 million more times of it than any one of the billion in Hell 2. It is not clear where the lines get drawn.

thirty-cent gain. This is because at this level, not very many steps down in income will lead to a lack of ability to survive. In other words, at and below the poverty line, and increasingly the further below, the disutility of a loss of a given sum experienced in welfare terms is much greater than is the utility value of a gain of the same sum expressed in welfare gains. This is clear when we think of what that sum could buy or no longer buy if lost. Going from two to three meals a day is an important benefit and could add some years to a person's life. But going from two meals a day to one will lead to serious malnourishment if not starvation and the loss of many years, perhaps all, of expected life.

Including the utility function and disutility function, expressed in welfarist terms of those in poverty, effectively weighs the consequences of gains and loss from microcredit in the way the prioritarian would want to. In Derek Parfit's original discussion of prioritarianism,[6] each unit of benefit is equal: if someone rises from 99 to 100, he benefits as much as someone who rises from 9 to 10. In the case of microcredit, and the provision of it to those in poverty, we are making the opposite assumption: that the law of diminishing marginal returns means that someone who rises from 99 to 100 does indeed get less benefit than someone who rises from 9 to 10; and that, more importantly, for the opposite burden, falling from 10 to 9 when 10 is already survival-critical has much higher disutility than falling from 100 to 99; and that when 10 is the poverty line, the disutility of a fall from 10 to 9 is greater than the utility of a gain from 10 to 11.

The welfare consequentialist would take the measures of the impact of microfinance in terms of household income (which combine to a net zero impact) and translate these gains and losses in income into the impact on the welfare of the borrowers.[7] At this level of poverty, the negative impact on welfare of the loss of even a relatively small sum of income is greater than the positive impact on welfare of the same sum gained, leaving the consequentialist also rejecting a distribution of the benefits and burdens of microfinance that includes significant losses as well as significant gains.

I argue, then, that an ethically acceptable distribution of benefits and burdens created by the use of microcredit is one where the totality of positive consequences outweighs the totality of negative consequences after the income gains or losses to the borrower are multiplied by their welfare impact, which itself reflects the utility or disutility of the gain or loss to her, given where she starts from in poverty terms. The disutility of a unit loss in welfare terms to someone already below the poverty line will be many times the equivalent gain in welfare to one well above it. On that basis, if the total positive consequences of welfare-adjusted utility outweigh the total negative consequences of welfare-adjusted disutility, then that distribution is ethically acceptable.

---

[6] Derek Parfit, *Reasons and Persons* (New York: Oxford University Press, 1984), 67–86.

[7] This book will not attempt to do so, but one obvious unit of welfare measurement that could be used here would be the number, or fraction, of quality-adjusted life years (QALYs) a marginal difference in income could effectively buy at each and every level of poverty, the idea being that a gain from 99 to 100 for a person already on 99 would buy fewer additional QALYs than a fall from 10 to 9 would cause a person already on 10 to lose.

So what do we know about the actual distribution of the benefits and burdens of engaging with microcredit?

2. Measuring How the Distribution of Benefits and Burdens in Microfinance Falls

We need to understand just how many "winners" and "losers" from microfinance there are, and by how much they win or lose, both financially and in terms of disempowerment. Unfortunately, this is where we run into the paucity of studies that follow up on dropouts to measure what the eventual impact on them of having engaged in microfinance was. There is also very little on what the impact of microcredit is by income level: the RCTs discussed earlier only give results for the mean of the "treatment" and "control" groups. But what information there is is discussed below.

It is tempting, but difficult, to try to estimate who might be "losing" from microcredit from the statistics that MFIs do report. There is no clear single number we can point to to measure the "losers" from those who take up microcredit. Candidates are the inverse of the repayment rate (i.e., what percentage of loans move into default); the different number of those borrowers who do, individually, in fact default; the numbers who drop out; and the numbers who (if we could only measure it accurately) become overindebted and choose or are forced to make serious sacrifices to repay their loans.

The inverse of the repayment rate[8] is not an accurate measure of "losers," because a greater number of borrowers than this in fact default, but their group then makes the sum up (even if it is sometimes coercively reclaimed from the borrower's assets). A better number would be the ratio of borrowers who do in fact default on their loan, whether made up by the group or not, but even that is not a pure measure (it may potentially overstate), because some borrowers may choose to default when in fact they could comfortably continue to pay. There are also some who may "strategically" default—they are able to repay their loans, but can see one or more members of their group who are struggling badly and who will be obliged to default, leading the MFI to call upon the savings of the more successful borrowers to make good the missed payments. If enough in the group are struggling, and it is early enough on in a repayment cycle that the sum of the nonstruggling borrowers' balances outweigh the savings they stand to lose, then a mass default by the whole group is a rational response by the nonstruggling borrowers to limit the damage to them personally. Such instances might be rare but can be expected to occur when there is a general repayment crisis, caused either by local events such as economic downturn, or failure of crops or even by government advice that it is not necessary to repay loans, as happened in Andhra Pradesh in 2010.

[8] That is, 100% − repayment rate, so where that is 98%, 100% − 98% = 2%.

However this may be, individual default ratios are not released by MFIs, so we cannot measure the number of "losers" this way. The next best option is the number who drops out: the proportion of borrowers who decide not to carry on borrowing with an MFI.

Although MFIs do not regularly disclose dropout numbers, some studies have been done, and as we saw earlier, ratios of 25%–60% were found in East Africa and around 15% in Bangladesh.[9] The dropout number then needs further modification before it can be our "losers" number, however. In theory, some borrowers will drop out because the MFI has served its purpose and the business has been so successful the borrower graduates to a full banking relationship with a bank. One rarely sees this great success however, though it would surely be broadcast by the MFIs whenever it did occur. More likely, some borrowers will drop out from an MFI's program because it disappoints in terms of its delivery, the loan officers are not liked, or the weekly meetings become too time consuming. These dropouts are not "graduates," but they are not necessarily "losers" either.

Some will also leave because they can get a better rate elsewhere. However, the number of dropouts will also *under*estimate because there may be many struggling borrowers who are losing money but do manage to stay within the group. They may sell assets or take in other borrowing just to avoid default and its consequences. Rosenberg and Schicks have tried to examine how many borrowers become overindebted and would have been better off if they had not availed themselves of microcredit, roughly what is being sought here as "losers" from the process[10]

Rosenberg and Schicks's own definition of indebtedness is that borrowers are overindebted "if they have serious problems repaying their loans," with "serious" fleshed out as when a borrower "is continuously struggling to meet repayment deadlines and structurally has to make unduly high sacrifices related to his/her loan obligations. Especially in the context of an industry that says its purpose is to help the poor, microborrowers who manage to repay only by sacrificing minimum nutrition levels or their children's education should be counted as over-indebted."[11] They note:

> Overindebtedness often implies heightened vulnerability and further impoverishment of borrowers. Material effects include reduced consumption levels, late fees, asset seizures, downward spirals of ever-increasing debt, and eventually, a loss of creditworthiness. There are sociological effects related to peer pressure and a loss of social position, as well as psychological effects on mental and physical health. In extreme cases, borrowers' desperation can even lead to suicide.[12]

---

[9] Wright, "Dropouts and Graduates," 14–16; and Hulme and Mosley, *Finance against Poverty*.

[10] Richard Rosenberg and Jessica Schicks, "Too Much Microcredit? A Survey on the Evidence of Over-indebtedness," CGAP Occasional Paper No. 19, 2011. Note though that they are not suggesting that microcredit is the only, or even primary, cause of the overindebtedness, recognizing that many overindebted microcredit borrowers will be borrowing from many sources.

[11] Rosenberg and Schicks, "Too Much Microcredit?" 23.

[12] Rosenberg and Schicks, "Too Much Microcredit?" 1.

Rosenberg and Schicks are not able to quantify the actual level of overindebtedness in most markets. But they are concerned because "today there is less confidence in assertions that microcredit can raise millions of people out of poverty. The actual benefits may be considerably more modest. If the quantum of benefit we expect is lower, then the potential downsides for clients that we're willing to tolerate should be lower."[13]

Indeed so. If the total positive consequences (increased income of successful borrowers multiplied by its welfare utility to them) are smaller than proponents of microcredit thought, total negative consequences (fall in income multiplied by its welfare disutility) need to be much lower to justify microcredit ethically. The problem is that at the same time as microcredit's positive consequences are being revealed to be less prevalent than thought, more evidence has emerged of its negative consequences.

Rosenberg and Schicks locate six field studies that try to quantify microcredit overindebtedness, summarized below. It is a skewed sample because the markets studied were chosen just because local observers were worried about overindebtedness problems. Even after discounting for this, they found the results worrying.

Gonzalez's study in Bolivia—using quite a wide definition of overindebtedness as drawing down on savings or working overtime at any point over a four-year period—found that 85% of people were overindebted.[14] That is a shockingly high number, but it is perhaps too wide a definition. Many people become temporarily overindebted and have to cut back on some item of consumption in the short term, but might conceivably benefit from borrowing in the long term. We are interested in chronic overindebtedness, where a borrower is consistently making sacrifices in order to repay, perhaps rotating debt between different lenders and falling into a debt spiral.

Grammling, defining overindebtedness as having to draw down on nonbusiness assets to keep up microloan repayments, found 12% of borrowers he studied in Ghana to be overindebted and 16% at serious risk of becoming so.[15] In a restricted-distribution study of a thousand microborrowers of half a dozen institutions in a country simply labeled X, overindebtedness was defined as debt-servicing costs in excess of 100% of net income. Seventeen percent were classified as overindebted and another 10% as at risk of becoming so, with the poorer clients the most at risk of becoming overindebted.

In a peculiar study in Karnataka, India, there had been several mass defaults, largely by Muslims, in certain particular towns where local Muslim organizations banned Muslims from continuing contact with MFIs.[16] Comparing the mass default towns to the

---

[13] Rosenberg and Schicks, "Too Much Microcredit?" 3.

[14] Adrian Gonzalez, "Microfinance, Incentives to Repay, and Overindebtedness: Evidence from a Household Survey in Bolivia," PhD diss., Ohio State University, 2008, 1.

[15] Mattias Grammling, "Cross-Borrowing and Over-indebtedness in Ghana: Empirical Evidence from Microfinance Clientele and Small Enterprises," technical draft for discussion, ProCredit Holding, Frankfurt am Main, 2009.

[16] Karana Krishnaswamy and Alejandro Ponce, "A Preliminary Analysis of Mass Defaults in Karnataka, India," presentation slides, 2009), quoted by Rosenberg and Schicks, "Too Much Microcredit?" 234.

nondefault towns, 21% against 3% said repayment was a burden; 34% against 2% said they had skipped important expenses, such as meals. Rosenberg and Schicks can only speculate as to how far these defaulters were acting opportunistically in an agitated political atmosphere and how far this skewed the defaulters' accounts of their sacrifices. Note, as mentioned earlier, these defaults may have been less opportunistic than rational if borrowers thought their savings were about to be called upon to make up others' defaults. Embarrassment about admitting that possibility as a motive may also have skewed the extent of the sacrifices they claimed to have been making.

Finally, Guérin and coauthors conducted a study in Tamil Nadu, India, that defined overindebtedness as a process of impoverishment through debt, distinguishing three different levels:

1. Transitional overindebtedness: debt servicing is high enough to prevent accumulation of assets, but no worse; average debt levels are 1.4 times annual household income.
2. Pauperization: despite asset sales, debt levels continue to rise, just to service existing debt and ensure household survival. There is no realistic prospect of the debt being met long term, but for a while it is continually recharged. Average debt levels are 3.2 times household income.
3. Extreme dependence: households have no prospect of repayment and rely on kin support and charity for daily survival.[17]

Of the original sample of 344 households, Guérin and coauthors then studied the most indebted 20% in detail. Of these, 19% were in "transitory overindebtedness," 38% were cases of "pauperization," and 43% suffered from "extreme dependence." If we exclude those who may only have been in transitional overindebtedness, then, of all of those surveyed, 16% would count as overindebted to the extent that sacrifices are being made every month to ensure repayments, and a debt spiral is in place or forming.

To be clear, however, it is not Guérin and coauthors' claim that microcredit alone is overindebting 16% of all its clients or even 16% of those in Tamil Nadu. The study is of total overindebtedness. Of all 344 households, 41.3% had microcredit, and the amount was low relative to the total debt (13.5% on average). The role of microcredit here is to *add* to overindebtedness, not necessarily to cause it. Their view is that microcredit is not used as an alternative to more expensive debt, but as an additional source of liquidity, as one more tool in the juggle of smoothing revenues and expenditures. Rosenberg and Schicks's own conclusion from Guérin's study, given that in addition to the most overindebted

[17] Isabelle Guérin, Marc Roesch, Venkatasubramanian, and Santosh Kumar, "The Social Meaning of Over-indebtedness and Credit Worthiness in the Context of Poor Rural South India Households (Tamil Nadu)," RUME Working Paper Series 2011–1, 2011, Institute de recherche pour le développement, Paris.

households are households that are also overindebted, just not the most overindebted fifth, is that "twenty per cent is therefore the absolute minimum estimate for overall over-indebtedness in the original sample."[18]

This is fair enough in analyzing the problem of overindebtedness as a whole, but only a portion of it is attributable to microcredit, so although microcredit *may* be adding to the problem here, it is not the case that these problems of overindebtedness are due to microcredit alone. If one considers that microcredit is adding to overindebtedness in about half of the cases here, then this study would be broadly in line with those earlier that find around 10% of microcredit clients overindebted.

The problem of "losers" is further compounded by some evidence that these burdens are relatively more likely to fall on those least able to bear them. Hulme and Mosley drew on a study of thirteen financial institutions in seven countries, in Asia, Africa, and South America.[19] They analyzed the impact of a loan on the income of a borrower and charted that impact against her starting level of poverty, that is, where she was relative to the poverty line at the point of taking out the loan. They found that the benefit of credit was greatest to those just above the poverty line (100%–150% of it), who saw improvements to income of around 10%. Borrowers who were "upper poor," with starting incomes 200% of the poverty line, saw much lesser gains. Most problematically, those who when they borrowed were below the poverty line saw their income *reduced*, and the poorer they were, the worse this was. The business failures (estimated at 15%) were disproportionately among those who were poorest to begin with and suffer the greatest disutility from any given loss.

Coleman's study of microcredit in villages in northeast Thailand also found very clearly that microcredit was of benefit to the better off in the villages, but of little benefit to the poorest.[20] Dividing borrowers into "committee members"—those who became the president, vice president, or treasurer of the borrowing group—and the "rank and file," he found that those who became committee members started out wealthier and did better from their loan, and very many used the names of members not currently borrowing to take out loans in their names to add to their own borrowings. "In the most extreme case, one village bank president (who was also the village chief's business partner and a moneylender for several villages in the area) used nine names to borrow." Coleman estimates that more than a third of loan volume was borrowed by someone other than the person whose name the debt was recorded against. These wealthier committee members benefited from their borrowing. But

[18] Rosenberg and Schicks, "Too Much Microcredit?" 28.

[19] David Hulme and Paul Mosley, "Finance for the Poor or Poorest? Financial Innovation, Poverty and Vulnerability," Discussion Papers in Development Economics, Series G, vol. 4, 1996.

[20] Brett E. Coleman, "Microfinance in Northeast Thailand: Who Benefits and How Much?" ERD Paper Series No. 9, Asian Development Bank, April 2002.

for the rank and file the results were largely insignificant—indeed the only results that *did* have a significant impact for them were all negative.[21]

As we have seen, high default rates cannot simply be read across to suggest overindebted borrowers, or the "losers" from microcredit, but clearly rising default levels can only be a bad sign. They have risen globally. A 2010 study summarizes recent problems: Chen, Rasmussen, and Reille report that delinquent loans rose from 2% to 7% between 2004 and 2009 in Bosnia-Herzegovina, and to 10% in Morocco, 12% in Nicaragua, and 13% in Pakistan.[22]

Taking the evidence then of the early Hulme and Mosley survey (15% business failures overall, disproportionately among those poorest to begin with, who saw income reduced), the indebtedness surveys (serious indebtedness of at least 10%, albeit in places known to be problematical), and the numbers that regularly drop out (10%–65%), it seems reasonable to suggest that there are at least 10% of microfinance borrowers whose lives go worse from having borrowed, with the percentage peaking at very much higher levels when credit has become too easily available in a market and overborrowing has occurred. Dropouts are certainly lower in Asia than Africa, and interest rates also lower, so it may well be that Asia would be at the lower end of this approximation, but given that, for example, loans past due or rescheduled at Grameen Bank are even today in excess of 12%,[23] that lower end may well hold good, even in Asia. Given that the RCTs that have been carried out that did include dropouts (as the Spandata study did) showed no overall positive net impact, and that we know that most enterprises do not flourish (because so few expand), it would follow that to offset the hidden losers, there are either more 'winners' than is apparent at first sight, or that there are indeed few, but that they are gaining more each than the 'losers' are losing.

Banerjee and coauthors' update of their Spandata study suggests just the latter (although it is not explicitly tested for).[24] Three to four years after the initial expansion of borrowing, the average business was still no more profitable than at the start, but there was an increase in profits at the top end; and it was not just any old increase.

After fifteen to eighteen months, at every quantile between the fifth and ninety-fifth percentile, there was no difference in the profits of a business. There was an increase in the average profits of businesses already in existence before microcredit is expanded, "but

---

[21] Coleman notes that in four of the eight treatment villages and three of the six control villages, at least one committee member engaged in moneylending to some degree, "and some non-members and rank and file members complained that committee members borrowed from the village bank, then lent the money at higher interest rates." This problem, that some of the higher-margin, more successful businesses that microcredit borrowers undertake are not necessarily quite what the lending institution originally had in mind, is discussed in chapter 7.

[22] Greg Chen, Stephen Rasmussen, and Xavier Reille, "Growth and Vulnerabilities in Microfinance," CGAP Focus Note 61, 2010.

[23] Past due, overdue, and flexible (rescheduled) loans as a percentage of the loan portfolio, calculated from Grameen's figures available at http://www.grameen-info.org, under Data and Reports tab, accessed August 19, 2014.

[24] Banerjee et al., "The Miracle of Microfinance?"

this is entirely due to very large increases in the upper tail." For businesses that existed before Spandata expanded, profits increase on average Rs 2,194 in treatment areas, double the control mean. But this is *entirely* contained in the upper tail, quantiles 95 and above, where the monthly profit is Rs 14,600.

It is all the businesses between the thirty-fifth and sixty-fifth percentiles that pulled the average down: these all showed "significantly lower profits in the treatment areas."

As we saw in chapter 2, the overall picture Banerjee and coauthors paint is that where there is an existing business and then microfinance is made available, the already successful borrow even more, lever up, and can do well—but there were very few of these, and businesses that were new or inexperienced saw no benefit to profits from microcredit. A picture is being suggested of microcredit's benefits and burdens, then, of nearly all of the gains from microcredit accruing to successes among the top 5%, possibly fewer; of a large "middle" where little difference is made or is negative, but only modestly so; and some number at the bottom that could be around 10% or more, where lives go worse from having engaged with microcredit.

Crépon and coauthors found much larger effects on profits from businesses that chose to use microcredit in Morocco, but found the same tendency for the top few businesses using credit to make a very high proportion of the profits that were made in total, and the smallest businesses (likely managed by those on the lowest incomes) to do the worst.[25] Their results suggested that 25% of businesses that used microcredit saw a negative impact on profits, balanced off by the high profits of the larger businesses. The authors do not explicitly link size of business to above- or below-median income, but it is likely that those on lower incomes would be seeking to borrow less than those with more assets and hence again that it is the lower-income groups who are doing the worst from microcredit under the blanket "overall, net zero" average.

The distribution of the benefits and burdens of microfinance, on the patchy evidence we have, appears to be that at least a significant minority, perhaps 10% or more, and still more in credit bubbles, are losing significantly, and these are typically poorer borrowers for whom disutility from the loss is highest. There is a large majority to whom not much difference is made, and a small number of "winners" who really do relatively well.

Most of the studies cited above were trying to establish the overall impact of microcredit on the average borrower, not explicitly which groups might do best or worst out of it. Angelucci, Karlon, and Zinman carried out a study of borrowing from Compartamos in Mexico to try to pick up who is "winning" and who is "losing" from borrowing at an APR of 110%.[26]

---

[25] Crépon et al., "Estimating the Impact."

[26] Manuela Angelucci, Dean Karlan, and Jonathan Zinman, "Win Some Lose Some? Evidence from a Randomized Microcredit Program Placement Experiment by Compartamos Banco," May 2013, available from the Poverty Action website at http://www.poverty-action.org/sites/default/files/ipa_winsomelosesome_release_0.pdf.

The authors conducted a randomized trial in north-central Sonora, Mexico, remeasuring after eighteen to thirty-four months. Overall, they concluded that microcredit caused "some good and little harm," increasing the size of some existing businesses but finding no effect on profits. If the "good" here, however, is simply a larger—but no more profitable—business, then this will not obviously have a positive welfare impact at all, so it is unclear that this adds to the total of positive consequences of microcredit. Like Banerjee and coauthors, they find very modest impact on average, with increases in business profits for above-median-size businesses, but losses for businesses below the median.

The authors then divided up borrowers into different subgroups: urban/rural, prior experience, income level, extent of education. Those on above-median income had little difference made to them. But the below-median income group had only one positive result and five negative. Overall, the authors do not think their study provides strong evidence that borrowing at these levels creates large numbers of "losers" as well as winners. But they are, rightly, concerned that those on lower incomes, and those without formal credit experience, suffer "negative treatment effects on balance."

This point could be made rather more strongly. Where the authors suggest that for the least well-off groups there are negative effects "on balance," they mean that of their measured outcomes, a majority were negative for this group. But this majority of negative effects include some of the most important outcomes measured, at least if we are trying to look at for whom microcredit alleviates poverty. Those on below-median incomes saw negative impacts "on profits, business problems, locus of control, trust in institutions, and life satisfaction."[27] Echoing Hulme and Mosley's work of the 1990s, this study shows that it is those on below-median incomes, who can least afford it, who do worst from their microcredit enterprises.

Since business profits are down and there are business problems with the below-median income group, it is likely that they are struggling to repay their debts, though this is not explicit. There are reasons to believe that those on below-median incomes are more vulnerable to falling into overindebtedness than those on above-median incomes. Stewart and coauthors in a systemic review of microcredit, microsavings, and microleasing suggest a very straightforward mechanism for why this should be so.[28]

Borrowers, they point out, have to make a considerable return (remember the interest rate tables in chapter 3) on a small capital investment very quickly—often within a week—to make their first loan repayment. Clients with above-median income are more likely to have a financial buffer to draw on to make that first and subsequent repayments, if sufficient income from

[27] Angelucci, Karlan, and Zinman, "Win Some Lose Some?" 25.

[28] Ruth Stewart, Carina van Rooyen, Marcel Korth, Admire Chereni, Natalie Rebelo Da Silva, and Thea de Wet, "Do Micro-credit, Micro-savings and Micro-leasing Serve as Effective Financial Inclusion Interventions Enabling Poor People, and Especially Women, to Engage in Meaningful Economic Opportunities in Lower and Middle Income Countries?" technical report, EPPI-Centre, Social Science Research Unit, Institute of Education, University of London, 2012.

the businessis not forthcoming with which to do so. For the poorest of the poor, "A failure to increase their income sufficiently will result in the loss of the collateral used to secure the loan in the first place and/or a requirement for further loans and a potential cycle of debt."

The better off may or may not be more successful in generating enough income from a loan-financed business so as to make the first repayment, but if they do not, they are more likely to have reserves to make the first repayment with instead, thus avoiding a debt spiral. As Stewart and coauthors add, "This is not to say that the poorest of the poor will necessarily face more difficulty in repaying proportionate loans, but that the risks to their quality of life are more severe if they are unable to make repayments."[29]

This leads Stewart and coauthors to suggest that MFIs should be very careful in lending to poor groups. They suggest that practitioners, as well as policymakers, need to be cautious when deciding whom to target with microcredit services. Microcredit ought only to be targeted at the poorest of the poor with considerable care because some clients will be made poorer as a result of taking out a loan, the consequences of which could be devastating. Services should be targeted at those who already have some financial security, such as savings or another source of income, which will allow them to make loan repayments even if their businesses do not generate a profit immediately.[30]

3. Shifting the Balance of the Distribution of Benefits and Burdens in Microfinance

Rigorous statistical evidence on the distribution of the benefits and burdens of microcredit is only just beginning to emerge. The studies discussed above suggest a pattern of a few winners, to whom most of the total gains accrue, and rather more losers. The majority experience little difference one way or the other, but the losers are most likely to come from the lower income groups, least able to bear the loss.

The BBC reporter Mukul Devichand observed this pattern anecdotally when he visited a joint liability group of ten women in the slum of Navodhya Nagar in Hyderabad. Of these ten, one was in severe debt, one's business was "a flop," and two had "man-trouble"—one woman's husband had run off with her loan and another's drank the money away. Five were not observing much difference in their lives. The remaining one who was had started a sari-trading firm and was now building a grand new home on the lake.[31]

The pattern that out of a group of ten, there might be one significant winner, five broadly nil effects, three negative experiences but not so severe as to suggest overindebtedness, and one very significant loser, is not a distribution that is likely to be acceptable

[29] Stewart et al., "Micro-credit, Micro-savings and Micro-leasing," 26.

[30] Stewart et al., "Micro-credit, Micro-savings and Micro-leasing," 7.

[31] "The Bankers and the Bottom Billion," broadcast on BBC Radio 4 FM at 8:00 p.m. on May 17, 2011.

to many. This is particularly so for welfare consequentialists if household income impacts are translated into welfare impact, at which point the net zero income impact would likely translate into a net negative welfare impact. Of course, this is not to suggest that the statistics yet back the one-off anecdote as to the precise distribution of benefits and burdens, but they are suggestive of a pattern close to it, and do give a worrying sense that microcredit is producing rather too many losers for the few winners that emerge.

When the National Institute for Health and Care Excellence (NICE) in the United Kingdom decides whether a new drug should be allowed to be prescribed by doctors working for the National Health Service (NHS), what is taken into consideration is the number of lives that will be improved by use of the drug in treatment, and by how much; the number of lives that are likely to be adversely affected by use of the drug treatment, and by how much; and the cost-effectiveness of the drug compared to the other treatments.

If microcredit were a drug up for approval by NICE for the treatment of poverty, what would shock those at NICE deciding on its approval or otherwise would first be the lack of evidence of numbers benefiting and by how much; and numbers being hurt, and by how much. At best, at the moment, the MFIs proposing microcredit would only be able to say, as industry consultant and critic Hugh Sinclair pithily puts it, "mostly ineffective, helps a slim minority, kills very few."[32] If anything, studying the work on overindebtedness—though recognizing that microcredit is only a contributory cause and not necessarily the dominant one—suggests an even less comfortable picture. The winners are a small minority of perhaps 5%; there are twice as many losers, more in times of bubbles; and the losers are concentrated amongst the poorest who can least afford to bear the loss. That, alas, would not be sufficient, one suspects, to pass NICE guidelines. What would certainly then fail it as a mass treatment for poverty would be its cost-effectiveness: what is the opportunity cost to the treatment purchaser (for NICE here, think USAID or DFID) of prescribing microcredit rather than some alternative that could be implemented? The implications of *that* are taken up in chapter 8.

This chapter started out asking what would be an ethically acceptable distribution of the benefits and burdens of microcredit, and whether it was it likely that microcredit as practiced meets that standard. It has been argued that *some* losses to a few, especially those who are least poor, whose welfare disutility in incurring them is least, might be acceptable if they were balanced by many gains, especially if they were enjoyed by the poorest, whose welfare utility from the gain would be the highest. Unfortunately, such evidence as there is suggests the reverse is the case: losers outnumber winners and are concentrated among those who suffer most welfare disutility from the loss. Microcredit could clearly improve

[32] Hugh Sinclair, *Confessions of a Microfinance Heretic* blog post, "Disguised Mediocrity—the Quest for POSITIVE Impact Results at Compartamos," August 27, 2013.

the ethical balance of its distribution of benefits and burdens if it could somehow lend only to those who turned out to be successes: easy to suggest, but rather more difficult to do. Picking who will be a successful entrepreneur individually is likely to be no easier for an MFI in developing countries than for a private equity firm scouring individual investment opportunities in developed countries. From Banerjee and coauthors' work, we can see that some conditions are likely to be helpful: the borrower who already runs a business, has already shown skills, and has some buffer from existing profits to make early repayments on a loan if the new or expanded business does not generate profits soon enough. This is a borrower who already understands the risks of debt and is actively and knowingly seeking more of it. It is a legitimate pool to seek to lend to: just not necessarily a very large one.

At the start of this chapter, I suggested that the questions we need to answer are how to secure sufficient client protection in microfinance that, though the causing of some harms may have to be accepted, they never go beyond a certain extreme; and how to ensure that total harms caused are only a small proportion of the total gains achieved.

The previous chapter proposed microfinance practitioners recognize a duty of care to their borrowers, and spelt out how this could be specified. If practitioners accept these measures, and in particular were prepared to accept higher levels of default or loan rescheduling when the borrower is in difficulties, it is likely some of the worst harms could be avoided. Practitioners can also actively seek to avoid lending to those with the worst risk/reward profile, as best we know it. These are those who are below the poverty line and who have never run a business before. Sometimes it is easier to recognize a common profile of likely "losers" than "winners," and Hulme and Mosley's, Stewart and coauthors', and Banerjee and coauthors' works suggest that this is so in microcredit.

It is unfortunate that the best way microcredit might improve its effectiveness at alleviating poverty may be by stopping trying to help the poorest of the poor, those its most altruistically minded practitioners want to help the most. But two things need to be accepted: first, the old medical dictum "First, do no harm" applies to extending microcredit too. And second, Yunus's dictum that every poor person in the world has the potential to be an entrepreneur (all she lacks in access to capital) is just simply false. The academic studies may not yet show us clearly what the distribution of the benefits and burdens of microcredit are. But they do show that the majority of businesses that are started with microcredit do not or only barely cover their costs, that few ever grow, and that the worst results come from those who are new to entrepreneurship.

Given this, the shortcut for microcredit improving its ethical balance is to refocus away from trying to lend, on a sustainable basis, to the poorest, and on the assumption that any poor woman can start and succeed in a business. There are two models it could follow in doing so. One is to keep the focus on the poorest, but provide grants, support, and basic welfare before attempting to lend, and accept that this will come at the cost of sustainability (BRAC and BASIX might argue that they exemplify such a model). The other model is to lose the focus on the poorest while keeping the aim of sustainability, by refocusing on the better off poor and SME lending, as ProCredit is trying to do, in the hope that this will improve local economies and that these benefits will eventually trickle down to the poorest. Either route means the bulk of microcredit moving away from the Grameen-style model that has been such a promotional success. But other models do exist, and whilst the subsidized, grant model and SME lending model represent two extremes, bifurcating the centre ground to either of these may be the only way for microcredit to shift its ethical balance such that it can have confidence that it actually does more good than harm.

All that glisters is not gold . . .
Gilded tombs do worms enfold
—SHAKESPEARE, *The Merchant of Venice*

7 Hear No Evil, See No Evil, Speak No Evil

MICROFINANCE AND THE INFORMAL ECONOMY

CHAPTERS 3, 4, AND 5 looked at ethical issues arising from the relationship between the MFI and individual borrower, in particular whether that relationship is exploitative, coercive, and lacking in a morally required duty of care from MFI to borrower. Chapter 6 broadened the perspective to the moral acceptability of the distribution of benefits and burdens of microcredit on its borrowers as a whole, as best we know it. The next chapter will assess the impact of microcredit on societies and economies as a whole, its macro impact on development. This chapter, however, looks at some of the more ethically challenging practices of microcredit borrowers themselves, the extent to which MFIs and MIVs are complicit in them, and the lack of transparency of MFIs with regard to the challenges of operating in the informal economy.

The vast majority of microloans that go into enterprises (as opposed to consumption) go into enterprises in the informal economy. They are mostly one-person businesses, typically unregistered, that do not pay tax and would struggle to comply with laws designed for large corporations. If MFIs took the stance that they would only lend to microenterprises that were operating on a fully legal basis in the formal economy, much lending would cease. It is the role of the state, not the MFI, to decide the extent to which it wants to enforce its regulations and tax laws. Nonetheless, MFIs do have some choice as to whether to support some of the illegal or unethical enterprises that some loans are used for.

The chapter is in three parts. The first examines some of the more questionable business uses to which some loans are put, from the brewing of high-ethanol alcohol, moneylending, and funding of illegal migration, to the illegal making and selling of charcoal or funding a cockfighting business. The second part looks at microborrowers' use of child labor. Some of these uses of loans and labor by borrowers are illegal, some are illicit, and some are unethical: some are all three. Here I ask what ethical principles should guide MFIs as to when a loan use should not be funded or child labor allowed, even if legal.

The third part of this chapter then broadens out the discussion from the widespread absence of transparent policies on permissible loan use and use of child labor in the microcredit industry, to its more general lack of transparency, including with regard to the true level of interest rates and its own efficacy. This lack of transparency has perhaps resulted from the tendency of microcredit to preserve the public facade of "doing good by doing well" at all times. The extremes of hyperbole beginning in the 1990s, when the industry was rashly overpromoting itself as a cure to poverty, may perhaps be over for now. But the industry is still reluctant to allow publicly that difficult ethical quandaries lie just below its surface. This needs to change, because if there is little or no published guidance on permissible loan use, use of child labor, acceptable loan collection practices, and so forth, in practice anything *may* go, and might again in the future.

It is true that even when there are published guides, they may not always be followed in practice: undeniably, money being fungible, a borrower may insist a loan is for one purpose and use it for another. But by having transparent codes on these matters, even if on occasion they are abused, MFIs have a standard to hold their loan officers to, and to be held to themselves. It is not enough that the industry has reduced the level of its overpromising: to eliminate unethical practices both by MFIs and by MFI borrowers, it needs to be transparent about what practices are and are not acceptable.

The business use a loan is put to, then, and the labor used in that business can be illegal, illicit, or unethical, or a combination of the three. The tricky areas for a board of an MFI trying to decide which loan uses should be allowed are those loans that are for purposes that are illegal but not necessarily illicit or unethical, and those for business usages that are perfectly legal but either illicit or unethical, or both.

It would be well to define the terms being used here. An illegal loan use is one that breaks the law of the country it is lent in. An illicit loan use is one that is often illegal, but not necessarily: rather it is disapproved of by the majority of the members of the society in which it occurs and tends to be secretive. An unethical loan use may or may not be illegal or illicit but is one that breaches a universal moral principle or at least one of a widely overlapping set of moral principles.

This last area can be problematical, especially where funders in the West regard a loan use or business practice as unethical, but local culture does not (i.e., it is not illicit). Examples would be loans to fund a cockfighting business or the growth of coca.[1] Any board

---

[1] Hugh Sinclair reports on the campaign of some Kivans to stop Kiva from financing cockfighting loans on grounds of animal cruelty and ponders the wisdom of providing loans to borrowers to grow and sell the leaves of coca while the US government funds coca eradication programs as part of the "War on Drugs," in *Confessions of a Microfinance Heretic: How Microfinance Lost Its Way and Betrayed the Poor* (San Francisco: Berrett-Koehler, 2012), 171.

of a Western-based MFI practicing in the developing world will have to be alert to the dangers of "us" patronizingly imposing "our" ethical standards on "them." But while such a board should be alert to that danger, using that danger as an excuse to simply adopt a guide that if a practice is not illegal or illicit, then it is permissible, or even that practices in the informal economy are no concern of an MFI board, will not do. A board doing that would be like a round-the-world yachtsman deciding that learning how to use navigational charts was just all too difficult and setting sail regardless of where the winds might blow him. Lending money to the poor and vulnerable who then put it to use among the poor and vulnerable entails a moral responsibility that cannot be disposed of quite so easily. There are some practices—moneylending at exorbitant interest rates being one—that are not illegal or necessarily illicit, but exploit the poorest and by any general standard would be deemed unethical. Alas, this loan use—a borrower arbitraging the rate at which she can borrow from the MFI, however high, to on-lend still higher—is not an uncommon one. Complex though the issues are to think through, cultural sensitivity cannot be used as an excuse for not doing so.

Happily, boards do not have to choose between whole ethical systems in order to determine an ethical guideline as to what business practices should be permissible among borrowers. The simplest solution is to use John Stuart Mill's "harm principle," which states, roughly, that people should be allowed to do as they please with their own talents, capital, and labor without interference—provided they do no harm to others in the process. This will enable distinctions to be made between permissible and impermissible loan and labor uses, and be equally acceptable to boards coming to ethics from consequentialist, absolutist, religious, or indeed just plain haphazard points of view. It is not as strong as Kant's categorical imperative[2] or the Christian Golden Rule, to always treat others as one would wish to be treated oneself, but it does not need to be: Boards do not need a complete guide to how to live an ethical life, but a practical rule as to what uses of loans are ethically permissible and which are not.

Mill states his principle in several different ways, but in *On Liberty* as follows: "The only purpose for which power can be rightfully exercised over any member of a civilised community, against his will, is to prevent harm to others . . . the only part of the conduct of any one, for which he is amenable to society, is that which concerns others."[3] It is the fact that this principle is the key to setting the boundary on how individuals may behave in the marketplace and in society, how to mark the trade-off between individual liberty and the impact of individual behavior on society, that makes it appropriate to guide decisions on what uses of a loan an MFI may make.

---

[2] In either of its formations, that one should always act in such a way that one can consistently will that everyone else act in the same way, or that one should never treat humanity in oneself or in others merely as a means but always also as an end.

[3] John Stuart Mill, *On Liberty*, in *Collected Works*, vol. 18, *Essays on Politics and Society* (Toronto: University of Toronto Press, 1977), 223.

Applying the harm principle to what uses of loan and labor an MFI should allow extends an MFI's responsibilities not just to recognizing a duty of care to its borrowers, but to protect those who are not even clients of the MFI from potentially harmful consequences of the MFI's clients' business activity. To some, that may seem to extend the MFI's responsibilities too far, but this book is about how to practice microfinance *ethically*. It is illegal in developed countries for financial institutions to knowingly lend to businesses engaged in illegal activities: that at least should be the same for MFIs. And for ethical MFIs, there is one step further: the ethical MFI should only lend to borrowers whose use of the loan itself does not involve harm to others.

One should be clear about the limits on what is meant by "harm." The harm Mill refers to here is not harm caused by offense to feelings based on individual views of morality or immorality. If lending to fund the production of high-ethanol alcohol (moonshine) is forbidden because it causes harm, it is not because the harm consists in the distress caused to those who believe all alcoholic consumption is immoral, but because moonshine consumption is linked to the spread of AIDS in sub-Saharan Africa and thus generates real harm to the welfare of partners of drinkers of moonshine. Nor is the type of harm referred to here that which is caused by fair economic competition knowingly entered into, such as a new entrant microcredit borrower selling tomatoes who puts an existing tomato seller out of business. That is an issue for the next chapter, which considers microcredit's impact on development as a whole. The harm referred to here is harm to welfare inflicted unilaterally (if sometimes unintentionally) on an innocent party.

What, then, are some of the business practices of borrowers from MFIs that need ethical exploration? Below are listed some challenging loan uses, some of which are illegal but some of which are not, and it will be seen how using the harm principle as an ethical guide can help a board determine where a business practice of a borrower might be unethical even where legal. The same approach is then taken to borrowers' use of child labor, before finally opening up wider issues of transparency in microcredit. I shall start with the example suggested above, the production and sale of illicit hard liquor, which is legal in some countries and illegal in others, illicit in most, and, I argue below, unethical in countries where it is closely associated with harm to others, most particularly sub-Saharan Africa.

1. Ethically Questionable Loan Uses

HARM TO OTHERS: MAKING AND SELLING MOONSHINE (HARD LIQUOR)

Most MFIs make it clear to borrowers that loans may not be used to pursue illegal activities, but where some of these illegal activities meet the cash flow requirements of the MFIs and are widely practiced despite their illegality, a blind eye may be turned. An example of this is the use of loans to produce and retail moonshine, high-ethanol alcohol, in sub-Saharan Africa. In this instance, very serious questions of harms to others are raised because of the link, especially strong in southern Africa, between alcohol use and the spread of HIV/AIDS, violence, and crime. This is particularly so where it is sold at informal gatherings and from, or from near, private homes, as is often the case when it is sold by microcredit clients.

Kalichman and coauthors in 2007 reviewed all the academic literature—about 80 studies—that examined the link between alcohol use and sexual risk behavior in southern Africa.[4] They observe that research has "repeatedly shown that alcohol use is related to sexual risks in several populations, especially among those with the highest rates of HIV infections."[5] As background, they note that two out of three people with HIV live in sub-Saharan Africa, where great quantities of alcohol are also consumed. They find that "like elsewhere in the world, alcohol use is often associated with sexual risks in southern Africa. However, unlike anywhere else, the implications of alcohol use on risks for HIV infection are greatest in southern Africa because HIV prevalence rates are highest."[6]

The studies surveyed show clearly that alcohol use is associated with STI (sexually transmitted infection) and HIV prevalence. The predominant risk behavior is among men who drink, who are more likely to have multiple sex partners, not use a condom, use prostitutes, and then transmit diseases to their partners at home. This is the link WHO refers to when it states (specifically here of Zambia): "Alcohol abuse constitutes one of the principal reasons for the propagation of AIDS especially among married women."[7] The Kalichman metastudy summarizes: "People who drink alcohol in southern Africa are at higher risk for HIV than individuals who do not drink. The association between drinking and sexual risks is also observed across a wide array of populations. Any alcohol use at all and drinking greater quantities of alcohol are closely associated with HIV transmission risks in southern Africa."[8]

Having established this, Kalichman and coauthors go on to look at factors that connect to alcohol use that can exacerbate its negative effects. Unfortunately, given my own personal experience in seeing the way in which the moonshine produced by women borrowers is sold in Malawi and Zambia (from shacks or from near their homes), the study then finds this to be a distribution method that further increases the risk of spreading disease. "Informal alcohol serving establishments, such as private homes where alcoholic beverages are sold and served, are also often the same places where sex partners meet."[9]

---

[4] Seth Kalichman, Leickness Simbayi, Michelle Kaufman, Demetria Cain, and Sean Jooste, "Alcohol Use and Sexual Risks for HIV/AIDS in Sub-Saharan Africa: Systematic Review of Empirical Findings," *Society of Prevention Research* 8 (2007): 141–151.

[5] In particular they cite Lance Weinhardt and Michael Carey, "Does Alcohol Lead to Sexual Risk Behaviour?" *Annual Review of Sex Research* 12 (2001): 125–157.

[6] Kalichman et al., "Alcohol Use," 141.

[7] See www.who.int/substance_abuse/publications/en/zambia.pdf

[8] Kalichman et al., "Alcohol Use," 146.

[9] Neo Morojele, Millicent Kachieng'a, Matsobane Nkoko, Kgaogelo Moshia, Evodia Mokoko, Charles Parry, Mwansa Nkowane, and Shekhar Saxena, "Perceived Effects of Alcohol Use on Sexual Encounters among Adults in South Africa," *African Journal of Drugs and Alcohol Studies* 3 (2004): 1–20.

Research conducted in South Africa has demonstrated the close association between patronizing shebeens and HIV risks. Weir and coauthors[10] mapped the linkages among places where people meet new sex partners and places where people drink alcohol. The study demonstrated a remarkable overlap among these venues: "Over 85% of the locations where people meet sex partners are alcohol serving establishments. . . . As many as 57% of men and 46% of women who drink at shebeens report having two or more sex partners in the past two weeks. Unfortunately, shebeens and other alcohol serving establishments, such as taverns and bottle stores, rarely have condoms available for their customers. . . . The number of days of the week that men drink correlates with their frequency of engaging in unprotected sex with casual partners. . . . Places that serve alcohol therefore appear uniquely linked to HIV transmission risks in southern Africa."

On top of the risks of HIV-AIDS transmission, Kalichman and coauthors summarize the evidence of a link between alcohol use and sexual coercion. (Note that the highest incidence of new HIV infections in Malawi is among girl adolescents [ten to nineteen years of age], 56% of whom report forced sex.)[11] Kalichman and coauthors summarize: "Sexual assault is prevalent in southern Africa and sexual violence is related to alcohol use and HIV transmission risks. Men who have a history of sexual violence are more likely to drink than men who have not been sexually assaultive. Likewise, alcohol use is associated with having been sexually assaulted among women. . . . The association between relationship violence and HIV risk is at least partly accounted for by alcohol use . . . it is clear that alcohol consumption and sexual violence are related."[12]

The question of whether a woman distilling and selling moonshine in southern Africa does so legally or not varies with each country, but usually turns on whether she has been licensed. In both Zambia and Malawi, for example, the production of moonshine (often called *kachasu* in Zambia, but it has a lot of nicknames in both places) for home consumption, for personal use, is legal. The sale of it, unless licensed, is illegal. The sale of it to those under age eighteen is illegal, whether licensed or unlicensed. (This is a serious problem in Zambia.)

Some provinces in Zambia have local bylaws regarding *kachasu* specifically that make the sale of it illegal even if licensed.[13] I have not yet met a woman borrower in either of

---

[10] Sharon Weir, Charmaine Pailman, Xoli Mahlalela, Nicol Coetzee, Farshid Meidany, and Ties Boerma, "From People to Places: Focusing AIDS Prevention Efforts Where It Matters Most," *AIDS* 17 (2003): 895–903.

[11] Anne Conroy, Malcolm Blackie, Alan Whiteside, Justin Malewezi, and Jeffrey Sachs, *Poverty, AIDS and Hunger: Breaking the Poverty Trap in Malawi* (Basingstoke: Palgrave Macmillan, 2006), 59–60.

[12] Kalichman et al., "Alcohol Use," 148.

[13] The law in this area in Zambia is summarized by Alan Haworth in *Moonshine Markets*, ed. Alan Haworth and Ronald Simpson (New York: Hove: Brunner-Routledge, 2004), 41–67. The main acts are the Liquor Licensing Act (Chapter 167 of the Laws of Zambia), the Traditional Beer Act, and the Markets Act, which forbids the sale of alcoholic beverages within markets. In Malawi, the main act that covers moonshine is the Liquor Act, 1979. Of course, there is widespread recognition that these laws are widely flouted and rarely enforced, although there are sporadic outburst of activity. For example, a team of forty-eight security officers rounded up *kachasu*

these countries who includes the cost of a license in her cost breakdown when asked. It is unlikely that licenses are even applied for, as the borrowers are operating in the informal sector and do not usually pay taxes. If they are not licensed, they are selling moonshine illegally. Production and sale of moonshine is frequently illegal in sub-Saharan Africa and often illicit. It is nonetheless a widespread activity and, ethics apart, suits the high short-term cash flow demands of a microcredit loan—it can be produced and sold and a profit turned even within a week. And an MFI can argue that sale of homemade moonshine has a long history in some cultures. Some MFIs in sub-Saharan Africa already ban it as a loan use, but not all; one MFI in Malawi the author is aware of regarded it as acceptable at the time, and loans to brew and sell moonshine then represented 40% of all loan uses (subsequently reduced). But it clearly fails the harm principle test for ethical permissibility.

Opinions may vary as to whether the consumers of the moonshine should be paternalistically prevented from harming themselves. But here we have harm to wholly innocent parties: the resultant rape victims and, notably, the wives of the drinking men who have caught STIs that their partners picked up from unprotected sex with prostitutes. It might be as well to be clear here that none of this is to suggest that microcredit itself plays a large part in the spread of AIDS in sub-Saharan Africa—the AIDS endemic is a much bigger problem than microcredit-financed production of moonshine could possibly account for. What *is* suggested is that it is very clearly an unethical loan use, and one that MFIs should make clear to borrowers is impermissible.

IMPERCEPTIBLE HARMS: ENVIRONMENTAL DEGRADATION

Not permitting loans to be used for the production of and sale of moonshine is a relatively straightforward case: it is, after all, often illegal and illicit as well as being unethical. I have dwelt on it because it is not illegal everywhere, so it is necessary to draw out the principle that what really makes it unethical and wrong to do or fund is the terrible harm it causes to others, who are innocent parties—not even the borrower or even her clients, but the wives of the latter. Whatever its legal status, it is the harm-to-others principle that really drives the ethical reasoning as to why this loan use should not be allowed.

There are more complex cases where the loan use is illegal but licit and the ethics are in dispute. Such loan uses might be for those microenterprises whose underlying activity is illegal for the good reason that, conducted on a large scale, it leads to environmental degradation, but where the individual microentrepeneur might claim that the tiny difference she makes is so insignificant as to be undetectable. Examples of such businesses might be the making and sale of charcoal where it is done unsustainably and leads to deforestation,

distillers in Mazabuka in August 2009—though it took them an hour and a half to arrest a woman in her sixties who threatened to bewitch any police officer who dared lift her. See http://www.zambian-economist.com/2009/08/inefficient-policing.html.

or fishing where the microloan is used to buy a net with a small mesh size, risking the overfishing of certain species.

The problem here is that while any individual microentrepeneur may make an imperceptible difference to environmental degradation, there are many hundreds of thousands of them. It is sometimes thought that an act that benefits one by creating a very tiny harm to a large number of people, so tiny that it is almost imperceptible, is a "victimless crime" and all but harmless. This is a failure of moral mathematics. All the tiny, near invisible harms need to be added together.

To see this, consider the moral philosopher Jonathan Glover's argument against the view that harm is not divisible:

> Suppose a village contains 100 unarmed tribesmen eating their lunch. 100 hungry armed bandits descend on the village and each bandit at gun-point takes one tribesman's lunch and eats it. The bandits then go off, each one having done a discriminable amount of harm to a single tribesman. Next week, the bandits are tempted to do the same thing again, but are troubled by new-found doubts about the morality of such a raid. Their doubts are put to rest by one of their number who does not believe in the principle of divisibility. They then raid the village, tie up the tribesmen, and look at their lunch. As expected, each bowl of food contains 100 baked beans. The pleasure derived from one baked bean is below the discrimination threshold. Instead of each bandit eating a single plateful as last week, each take one bean from each plate. They leave after eating all the beans, pleased to have done no harm, as each has done no more than sub-threshold harm to each person. Those who reject the principle of divisibility have to agree.[14]

Malawi lost 13% of its total forest cover to firewood collection and subsistence commercial agriculture between 1990 and 2005.[15] Throughout this time, charcoal production was illegal, but it is estimated that it employed 93,000 people as producers, transporters, and roadside vendors. Ironically, if it were legalized it could then be regulated and made sustainable. But while it is illegal, no reforestation takes place, and so the harm to future generations of the loss of this resource caused by all these tiny individual harms (only some of which are financed by microcredit, of course) will be considerable. Microcredit by no means takes the sole blame for this: but lending for charcoal production certainly adds to the problem, and on the harm principle must be deemed an unethical, impermissible loan use.

---

[14] Jonathan Glover, "It Makes No Difference Whether or Not I Do It," *Proceedings of the Aristotelean Society Supplementary* 49 (1975): 174–175.

[15] See "Malawi: Charcoal Is a Burning Issue," IRIN Humanitarian News and Analysis, available at http://www.irinnews.org/report/80816/malawi-charcoal-is-a-burning-issue.

This is written cautiously, however, knowing the borrowers here are trying to eke out a living with few opportunities to choose from, and preventing their miniscule contribution to environmental damage will not of itself stop others simply taking their place. But the answer to that dilemma is not to permit permanent damage to be done, but for the state to provide a better route to sustainability of its forests than simply criminalizing its poor.

ARBITRAGED HARM: MONEYLENDING

The above two loan uses are, largely, illegal as well as unethical. The next example is of a dubiously ethical loan use that is frequently legal and licit, as well as common—moneylending.

Chapter 3 argued at length that many microcredit rates themselves are exploitative and exorbitant, certainly where they are multiples of the formal rate. Where a microcredit is being arbitraged by a borrower, the rate at which it is on-lent will be even higher, even more exorbitant. It is obviously hard to estimate how many microcredit loans are used to on-lend: borrowers will not typically state, nor MFIs record, that a loan is to be arbitraged and lent on, that microcredit has become the banker to loan sharks. Yet this could indeed be widespread.

Jude Fernando studied Grameen and ASA in Bangladesh and observed that in the stage of the NGO establishing itself in a village, nine out of twelve with whom the NGO first had contact became group leaders.[16] Group leaders typically were women whose husbands played a leading role in local economics and politics. Strikingly, seven out of the twelve came from families who lent money. NGO officers noted to Fernando that the fact that some group leaders function as moneylenders made it easier for the NGOs to assess the profitability of lending. Of Fernando's twelve groups, six group leaders used the loan to become moneylenders. And as we saw with the case of Jahanara Begum in chapter 4, local microcredit borrowers who turn moneylender can be among the most coercive in terms of loan collection.

Moneylending is not necessarily either illegal or illicit. It is likely to be unethical if money is lent at exorbitant rates, as being likely to do more harm than good to its borrowers. It can be illegal if it is lent at a rate higher than that set by an industry regulator. If an MFI has finite lending resources and is operating in a country or state where the rate is actually or effectively capped (Andhra Pradesh now), there must be quite a good chance the MFI will ration credit to the most creditworthy borrowers, and some of them will use their network in the informal sector to on-lend at higher rates.

There is an additional problem with a microloan being used for moneylending, on top of its failing the harm principle test. The MFI has raised money on the premise that it is

[16] Jude L. Fernando, "Microcredit and the Empowerment of Women," in *Microfinance: Perils and Prospects*, ed. Fernando (New York: Routledge, 2006), 214.

lending at rate x to the poor. If in fact that money is being funneled through to the poor at rate y, x plus a margin, those who provided the funding have been, however unintentionally, misled. In fact the donor may be doubly misled if she has donated to an MFI believing it is lending at a quoted 5% per month, not knowing that with compulsory savings, using a flat rather than declining balance for interest rate calculation and possibly also fees, this is well over 100% per annum. The double misleading is that she is not lending to the poor at even that rate: her money is being on-lent to the poor at an even higher one. She has set out to provide what she believes is capital to the poor at a reasonable rate and ends up enabling the poor to exploit the still poorer. If this were better understood, it could put some donors off supporting the sector altogether.

HARM TO NONHUMANS: ANIMAL CRUELTY

A board writing a code of ethics to guide management as to what loan uses are permissible and using the harm principle as its guide rather than (or as well as) the legal status of the activity will have ruled out moonshine production, environmentally degrading practices, and moneylending as acceptable activities. The example of loans being used for cockfighting in Peru would be ambiguous on the harm principle test, which only considers harm to other human beings, not animals. Sinclair cites Kiva's then-CEO, Matt Flannery, as arguing that Kiva should not be deciding which loans are ethical, but should rather leave that to donors to decide through their funding only those Kiva loans that are in line with their ethical beliefs.[17] A true peer-to-peer lending platform can make that argument, but that is not the position of most of those who finance MFIs, who fund the MFI as a whole, not individual loans.[18]

The principle of avoidance of harm to others is one that pretty much every ethical system accepts and so works for an MFI to adopt as its guide in deciding loan use permissibility. Avoiding harm to animals has much less widespread acceptance. What MFIs could do here is be very transparent in publishing their code of permissible loan uses and state their position on loan uses involving animal cruelty. This might not be a perfect solution but would help funders to make their own choices.

UNCLEAR HARMS: BORROWING TO FUND ILLEGAL MIGRATION AND ILLEGAL HOUSING

The harm principle has so far been used to pick out loan uses that MFI boards should make impermissible even where they are legal. There is also, of course, the contrary possibility of a loan use being illegal but only arguably actually causing harm to others.

---

[17] Sinclair, *Confessions.*

[18] This is effectively also true for Kiva, as by the time a Kivan clicks on a picture of a particular client to lend to, the borrower may well have already had her loan disbursed by the MFI: so the loan simply goes to the MFI.

The first example of this is a loan taken out to improve or even build a house on an illegal settlement. It is hardly unusual in the developing world for shantytowns or squatter settlements to start up on the periphery of cities and for the residents to work together to improve them and even for them eventually to become recognized, middle-class suburbs. Since the occupant will not have legal title to his shack, an MFI lending to him to improve it will be funding an illegal purpose. Yet where is the harm being done here, especially in terms of harms to others? There is arguably some harm done to the ultimate owner of the land the shantytown arises on, but this is not on the scale of the harms to others inflicted in previous examples.

The issues are even more difficult when loans are used to fund illegal migration. In his book *El Norte or Bust!* David Stoll describes in detail the process of borrowing from credit unions, MFIs, and banks in Nebaj, Guatemala, to recruit local Nebaj who want to migrate, pay smugglers to take the migrants north (usually a down payment followed by the balance once successful), and repay via remittances from the migrant.[19] If the remittances stop for any reason, those taking out the loans can become very overindebted. On the other hand, if it succeeds, with wages in the United States ten times those in Guatemala (if work was available), this was the only way to be able to afford to buy a plot and build a house.

The MFIs never explicitly lend to borrowers for this purpose, but, interviewing those in the migrant smuggling industry, Stoll was convinced that loan officers knew the true purpose of the loan but felt better recording it as for "pig-raising" or something equally anodyne.

Clearly no MFI that expects to retain a license is going to record a loan as being for people smuggling, when the activity is clearly illegal. But it is not necessarily illicit—the practice is widely morally condoned in Nebaj—and while aspects of it in practice will be unethical (occasions where the people smugglers desert their would-be migrants, or possibly the punishments incurred by would-be migrants if they are caught by the Border Patrol), whether illegal migration itself is regarded as unethical or not will be a truly complex equation turning on how its harms are weighed against the benefits to migrants, and how heavily to weigh harms to those relatively well-off who may see lower overall wages against the considerable gains (when successful) to the relatively very worst-off. Stoll himself argues that individuals have human rights to cross borders to try to improve their lives and support their families, and laws that prevent that are unjust and unfair laws: in which case, a loan to facilitate breaking such a law would not be unethical. I am not here trying to defend that position: the point is to show that the case for an ethical but illegal loan use can be made, and those responsible for making the loans need to think through their own ethical positions carefully.

---

[19] David Stoll, El Norte or Bust! How Migration Fever and Microcredit Produced a Financial Crash in a Latin American Town (Lanham, MD: Rowman & Littlefield, 2013).

The cases of lending used to support illegal settlements and illegal migration are difficult. Here, the law is clear—these are illegal—and on those grounds the MFI should not lend to them—but the harm to others that they cause is more debatable. The harm done to others caused by these laws being broken might not seem very great compared with the benefit the borrower derives when he successfully migrates and gets work; but of course the opposite can also happen. An illegal migrant who dies en route or is unable to work when he reaches his destination and send remittances home incurs great harm himself and harm to the family back home, left saddled with the debt repayments and no remittances to pay them with.

The problem here is, if the law itself is unfair and discriminatory toward the landless and jobless, is the MFI justified in ignoring it? There is no obvious single answer here, not least because there will be different views on when a law *is* discriminatory. Though since even the "best" cases for doing so are themselves not clear-cut, the simplicity of a "no illegal activities" rule is attractive. That response is something of an ethical cop-out. Perhaps it is better to say that it is conceivable that there could be cases where an MFI was ethically justified in lending to an activity that was illegal, uncomfortable as it sounds. Imagine a country whose government forbade lending to certain ethnic groups but not others. So perhaps conceivable: but as a practical matter, for MFIs that hope to stay in business, a policy of not lending to illegal business uses is likely to be at the very least pragmatic.

2. Child Labor

If the harm principle can be useful to MFI boards in resolving an ethical code for loan use, it can equally be useful in resolving the vexed question of when microborrowers' use of child labor should be regarded as permissible.

One of the oft-repeated claims of MFIs is that their clients use, or intend to use, the profits from their enterprises to send their children to school. There is no need to doubt the honest intent of that claim: but, as has been seen throughout this book, the impact of microfinance can be very different from its practitioners' intent. In particular circumstances, it turns out that microfinance can lead to an increase in children being taken out of school, either to work in the microenterprise or to substitute for the domestic labor of the female microentrepreneur.

This is not to claim that the overall impact of microcredit on child labor is to increase it: the evidence on that is mixed.[20] It is, rather, to suggest that there are predictable,

[20] A number of impact studies have attempted to measure the effect of microfinance on schooling rates and child labor among borrowers' children. The strengths and weaknesses of such impact studies were discussed in chapter 2. We can note here, however, that they are divided somewhat evenly between those that observed reduction in child labor and those that found an increase. The evidence from the randomized studies discussed in chapter 2 is also mixed.

foreseeable circumstances in which microcredit *is* very likely to increase child labor and that, with these, it is incumbent on MFIs and their boards to ensure that there are policies in place to prevent or at least minimize that effect. It is not to demand that MFIs monitor every client to check if she uses child labor, which might be too much of a counsel of perfection. It is rather to suggest that the MFI proactively recognize when circumstances are likely to transpire to cause a borrower to be tempted to increase use of child labor, and that the MFI then makes clear to the borrower that it will cut her some slack in repayment in those circumstances rather than see child labor increase.

The International Labour Organization (ILO) regards child labor as "simply the single most important source of child exploitation in the world today."[21] It reduces the child's current welfare and, through loss of schooling, future welfare. According to estimates by the ILO, there were 215 million child laborers in 2008,[22] with the highest child labor force participation rates being in sub-Saharan Africa, even in countries where it is technically illegal.[23] The aim here is to examine the marginal impact of microcredit on the attendance of borrowers' children at school: it is not suggested that microcredit is a major cause of child labor itself.

In countries where those under fourteen are around half the total population (typically, where the adult population has been badly reduced by AIDS), child labor will inevitably be higher.

According to the ILO, children are frequently taken out of school in order to boost family income when the family meets with an unexpected negative income shock, such as the male head of household becoming unemployed; "child labour is used as a buffer against economic shocks."[24] As the authors point out, once children are taken out of school and integrated into the labor market, they tend to stay there; transition back to school is difficult.

Microcredit can be an aid to solving this problem if a short-term loan can cover the immediate shock without the child having to be taken out of school and a return can be made with the capital. It adds to the problem where the enterprise undertaken is a labor-intensive one that is only just profitable, certainly not profitable enough to cover the cost of another full-time employee: here it may make most economic sense for the family to employ the child at no cost to increase productivity and thus profit. Further, if it is the microentrepreneur who is temporarily unable to work, the need to keep up the

---

[21] "Child Labour: Targeting the Intolerable," Eighty-Sixth Session, International Labour Conference, International Labour Office, Geneva, 1998.

[22] "Accelerating Action against Child Labour, Global Report under the Follow-up to the ILOP Declaration on Fundamental Principles and Rights at Work," International Labour Office, Geneva, 2010.

[23] For example, in 2005 in Malawi, where laws prohibit child labor under the age of fourteen, there were 3.2 million children working (Malawi Ministry of Economic Planning and Development) out of a total population of 13.5 million, 6.1 million of whom were aged fourteen and under (US Census Bureau, International Database).

[24] Jonas Blume and Julika Bieyer, "Microfinance and Child Labour," Employment Working Paper No. 89, International Labour Office, 2011.

discipline of making the weekly repayment of interest may make taking the child out of school to keep the enterprise going the obvious first solution.

In some situations, microcredit leading to an increase in child labor is fairly predictable. Hazarika and Sarangi found that access to credit raised borrowers' children's propensity to work in rural Malawi during the peak harvest season.[25] Essentially, in a country dominated by subsidence farming, if a woman takes out a loan to run an enterprise, for much of the year she will juggle that and completing the household domestic work to keep the household going: but at harvest time she cannot do all three—help bring in the harvest (which will be the urgent priority), run the household, *and* run the enterprise (where the weekly repayments will also demand priority). Children are then taken out of school to fulfill one of these functions in her place, usually that of domestic household work.

It can be argued that it is not the MFI that is creating the harm here: that if anyone is guilty of exploiting child labor, it is the parents who exploit their children, rather than the MFI. And indeed it is the parents who are taking advantage of their children's vulnerability; it is not, after all, as if the MFI is making the loan to the children. All this is true, but yet the role of the MFI in child labor is clear, even if it is not technically the exploiter. It is the MFI's demand for consistent loan repayment when a family endures a negative income shock or needs to temporarily cease the microactivity while the harvest is brought in that adds an extra incentive to take the borrower's child out of school to act as economic buffer. It is not argued here that the net impact of microcredit *overall* on borrowers' children's school attendance is negative—that is not clear—but rather that, in the particular circumstances of negative economic shocks and harvest season in rural, subsistence farming economies, the impact of microcredit can predictably be to exacerbate an existing tendency for households to use their children to solve their labor shortage.

The MFI, of course, has the most power to prevent the exploitation of child labor in these countries. Allowing deferral of interest payments on a loan for a grace period while a client recovers from an economic shock,[26] or allowing the borrower to "rest"—not take out a loan—during harvest season in rural, subsistence economies, without penalizing her by lending a smaller amount or at a higher rate when she returns, would be steps MFIs could take to minimize the risk of credit pressuring parents into using their children as labor. Indeed, it could be argued that where the MFI has been on the ground long enough to understand these mechanisms but, instead of allowing a grace period or a rest in the harvest season, incentivizes loan officers to have clients keep rolling over their loans (because that way the MFI maximizes the number of interest payments it receives from the borrower), the MFI in fact becomes complicit in the use of child labor.

---

[25] Gautam Hazarika and Sudipta Sarangi, "Household Access to Microcredit and Child Work in Rural Malawi," *World Development* 36, no. 5 (2008): 843–859.

[26] As, in fairness, some MFIs do, notably Grameen Bank.

Most straightforwardly, of course, MFIs could decline to extend loans to borrowers who use child labor to conduct their enterprises or could let it be known that loans will not be renewed to those who use child labor. Such a lending policy is very rare, however.

A board using the harm principle to drive its code of ethics would recognize the harm to the child's welfare of losing schooling through that labor and suggest a policy of not lending to borrowers who use child labor in their business. Or it could be a little more subtle than that: it might be the case that *some* child labor, particularly if just an hour or two *after* school, is not harmful to the child. In that case, the board can write into its code of permissive practices that it will not lend to borrowers who use *harmful* child labor in their businesses. What is harmful could then be specified further, at the country level, and might well be in line with countries' own laws, many of which are quite subtle about how much child labor is legal, rather than stating that it is *all* illegal. If a board is doubtful about its ability to specify what is harmful child labor, it could, as a minimum, specify obeying a country's own local laws on use of child labor.

3. Transparency in Microfinance

Wider issues of corporate governance in microfinance are discussed in chapter 9. This chapter will keep to the issue of the transparency of MFIs and MIVs with regard to their own lending practices, their own efficacy, and the loan use and child labor practices they will tolerate from their own borrowers.

As noted at the start of this chapter, few MFIs are transparent as to their policy, if any, on what loan uses are impermissible and whether child labor is allowed. There are honorable exceptions (e.g., VisionFund, ProCredit), but far more could be done. Indeed, this is a point that should be made at every link along the chain of funding: not only should MFIs have transparent loan and labor use policies, but so should the MIVs that provide funding to them, so that MFIs funded by MIVs know what is expected from them, and development agencies funding MIVs, in turn, know what to expect from them. That argument taken one step further would suggest that the development agencies themselves might make their own policies on these matters transparent, too. So it is good to report that some do (e.g., MIVs such as Blue Orchard and Oikokreditbank).

One such funder to the microcredit industry, the Norwegian MicroFinance Initiative, has produced such a code of what it expects those MFIs it funds not to tolerate, and this is reproduced in table 7.1.[27]

[27] The NMI is a partnership between public authorities and private investors in Norway to invest in microfinance. It comprises three funds: Global Fund, NMI Frontier Fund, and NMI Fund III. The Global Fund invests in older and larger MFIs, largely through MIVs. The NMI Frontier Fund invests directly in younger MFIs in sub-Saharan Africa and South Asia. NMI III has the same geographic focus but invests in MFIs that have reached, or nearly reached, financial sustainability. The three funds total approximately US$130 million; see www.nmimicro.no/about-nmi/nmi-overview.

TABLE 7.1

NORWEGIAN MICROFINANCE INITIATIVE

MICROFINANCE EXCLUSION LIST

1. Production or activities involving forced labor[1] or harmful child labor.[2]
2. Production or trade in any product or activity deemed illegal under host country laws or regulations or international conventions and agreements.
3. Production or trade[3] in: (i) weapons and munitions; (ii) tobacco; or (iii) hard liquor
4. Gambling, casinos or equivalent enterprises.[4]
5. Any business relating to pornography or prostitution.
6. Trade in wildlife or wildlife products regulated under CITES.[5]
7. Production or use of or trade in or storage of hazardous materials such as radioactive materials,[6] unbounded asbestos fibers and products containing PCBs.[7]
8. Cross-border trade in waste and waste products unless compliant to the Basel Convention and the underlying regulations.
9. Drift net fishing in the marine environment using nets in excess of 2.5 km in length
10. Production, use of or trade in pharmaceuticals, pesticides/herbicides, chemicals, ozone depleting substances[8] and other hazardous substances subject to international phase-outs or bans
11. Significant[9] conversion or degradation of Critical Habitat.[10]
12. Significant alteration, damage, or removal of any critical cultural heritage.[11]
13. Production or activities that impinge on the lands owned, or claimed under adjudication, by Indigenous Peoples, without fully documented consent of such peoples.

[1] Forced labor means all work or service, not voluntarily preformed, that is extracted from an individual under threat of force or penalty.

[2] Harmful child labor means the employment of children that is economically exploitive, or is likely to be hazardous to, or to interfere with, the child's education, or to be harmful to the child's health, or physical, mental, spiritual, moral, or social development.

[3] This applies when these activities are a substantial part of a project sponsor's primary operations.

[4] This applies when these activities are a substantial part of a project sponsor's primary operations.

[5] CITES: Convention on International Trade in Endangered Species or Wild Fauna and Flora. A list of CITES listed species is available from their website: www.cites.org.

[6] This does not apply to the purchase of medical equipment, quality control (measurement) equipment and any equipment where NMI considers the radioactive source to be trivial and/or adequately shielded.

[7] PCBs: Polychlorinated biphenyls—a group of highly toxic chemicals. PCBs are likely to be found in oil-filled electrical transformers, capacitors and switchgears dated from 1950–1985.

[8] Ozone Depleting Substances (ODSs): Chemical compounds which react with and deplete stratospheric ozone, resulting in the widely publicized "ozone holes." The Montreal Protocol lists OCDs and their target reduction and phase-out dates.

TABLE 7.1 CONTINUED

[9] Significant conversion or degradation means the (i) elimination or severe diminution of the integrity of a habitat caused by a major, long-term change in land or water use; or (ii) modification of a habitat that substantially reduces the habitat's ability to maintain viable population of its native species.

[10] Critical habitat is a subset of both natural and modified habitat that deserves particular attention. Critical habitat includes areas with high biodiversity value that meet the criteria of the World Conservation Union (IUCN) classification, including habitat required for the survival of critically endangered or endangered species as defined by the IUCN Red List of Threatened Species or as defined by national legislation; areas having special significance for endemic or restricted-range species; sites that are critical for the survival of migratory species; areas supporting globally significant concentrations or numbers of individuals of congregatory species; areas with unique assemblages of species or which are associated with key evolutionary processes or provide key ecosystem services; and areas having biodiversity of significant social, economic or cultural importance to local communities. Primary Forest or forests of High Conservation Value shall be considered Critical Habitats.

[11] Critical cultural heritage consists of (i) the internationally recognized heritage of communities who us, or have used within living memory the cultural heritage for long-standing cultural purposes; and (ii) legally protected cultural heritage areas, including those proposed by host governments for such designation.

There could be a number of reasons why most MFIs and MIVs do not publish an exclusion list like this. It is possible their boards have not recognized the ethical issues involved and appreciated that this ought to play an important part in their governance. It is possible they do recognize the ethical issues involved but think that their funders may have differing views and so duck the issues for fear of offending some: or possibly that they do not know how to respond to the ethical issues raised, not having clear principles to guide them between what is ethical and legal and what could be enforced anyway. If either of these reasons were true, use of the harm principle to guide policy would resolve a number of the problems.

But it may be the case that a common lack of transparency with regard to permissible use of loans and labor is simply part and parcel of an attitude of the industry as a whole toward keeping an extremely positive public image at all times. Microfinance is not unusual among other development efforts in playing down issues of occasional fraud, of loan officers or group leaders sometimes running off with a group's funds.[28] While it might be better if MFIs were open about this when it occurs, and how they deal with it, many agencies working in aid would regard such disclosure as quite heroic.

But the microfinance industry's approach to promoting its public image goes much further than not discussing such fraud when it occurs. David Roodman notes that when he surveyed the websites of American microfinance groups in 2009, the projection of confidence that microfinance 'worked' was universal:

> Kiva invited me to 'lend to a specific entrepreneur in the developing world-empowering them to lift themselves out of poverty.' FINCA had launched a

[28] For example, see Katie Wright, "The Darker Side to Microfinance: Evidence from Cajamarca, Peru," in Fernando, *Microfinance*, 133–148.

'historic campaign to create 100,000 Village Banks and lift millions out of poverty by 2010.' The Microcredit Summit Campaign had set a goal to 'help 100 million families rise above the . . . $1 per day threshold by 2015.' Opportunity International stated simply, 'Microfinance: A Solution to Global Poverty.'[29]

Its overwhelmingly positive, win-win image was key to the hundreds of millions of dollars raised from development agencies, corporates, and the public. Having sold itself on such an ethical ticket, it is hard now for the industry to be truly transparent as to its underbelly: the actual levels of interest charged, coercive loan collection techniques, its actual efficacy in delivering empowerment or enrichment, overindebtedness, some dubious loan uses, and use of child labor.

It is less bad than it was. The excessive hype has ceased and the Microfinance CEO Working Group published a letter in March 2012 stating just that,[30] that microcredit was not a "silver bullet" to end all poverty, and that the leaders of the industry had known for some time and the industry had been moving in that direction for many years (which is surprising, since the quotes from their websites noted above were from 2008 and 2009, so if the leaders knew it, they were holding this knowledge back from their marketing people). But moving from hyperbole to silence, while progress, is not enough. Transparency is needed as to what measures exist to prevent overindebtedness, coercion, illegal and/or unethical loans, and child labor use.

The industry has developed initiatives to increase its transparency and levels of responsibility, such as the Smart Campaign, with its client protection principles. But as we saw in chapter 5, the specification of these principles is very weak. It is not enough to say that interest rates should be transparent: an APR must be disclosed. It is not enough to plan to monitor effectiveness in achieving client outcomes if dropouts are not counted and monitored thereafter as well. It is not enough for an MFI to claim to lend responsibly, but have no list of impermissible loan uses or a policy on child labor.

Optimistically, at least the existence of the Smart Campaign lays the ground for something better, for a full and comprehensive specification of it. But if Smart does remain shallow rather than specified, the industry risks not only deceiving the public about the level of its ethical practices, but deceiving itself as well. If it does that, and as a result does not tackle its more ethically challenging areas, it risks more crisis brewing and boiling over, which could lose it all its support.

Ironically, in his introduction to the presentation of the 2014 industry report *Banana Skins*, David Lascelles argued that the biggest risk to microfinance was skepticism about its effectiveness (a risk not mentioned in the report). This may well be so, from the point

[29] Roodman, *Due Diligence* 140.

[30] "'The Hype is Long Over'—Microfinance CEOs Respond to Washington Post article 'Microfinance Doesn't End Poverty, Despite All the Hype,'" March 23, 2012, posted on Centre for Financial Inclusion website.

of view of the MFIs, but the opaqueness of the industry on its efficacy and loan and labor use policies is part of what is contributing to this skepticism.

If the industry were more transparent and explained the nuances of working in the informal economy now, it might lose some supporters. If it continues to be opaque and the public comes to understand with a shock that it has been deceived, sometimes deliberately so, the industry might see an avalanche of revulsion and withdrawal of funding.

The industry needs to keep the publicity clean because governmental or supranational developmental agencies—such as the International Finance Corporation, European Investment Bank, CDC, KfW, Norwegian Microfinance Initiative—are probably still the largest drivers of funds into microfinance.[31] These are sophisticated investors who will understand the complexity of lending in the informal economy, but they in turn rely on the taxpaying public for what they in turn support. If microfinance came to be seen by the public as containing many unethical practices, rather than being the silver bullet to end poverty, funding implications are not just the loss of the public's donations, but what the public will tolerate from its development agencies. The industry might consider whether devoting greater resources to *in fact* ending some of its less ethical practices, as opposed to the presentation of itself as being in control of them, might not be a wiser balance to strike.

[31] For an overview, see Marcus Fedder, "Microfinance from an Investor's Perspective," in *Microfinance: A Practitioner's Handbook*, consulting ed. Ranajoy Basu (London: Globe Law and Business Publishing, 2013), 103–104.

For every complex problem, there is a simple solution. And it's always wrong.

—H.L. MENCKEN

8 The Macro Impact of Microfinance

THE MAJORITY OF this book has considered the ethics of microfinance at the micro level: at the level of the relationship between individual and MFI or between borrowers. This chapter looks at the ethics of microfinance from the macro point of view—what impact does microcredit have, not just on its borrowers, but on the wider community in which it operates? Although microfinance has not been shown, in general, to lift most borrowers out of poverty, has it had impact, positive or negative, on development more widely? What is, or should be, its role in financing public services we take for granted in developed countries but the state does not provide in some developing countries?

Before microfinance made its central claim one of poverty alleviation for its clients, it made its central ethical claim that it was good for development: that from a macroeconomic stance, it was a key part of the toolkit for less developed countries to emerge, if not the sole silver bullet by which they could do so. So this chapter will look for the historical evidence of that macroeconomic benefit, before examining the charge leveled against microfinance that it will, theoretically, never help an economy develop because it is guilty of the "fallacy of composition." This is the claim that microfinance makes the mistake of supposing that just because one microentrepreneur can start up and successfully run a petty trading business, very many microentrepreneurs in the same local economy can do so as well. Rather, it is suggested, microfinance simply displaces economic activity with no net gain: it just redistributes the existing level of poverty.

This chapter then goes on to critique the concern that microbusinesses set up by microentrepreneurs lack scale, that as a result entrepreneurs seldom develop into small- to medium-sized enterprises (SMEs), which are the true engine of development, and that microcredit has diverted developmental aid that could otherwise have gone productively into developing SME sectors in impoverished countries.

There is an argument that even if microfinance has not established businesses that grow into SMEs, at least it has established microfinance institutions globally, which will be able to offer the prospect of financial inclusion—of savings, perhaps of insurance—to the many in the future and act as a catalyst to the mobilization of savings. But unless these microfinance institutions are able to offer financial inclusion without the use of these services being dependent on participating in their expensive offering of microcredit, then the bulk of any benefit derived will accrue only to the microfinance institutions themselves, and mobilizing savings will only be of developmental benefit if the MFIs change their lending policies beyond recognition (from microentrepreneur and consumption lending to SME lending).

A last strand of microfinance's impact on development that will be considered is the use of microfinance for the poor to be able to pay for the provision of such public services as education, health, water, and sanitation. There are a couple of issues to be unpacked here—whether microfinance can ever be as effective an instrument for providing such collective goods as a single monopoly supplier, such as the state, could be, and whether, efficiency aside, it can be ethical to ask the poor to indebt themselves in order to buy goods that might be thought to be within their human rights to receive.

1. The Historical Argument

The argument that microfinance has no positive macro impact and, worse, that it has a negative macro impact and actually acts as a poverty trap has been put forward most strongly by Milford Bateman and Ha-Joon Chang.[1] Critics have focused on Bateman's accompanying critique that microfinance is part of a neoliberal agenda, but his and Chang's macro arguments stand independently of that controversy and have not been answered. The large randomized control trial and follow-ups of Banerjee and coauthors in Andhra Pradesh seem, rather, to support them.

The macro argument comprises a historical analysis of how development has actually taken place and whether microfinance has ever successfully featured in it; moves on to suggesting that microfinance is guilty of the "fallacy of composition" and, in the absence of effective demand, leads simply to displacement effects; and concludes that few microenterprises ever grow into SMEs because of their lack of scale and therefore profitability.

[1] Bateman in *Why Doesn't Microfinance Work?*; Bateman and Ha-Joon Chang, "The Microfinance Illusion," working paper, University of Jurag Dobrila Pula and University of Cambridge, and "Microfinance and the Illusion of Development: From Hubris to Nemesis in Thirty Years," *World Economic Review* 1 (2012): 13–36; and Chang, *23 Things*, 157–167.

Indeed it has been argued that microfinance serves to undermine the growth of SMEs (seen as the true engine of development) through diverting the resources that might otherwise have supported productive SME growth, to unproductive microfinance activities.

Bateman and Chang start the historical argument by noting that the dominant microfinance model (that is, Grameen Bank–style replicators) has not unambiguously resulted in a sustainable poverty reduction and economic development episode anywhere. Indeed, exhaustive analysis of those countries that reached developed status in the 1800s and early part of the last century (the United States, Western Europe, and Japan) and the fastest-growing countries of the last thirty years or so (China, Taiwan, South Korea, Thailand, India, Malaysia, and most recently Vietnam) shows that the microfinance model has played no role whatsoever.[2]

Bateman and Chang are supported in this conclusion by Thomas Dichter,[3] who has looked at how the "northern" developed countries first used widespread formal credit and finds that this was not how entrepreneurship got started. The pattern he describes is of entrepreneurs using their own savings, then that of friends and family, as "soft" capital to develop a start-up that is known to be risky and could not withstand a sudden or high loan repayment demand. Only when the business is "cruising," has some critical mass and cash flow is formal credit applied for.

When credit became available to the poor, however, it was linked to consumption. For the poor, savings came first. "From the English 'friendly societies' of the late 18th century to the early German credit union movement associated with Herman Scholze-Delitzch in 1850 and Frederick Raiffeisen in 1864, to the postal savings systems, experiments in formal systems aimed at the poor were based on savings."[4] The sequence was, first, economic development (following industrialization in the North), then access by the poor to formal savings (now that there were enough working poor in concentrated areas to be worth being reached out to by financial institutions offering savings), and only after that access to credit for consumption.

In sum, Dichter notes the following:

- Earlier forms of microcredit never played a significant role in business start-up or small-business development.
- The first effects of democratizing financial services were almost entirely savings and "thrift" based.
- Economic development in fact came before (or at least alongside) the movement to democratize financial services.

---

[2] Bateman and Chang, "The Microfinance Illusion," 5.

[3] Thomas Dichter, "The Chicken and Egg Dilemma in Microfinance: An Historical Analysis of the Sequence of Growth and Credit in the Economic Development of the 'North,'" in Dichter and Harper, *What's Wrong with Microfinance?* 179–92

[4] Dichter, "Chicken and Egg Dilemma," 186.

- When credit for the poor did come along, it *followed* the savings movement, and developed almost entirely in relation to consumption.[5]

Having been unable to establish a role for microfinance in those countries that *have* developed, Bateman turns his attention to Bangladesh, where microfinance has been a major tool for development.

> Crucially, Bangladesh as a whole stands out as having been almost entirely left behind by its rapidly growing East Asia "tiger" economy neighbours. This is not a coincidence, but a result of policy choice. By and large, the successful "tiger" economies all opted to deploy a pro-active, subsidised, policy-based but nevertheless well-managed local financial model radically different to the Grameen Bank microfinance model that today dominates in Bangladesh. . . . Simplifying, the heterodox East Asian local financial model is marked out by the provision of affordable financial support for scaled-up formal sector small businesses and family firms that can efficiently link up with other sectors of the economy (i.e. with state companies, larger private businesses, marketing co-operatives . . .).[6]

The argument is, then, that the successful "tiger" economies have developed without microfinance and on a model very different from it. Bateman goes on to argue that where the Grameen Bank microfinance model has been most faithfully replicated, development has also failed to occur: he states that "Bolivia, Mexico, Cambodia, Nicaragua, Morocco and, most stunning of all, the Indian state of Andhra Pradesh in late 2010, all are now viewed as how microfinance can seriously destabilise and undermine the local economic and social structures of most benefit to the poor, not strengthen them."[7]

What, then, are the mechanisms through which, according to Bateman and Chang, microfinance fails to deliver development and might even undermine it?

2. The Fallacy of Composition

Bateman argues that from the very beginning Yunus fell victim to the fallacy of composition: the belief that simply because microfinance could work for one client, it could work for an infinite number of clients. He quotes Yunus as stating that a "Grameen-type credit program opens up the door for limitless self-employment, and it can effectively do it in a pocket of poverty amid prosperity, or in a massive poverty situation."[8]

---

[5] Dichter, "Chicken and Egg Dilemma," 180–181.

[6] Milford Bateman, "Confronting Microfinance Myths and Legends in the Western Balkans," *Indian Microfinance Business News*, August 22, 2011.

[7] Bateman "Confronting Microfinance Myths".

[8] Quoted in Bateman and Chang, "Illusion of Development," 22.

This is to suggest that if you have a local economy with so many tomato sellers already, you can introduce half a dozen more, financed with microloans, and the extra supply will have no effect on the existing suppliers or price of tomatoes; the demand for tomatoes will rise to meet the extra supply. But of course this is not so. It does not follow from the fact that some people can succeed with one particular type of business that everyone else can do the same. As Bateman and Chang put it, "Other things being equal, new and expanded microfinance-induced microenterprises do not raise the *total* volume of business/demand so much as redistribute or subdivide amongst market participants the prevailing volume of business/demand."[9]

It was not as if there had not been microenterprises in the informal economy before microfinance arrived: in Yunus's story of Begum, she is already weaving baskets before he steps in to undercut the price at which she borrows from the *paikars* to do so. As Bateman and Chang argue again:

> The reality in virtually all developing countries is that local economies have been saturated with simple informal microenterprises for many years: indeed, an informal microenterprise has long been the default activity for those without any type of formal employment or income—the vast majority in some countries. . . . The scale and scope of the local informal sector was and is mainly determined by local demand. With the arrival of microfinance in the 1980s, however, an artificial supply-side MFI-driven increase in the numbers of informal microenterprises was stimulated without any compensating intervention on the demand side. This inevitably created hyper-competition at the local level, which in turn precipitated reduced turnover in existing individual microenterprise units and downward pressure on local prices and incomes in general (thus negatively affecting both new and incumbent microenterprises). As a result, we find, not surprisingly, that from the 1990s onwards, incomes, wages, profits and work-life conditions for those struggling in the informal microenterprise sector began to deteriorate quite markedly across the globe.[10]

They argue that the result of this increase in supply with no increase in effective demand is community-wide job and income displacement, together with higher levels of exit by those who were producing before microfinance arrived. New entrants, absent an increase in demand, may just reduce the margins for all, the increase in supply driving down prices, and may push existing producers out of business. The lower prices may have benefits for consumers, but additional jobs or income at the community level are unlikely to be produced.

---

[9] Bateman and Chang, "Illusion of Development," 22.

[10] Bateman and Chang, "Illusion of Development," 22–23.

Just occasionally, a new technology or innovation *will* create a source of new demand, but even then these effects eventually come into play. Chang describes the following example:

> When a microfinance institution first starts its operation in a locality, the first posse of its clients may see their income rising—sometimes quite dramatically. For example, when in 1997 the Grameen Bank teamed up with Telenor, the Norwegian phone company, and gave out microloans to women to buy a mobile phone and rent it out to villagers, these "telephone ladies" made handsome profits—$750–$1200 in a country whose annual average per capita income was around $300. However, over time, the businesses financed by microcredit become crowded and their earnings fall . . . by 2005 there were so many telephone ladies that their income was estimated to be only $70 per year, though the national average income had gone up to $450.[11]

The project was a significant financial success for Telenor, but after the initial beneficial impact on poverty reduction, this impact quickly evaporated. According to Bateman, the intention was initially to have 50,000 telephone ladies, but with none being given their own exclusive territory, a few telephone ladies in each village became dozens, totaling 280,000 operating alongside each other in "telephone streets."[12]

Chang notes that this would not matter if new businesses existed that could keep replacing the old ones—if, phone renting having become unprofitable, the microentrepreneurs could make mobile phones or develop software instead.

> You will obviously have noticed the absurdity of these suggestions—the telephone ladies of Bangladesh simply do not have the wherewithal to move into phone manufacturing or software design. The problem is that there is only a limited range of (simple) businesses that the poor in developing countries can take on, given their limited skills, the narrow range of technologies available, and the limited amount of finance that they can mobilize through microfinance. So, you, a Croatian farmer who bought one more milk cow with a microcredit, stick to selling milk even as you watch the bottom falling out of your local milk market thanks to the 300 other farmers like you selling more milk, because turning yourself into an exporter of butter to Germany or cheese to Britain simply isn't possible with the technologies, the organisational skills and the capital you have.[13]

---

[11] Chang, *23 Things*, 164.

[12] Bateman, *Why Doesn't Microfinance Work?* 69.

[13] Chang, *23 Things*, 164–165.

Bateman and Chang observe the same increase in "poverty-push" microenterprises financed by microfinance in Mexico, and conclude: "The proliferation of MFI-financed microenterprises simply *redistributes* poverty within the poorest communities, if indeed it does not *exacerbate* it: it certainly does not *resolve* it."[14]

Increasing supply with no increase in effective demand will first of all reduce margins and revenue, and then many of the microentrepreneurs will go on to fail. Bateman and Chang quote the case of Bosnia, where 50% of microenterprises failed within a year of their establishment, according to one report.[15] This, of course, is likely to deepen the poverty and insecurity of the microfinance client who fails, as she will lose any other assets or savings she has invested in the enterprise or be forced to divert other sources of family income or sell off assets cheaply to repay the loan.

There is a further ethical problem hidden behind the relative success, at least early on, of the Grameen telephone ladies. Grameen has cooperated with other transnational corporations (TNCs), such as Danome, to bring the TNC's products to the market of Bangladesh, and others have replicated the model (for example, the distribution of "Living Goods" in Africa).

The model is that the TNC devises a product for a mass market that it believes is cheap enough for the poor in that country or countries to buy. In the case of the two products above, the intention is to sell products that will also improve the health of the purchasers, on attractive terms.

But if we step back from all the best intentions here, what is actually happening is that the transnational essentially sells its products en bloc to the MFI client, who borrows from the MFI to purchase them and who then, hopefully, sells them in the market at a profit. Assuming the best case, that the interest rate on the loan is priced so as to be lower than the margin the borrower turns on the product, so that a profit is guaranteed her if she sells, the borrower has still assumed all the risk that the product, in fact, fails to find a market. Designing products for the mass market of the poor is not easy, and the major risk to a transnational attempting this is not just the wasted cost of manufacturing the product if it does not sell, but all the costs of distributing the product—the transport, salaries, commissions.

Under this model, all that risk is taken on by the poor borrower, who in Africa may be borrowing at 70% interest and up. If the TNC has misjudged its market and she fails to sell, she still has to repay the loan. Projects such as these start off with the best of intentions and an apparent win-win but can easily end up as another case of the (possibly unintended) exploitation of the borrower.

---

[14] Bateman and Chang, "Illusion of Development," 23.

[15] Asli Demirgüç-Kunt, Leora Klapper, and Georgios Panos, "The Origins of Self-Employment," Development Research Group, World Bank, February 2007.

To be clear, there are those who object to companies ever making a profit from selling goods to the extremely poor. This is not that objection: I do not argue that it is unethical per se to try to sell products to the poor or to make a profit doing so. What is dubious here is asking the extremely poor to take on the financial risk of failure of the new distribution effort. Selling yoghurt to the poor is unobjectionable. Employing the poor to sell yoghurt for you would be a welcome source of jobs, and hiring the poor to sell yoghurt for you on a commission basis is acceptable. But asking the extremely poor to *borrow* to buy the product from you to sell transfers the risk of product failure from you to them, who are least able to bear it.

For microfinance to actually contribute toward development, a proportion of its microenterprises need to grow out of the informal sector into the small- to medium-sized enterprise sector, where they can increase employment and become engines of growth for the future. There are a number of reasons why this is not happening, but the effect of it not doing so is more pernicious than simply microenterprises not flourishing. If microfinance is taking up the development finance that might have gone into SME building, it is actually making things worse.

3. Too Few Microenterprises Grow

First among the reasons that so few microenterprises become SMEs is that they are not profitable enough to retain earnings with which to grow. They are not profitable enough because of all the reasons given above: too many represent an increase in supply of existing businesses without a matching increase in effective demand. Karnani quotes a study by the George Foundation (an NGO targeting poverty alleviation in India) of fifty microcredit programs in seventeen villages in South India where less than 2% of the microenterprises continue past the first three years.[16] Emran and Stiglitz explain that most microenterprises financed by microfinance only seem profitable because they do not value the time and labor of the microentrepreneur.[17] Hence a poor microentrepreneur can use a loan to buy a goat and sell the milk, but she can never grow because as soon as she takes on the cost of hiring someone at a market wage, her enterprise becomes unprofitable.

We should also bear in mind that perhaps the majority of those taking out microloans do not *want* to become full-time entrepreneurs running SMEs. In their latest piece of research revisiting the Hyderabad Spandata study, Banerjee and coauthors divide microentrepreneurs into "gung-ho entrepreneurs" and "reluctant entrepreneurs."[18] Gung-ho entrepreneurs are those who, in the Spandata study, had already set up a small business

[16] Aneel Karnani, "Undermining the Chances of Sustainable Development in India with Microfinance," 83–95. in Bateman, *Confronting Microfinance*.

[17] Shahe Emran and Joseph Stiglitz, "On Selective Indirect Tax Reform in Developing Countries," *Journal of Public Economics* 89, no. 4 (2005): 599–623.

[18] Abhijit Banerjee, Emily Breza, Esther Duflo, and Cynthia Kinnan, "Do Credit Constraints Limit Entrepreneurship? Heterogeneity in the Returns to Microfinance", quoted with authors' permission

and when microfinance was introduced, took advantage of it to expand, having previously been constrained by lack of capital. Reluctant entrepreneurs are those who set up a business for the first time when microfinance became available and are content with a very much smaller business.

It will be recalled that overall, Banerjee and coauthors were unable to locate major impacts from microfinance but did find some business impacts. These business impacts were not spread evenly among microentrepreneurs, but were concentrated among a very small minority. They are experienced "almost entirely" by those who already had a business before microcredit became available. Microcredit is not creating hordes of successful entrepreneurs, but if one was a successful entrepreneur already without microfinance, new access to microcredit has significant effects: "Self-employment hours increase almost 20%, the stock and flow of business assets increase by 35–40%, business expenses increase by 80% and revenues more than double" (all relative to already-established entrepreneurs in the control group without access to microcredit).[19] Banerjee and coauthors thus suggest that there is a case for, instead of handing out credit indiscriminately, identifying which entrepreneurs are gung-ho and which reluctant, and helping the former to grow (while, implicitly, cutting off or reducing credit to the rest). At least for a subset of these, the "gung-ho entrepreneurs," there is some increase in consumption after access to microcredit.

The authors reflect that "one of the most disappointing features of the first wave of microfinance impact evaluations is the lack of a positive effect on household consumption. . . . Our results point to some optimism, at least when microfinance is directed toward gung-ho entrepreneurs."[20] A pity, then, that much microcredit is given out in accordance with the Grameen Bank model, which assumes that *any*one can be a successful entrepreneur. There are some notable exceptions to this, such as ProCredit, that aim to be the "'house bank' for very small, small- to medium-sized businesses, as well as to provide simple savings services for ordinary people."[21] But these are, unfortunately, the exception rather than the rule.

There has to be doubt, though, that even if microfinance poured all of its resources into those most likely to grow their businesses (identified by already successfully running one without microcredit), these would still grow into SMEs in the formal sector. This might be the right thing to do from the point of view of microfinance, because this small subset is the only group Banerjee and Duflo can find any evidence of gaining in consumption through exposure to microfinance, but not from the point of view of development.

La Porta and Schleifer took three sets of surveys conducted by the World Bank in the 2000s: "enterprise surveys," which covered small, medium, and large registered firms

[19] Banerjee et al., "Do Credit Constraints Limit Entrepreneurship?"3.

[20] Banerjee et al., "Do Creit Constraints Limit Entrepreneurship?" 17.

[21] As stated on their website at http://www.procredit-holding.com/en/about-us/procredit-today.html.

in nearly one hundred countries; "informal surveys," which covered mostly unregistered but also some registered firms in a dozen countries; and "micro surveys," which covered mostly registered, but also some unregistered, small firms in a dozen more (mostly different countries).[22] Taken together, the surveys enabled the authors to make comparative statements about size, impacts, management characteristics, and, roughly, productivity of both official and unofficial firms. They had enough data to compare the informal economy to formal in developed countries but note that the microentrepreneurs that microfinance typically finances are below this level. Eighty-five percent of the observation in the informal and micro surveys had two employees or more, in addition to the entrepreneur: this is decidedly *not* the case with most microfinanced entrepreneurs, who seldom employ even one. The authors note: "The informal firms in our sample are likely to be substantially more productive than the own-account workers of Banerjee and Duflo."[23]

Nonetheless, there is at least a *possible* pathway to development here that runs successful microentrepreneur graduates to small informal enterprise, which graduates into a small- or medium-sized enterprise in the formal economy, productivity and contribution to development rising with each step. Is there any evidence of this?

La Porta and Schleifer outline three views of the role of unofficial firms in development: the romantic view, the parasite view, and the dual-economy view. The romantic view, which they associate with de Soto,[24] runs that unofficial firms are actually very productive but are held back by government taxes and regulations and lack of secure property rights and access to finance: lower the barriers and fund through microfinance, and they will be the sparks for economic growth.

The parasite view and dual-economy view both hold that the unofficial firms lack the scale to produce efficiently, but with the difference that the parasite view also holds that the cost advantage obtained by avoiding taxes and regulations enables unofficial firms to undercut the formal sector and so harm growth because they take market share from more productive enterprises.

The dual-economy view does not see the unofficial firms harming the formal sector in this way because it views them as so inefficient they are unable to undercut: they operate in different markets with different customers. The authors associate the dual view with traditional development economics that sees the transition from an informal/preindustrial economy to a formal/industrial one as key to economic development.

The authors' analysis of all the surveys supports, broadly, the dual view. They found that "high productivity comes from formal firms, and in particular large formal firms.

---

[22] Rafael La Porta and Andrei Schleifer, "The Unofficial Economy and Economic Development," NBER Working Paper No. 14520, December 2008.

[23] La Porta and Schleifer, "The Unofficial Economy," 13.

[24] Hernando de Soto,The Other Path: The Invisible Revolution in the Third World (New York: Harper and Row, 1989) and *The Mystery of Capital: Why Capitalism Triumphs in the West and Fails Everywhere Else* (New York: Basic Books, 2000).

Productivity jumps sharply if we compare small formal firms to informal firms, and rises rapidly with the size of formal firms. To the extent that productivity growth is central to economic development, the formation and growth of formal firms is necessary for economic growth."[25]

There was very little support for the romantic view; indeed, "The differences in productivity between the formal and informal firms are so large that it is very hard to believe that the registration of unregistered firms would eliminate the gap."[26] They expand: "Despite de Soto's emphasis on access to credit as the key to igniting the growth of unregistered firms, lack of external finance appears to be an attribute of all small firms in poor countries—not just of unregistered firms. In sum, the limitations of unregistered firms appear to be far more severe than acknowledged by proponents of the romantic view."[27]

Happily, there was not much support for the parasite view either. Crucially for the issue of whether microfinance and the informal sector could ever drive development, La Porta and Schleifer not only found no evidence that informal firms become formal as they grow, they found that "virtually none of the formal firms had ever been informal." The authors did not examine how many microentrepreneurs progressed to their informal surveys by employing one or two people, but we know from Banerjee and Duflo that few do. They *did* find that almost no informal firms become formal. "The vast majority of informal firms appear to begin and end their lives as unproductive informal firms."

They conclude: "The recipe for productivity growth is through the formation of official firms, the larger and the more productive, the better. Such formation must perhaps be promoted through tax, human capital, infrastructure, and capital markets policies, very much along the lines of traditional dual economy theories. From the perspective of economic growth, we should not expect much from the unofficial economy, and its millions of entrepreneurs, except to hope that it disappears over time."[28]

Bateman and Chang argue that the microfinance model ignores the crucial role of scale economies. They suggest that the microfinance industry seems to think that it is the number of microenterprises that are established that matters, rather than their size. But, they argue, this is not true: there is a minimum efficient scale of production that needs to be met. They point out that if the share of GDP taken up by the many microentrepreneurs in the informal economy were the key to growth, Africa should be booming: the share of the informal economy in GDP in Kenya is 72%, and Zambia 58%.[29] India too has a "missing middle" of SMEs, with growth for microfinance funding having been sourced from areas that previously would have funded SMEs. Bateman and Chang quote

[25] La Porta and Schleifer, "The Unofficial Economy," 35.

[26] La Porta and Schleifer, "The Unofficial Economy," 4.

[27] La Porta and Schleifer, "The Unofficial Economy," 22.

[28] La Porta and Schleifer, "The Unofficial Economy," 37.

[29] They quote Robert Rolfe, "The Viability of Micro-enterprise in South Africa," paper presented at the conference "Entrepreneurship in Africa," Whitman School of Management, Syracuse University, Syracuse, New York, April 1–3, 2010.

Karnani's concern that "the average firm size in India is less than one-tenth the size of comparable firms in other emerging economies. The emphasis on microcredit and the creation of microenterprises will only make this problem worse."[30]

Karnani observes: "Rather than lending $200 to 500 women so that each can set up a microenterprise manufacturing garments, it is much better to lend $100,000 to an entrepreneur with managerial capabilities and business acumen and help her to set up a garment manufacturing business employing 500 people. Now the business can exploit economies of scale, deploy specialized assets, and use modern business processes to generate value for its owners and employees."[31]

The same situation of financing being relatively easily available for microcredit but not for the more productive SME sector is observed in Bangladesh. Here Bateman and Chang quote the Department for International Development (DFID):

> The financial system—including banks, capital markets and the micro-finance sector—is inadequate to support long term investment financing for growth. Smaller firms, responsible for the lion's share of employment, have severely limited access to financial resources. Rural areas, with the highest potential for lifting low income groups out of poverty, are cut off from most financing mechanisms.[32]

As they comment,

> If what the DFID study calls "smaller firms" (that is, small firms that are not microenterprises) are finding it difficult to access financial support in the rural areas of Bangladesh, areas where the country's famed MFIs are increasingly in a desperate search for new microenterprise clients in order to keep themselves alive, then the "smaller firm" funding situation is clearly very bad indeed. Informal microenterprises and poor individuals can very easily access—in fact, they are being *pushed* to access—far more funding than they can repay, while "smaller firms" are increasingly being left without any finance to get established or to grow . . . the massive microfinance industry in Bangladesh has turned out to be a major *obstacle* in terms of supporting the development of the enterprises operating at or above minimum efficient scale that Bangladesh very urgently needs in order to sustainably develop and reduce poverty.[33]

---

[30] Aneel Karnani, "Microfinance Misses Its Mark," *Stanford Social Innovation Review*, Summer 2007.

[31] Karnani, "Undermining the Chances."

[32] Department for International Development, "The Road to Prosperity through Growth, Jobs and Skills," discussion paper, DFID Bangladesh, Dhaka, Bangladesh.

[33] Bateman and Chang, "Illusion of Development," 19–20.

The bleakest assessment of the macro impact of microfinance comes from the Inter-American Development Bank, which assessed the role of microfinance in Latin America, particularly Mexico.[34] It reports that here, too, many scarce financial resources have flowed into low-productivity informal microenterprises and self-employment, and not enough into small- to medium-sized enterprises in the formal sector. They conclude that this has been true throughout Latin America, not just in Mexico; Bateman and Chang sum up:

> In other words, the massive micro-finance induced proliferation of informal micro-enterprises that has taken place in Latin America since the 1980s has not been the economic and social saviour . . . but a factor that actually lies at the very *root* of that continent's recent economic and social malaise. As the IDB summed up . . ., "the overwhelming presence of small companies and self-employed workers is a sign of *failure* (in Latin America), not of *success*."[35]

As Harper reports: "Arguing that the root cause of poverty and underdevelopment in Latin America is the growing tendency of largely unproductive microenterprises and the self-employed to absorb the country's scarce financial resources, while the far more productive small- to medium enterprise sector goes without, the IDB effectively pulled the rug from under the microfinance industry. For the first time, a mainstream international development agency was arguing that a major misallocation of capital has taken place in Latin America these last two to three decades, and the situation needed correcting fast."[36]

4. Has Microfinance Led to the Misallocation of Capital?

The critical point that Bateman and Chang make is that development is not only *not* associated with the expansion of the informal microenterprise sector, but may well be undermined by it. Growth comes from high-productivity businesses, which typically require technology and skills the informal microenterprises do not possess and will likely never possess while remaining individual enterprises rather than collective. In *23 Things They Didn't Tell You about Capitalism*, Chang hammers home the point that it is collective endeavors that bring about growth, arguing that what really makes the rich countries rich is their ability to channel individual entrepreneurial energy into collective

[34] Carmen Pagés, ed., *The Age of Productivity: Transforming Economies from the Bottom Up* (Washington, DC: Inter-American Development Bank; New York: Palgrave Macmillan, 2010).

[35] Bateman and Chang, "Illusion of Development," 20.

[36] Malcolm Harper, "The Commercialization of Microfinance: Resolution or Extension of Poverty?" in *Confronting Microfinance: Undermining Sustainable Development*, ed. Malcolm Harper (Sterling, VA: Kumarian Press, 2011), 54.

entrepreneurship, and pointing out that the course of capitalist development is marked by entrepreneurship becoming an increasingly collective endeavor:

> To begin with, even exceptional individuals like Edison and Gates have become what they have only because they were supported by a whole host of collective institutions . . . the whole scientific infrastructure that enabled them to acquire their knowledge and also experiment with it, the company law and other commercial laws that made it possible for them subsequently to build companies with large and complex organisations; the educational system that supplied highly trained scientists, engineers, managers and workers that manned these companies; the financial system that enabled them to raise a huge amount of capital when they wanted to expand; the patent and copyright laws that protected their investments; the easily accessible market for their products; and so on.[37]

On top of this, he argues, in rich countries enterprises cooperate with each other: in Denmark, Netherlands, and Germany, the farmers organized themselves, with state help, into cooperatives and jointly invested in processing facilities and overseas markets. The farmers in the dairy sector in Bosnia have all tried to go it alone and thus not succeeded despite quite a lot of microcredit. The typical developing country does not invest in research and development or export marketing because it does not have a collective mechanism.

> If effective entrepreneurship ever was a purely individual thing, it stopped being so at least for the last century. The collective ability to build and manage effective organisations and institutions is now far more important than the drives or talents of a nation's individual members in determining its prosperity. . . . Unless we reject the myth of heroic individual entrepreneurs and help build institutions and organisations of collective entrepreneurship, we will never see the poor countries grow out of poverty on a sustainable basis.

There are grounds, then, for concluding that microfinance has not, historically, helped economies to develop; that it is theoretically unlikely to ever do so outside of a separate and sustained increase in effective demand; and that as the mistaken poster-child of development, it may have hindered development by soaking up resources that might otherwise have lent to more productive SMEs.

The scale of that opportunity cost is hard to quantify. Karnani argues that funding for the SME sector in India has been squeezed by the Indian banks' preference to fund either large Indian and foreign companies (low risk) or microfinance and self-help groups (previously also seen as low risk but with higher margins).[38] Bateman and Chang think it may

[37] Chang, *23 Things*, 165–166.

[38] Aneel Karnani, Fighting Poverty Together: Rethinking Strategies for Business, Governments and Civil Society to Reduce Poverty (New York: Palgrave Macmillan, 2001).

be worse still in Bangladesh, noting DFID's assessment: "Smaller firms, responsible for the lion's share of employment, have severely limited access to financial resources."[39]

But in fairness, it is not possible to say more than that enthusiasm for microfinance *may* have diverted resources that would otherwise have flown into SMEs. Microfinance as an idea was so attractive to such a broad spectrum for a while that it attracted funding that was specific to its promises alone (e.g., the Omidyar $100 million endowment gift to Tufts University, which may only be invested in microfinance initiatives) and would simply not have been forthcoming for other types of development finance.

The one thing that *is* being built when microfinance floods a country is microfinance institutions themselves. Roodman argues in *Due Diligence* that this in itself is a step on the road to development. In his chapter "Development as Industry Building" he ponders whether the building of a number of large, successful institutions that lend money to the poor can, of itself, count as development. He considers whether microfinance could be deemed the "hero behind the hero of capitalism," the financier behind the heroic micro-entrepreneur, and decides probably not. So long as most microcredit is invested in consumption or low-tech subsistence activities such as retail, he concludes, this development will not occur. There is a success story for the financial institutions, but not for the clients.

Where Roodman thinks microfinance *can* contribute to economic development is through microfinance institutions mobilizing savings. He suggests "the microfinance industry will probably never play a crucial role in the transformative economic processes that increase productivity, create jobs, and lift people from poverty. But the example set by the mainstream financial system is, broadly, the one to follow: microfinance institutions will contribute most to economic development when they become full intermediaries, taking funds from some locals and placing them with others."[40]

Unlike for credit, Roodman is able to quote at least one randomized study that found being offered a commitment savings account raised spending among female clientele. As observed earlier, provided the savings are *safe*, certainly the potential for *harm* is not there in the same way as it is for credit. But while the expansion of microsavings and other forms of financial inclusion such as microinsurance is to be welcomed, it is still tiny compared to microcredit. India forbids microcredit firms from taking savings; in most countries it is necessary to become a regulated bank in order to do so, and while the largest have the capital to do that, for the many small microfinance institutions that are barely profitable, this would be a real problem. In any event, development would only follow if the savings so mobilized were then lent to productive enterprises, probably in the formal economy. Enabling microfinance institutions to take deposits might be a good thing of itself, provided the regulation is adequate to protect those deposits: but this, if it came about, would not lead to economic development unless how those savings were lent out also changed.

---

[39] Department for International Development, "The Road to Prosperity."

[40] Roodman, *Due Diligence*, 251.

Microfinance started out being promoted as a tool for development, before (in the absence of much evidence that it did work as such) moving on to make poverty alleviation its central claim. The absence of evidence for that also may have motivated the change in emphasis to financial inclusion. But that aside, there is a separate risk, so far unconsidered, that microfinance might be inimical to development where it is advocated as a substitute for the state in the provision of essential public goods.

5. Microfinance and Human Rights

It is generally accepted that the poor suffer disproportionately from failures in public services. Karnani argues that the role of government in providing basic public services must be emphasized because of the direct and significant impact it has on productivity and thus on development.[41] Where, then, microfinance, which by its nature cannot be as effective in delivering public goods as a monopoly supplier, is substituted for the state in the provision of public goods, that substitution may in fact harm development. This all quite apart from the question of whether it can be ethical to ask the poor to pay for delivery of public services.

Mohammed Yunus has been an advocate of using microfinance to fill the gap that he believes *should* be left by states providing certain public goods. He writes: "Government, as we now know it, should pull out of most things except for law enforcement, the justice system, national defence, and foreign policy, and let the private sector, a 'Grameenized private sector,' a social consciousness-driven private sector, take over their other functions."[42]

Yunus's position is an odd one. He suggests that he tries to avoid grandiloquent philosophies and theories and "isms,"[43] but believes in free markets while accepting that they (as currently constituted) provide neither economic opportunity nor access to health or education services for all. Since he believes governments should pull back further, he seems, on the face of it, not to believe that there are human rights to food, shelter, or health[44]; but does claim that there is a human right to credit.

He seems to believe that the provision of credit to the poor is so powerful a tool to give them that it is all that is required for the poor to earn enough to buy health, education, and clean water. It may be that he thinks the role of microfinance is so critical in securing these goods that the importance of that role is what gives a right to credit the status of a human right.

---

[41] Karnani, "Undermining the Chances."

[42] Muhammad Yunus with Alan Jolis, *Banker to the Poor: The Autobiography of Muhammad Yunus*, rev. ed. (New York: PublicAffairs, 2003), 204.

[43] Yunus, *Banker to the Poor*, 205.

[44] which are, however, laid out in Article 25 (1) of the Universal Declaration of Human Rights

But if microcredit were justified as a human right through being the critical component for everyone being able to earn an adequate standard of living, then it needs, empirically, to be shown to do so. We have seen in chapter 2 that the claim that microcredit is enough to enable everyone, everywhere, to achieve an adequate standard of living fails. Indeed, the work of Hulme and Mosley, and Banerjee and coauthors, quoted in chapter 6, suggested that it may even deepen poverty for the poorest and certainly that they were least able to take advantage of it, where advantage was to be taken at all.

According human rights status to microcredit, then, fails, and there is no obvious reason to think that even if it succeeded, that an assortment of uncoordinated NGOs, for-profit banks, and not-for-profit microfinance institutions would be the proper institutions to bear the duty of providing that right, rather than the state or state-owned or heavily regulated providers. The state could, of course, be the duty bearer and *delegate* that duty (with appropriate regulation) to banks and microfinance institutions, as it chose: but that is not Yunus's argument.

Yunus's suggestion that microcredit is a human right, then, should be rejected.[45] But are matters more complicated than this? By using microfinance to substitute for state provision of certain public goods, do we risk undermining actual human rights? This is Phil Mader's argument with respect to using microcredit to provide clean water and access to sanitation.[46]

Mader is concerned that if microcredit is used to lend to the poor to provide themselves with clean water and sanitation, their human rights to these goods are undermined, because we have relieved the natural duty-bearer, the state, of its responsibilities in this area. He is also concerned that using microcredit to deliver public goods is inefficient and will therefore also undermine the fulfillment of the right to these goods. He also questions the ethics of requiring the poor to borrow to pay for goods that ought to be secured to them by their own basic human rights.

Mader accepts that those who advocate the use of microfinance for wide-scale access to clean water do not necessarily call for the privatization of water. Nonetheless he argues that by making access to water and sanitation dependent on private credit, this model privatizes what *matters* to the poor—access to water and sanitation, not the physical water and sanitation system.

---

[45] Individuals, of course, could have a right to microcredit in the much weaker sense of a right to apply for it without encountering discrimination, without fear of being refused it on grounds of gender, caste, or education level. They may have rights not be to refused access to a service on discriminatory grounds, but this would not be a human right guaranteed by international law, but a right claimed by a citizen to equal status to be allowed access to credit within her own country. This would not be a claim to a universal right, but to a civil right due to a citizen of that state.

[46] Phil Mader, "Making the Poor Pay for Public Goods via Microfinance: Economic and Political Pitfalls in the Case of Water and Sanitation," MPIfG Discussion Paper No. 11/14, 2011.

Holding back the ethical question just for now, the efficiency of trying to provide collective public services through microloans has to be challenged. Advocates for microfinanced provision of access to water and sanitation services seem to ignore the fact that the bulk of their cost comes in building and operating a network to tap into, rather than the marginal additional cost of an individual household's access. Mader quotes Hall and Lobina:

> Water services depend on an extensive network of pipes, pumping stations, treatment plants, and reservoirs. As a result, a very high percentage of the cost of water systems is the cost of investments in this network, and so water is a very capital-intensive sector. Extending water services to all requires a lot of capital to finance the new networks, and it is very expensive. Those still needing connecting are poor, and the resources required to connect them cannot be provided by the poor themselves. There has to be distribution from those with greater incomes.[47]

Advocates of microfinance for public services such as water, sanitation, health, or education tend to look only at the marginal cost of paying for one more child to attend an existing school system or one more household tapping into an existing water pipework network. But first, of course, the educational system and water pipework network have to exist, and their cost is vastly more than the marginal cost of one additional user, and very possibly very much more expensive when produced by a million individual efforts rather than by a natural monopoly supplier.

Mader argues that private credit interventions are in no position to generate *inclusive* access to goods and services such as education, water, and healthcare—and also that if we understand the theory of public goods and problems of collective action, we must doubt that individuals or households using credit to fund this service provision are capable of doing it on a market basis.

For microfinance to work in theory to provide water and sanitation services, Mader argues, households need to be able to recognize, internalize, and capitalize the benefits of water and sanitation. They must recognize the value of water and sanitation services to incentivize them to borrow and work to pay that borrowing back; they must internalize the benefit by reaping enough benefit as a *private* gain to make it worthwhile as an investment; and they must capitalize those benefits: that is, make enough money from the loan so as to be able to repay it and interest (for example, by having fewer days off working as a result of illness after sanitation is installed, and so being able to earn enough on those extra days to cover their capital and interest payments).

---

[47] David Hall and Emanuele Lobina, "Water as a Public Service," report commissioned by Public Services International, 2006, 17.

Mader has studied using microfinance to fund water and sanitation provision in Vietnam and India. Particularly in India, he found little recognition of the benefit water and sanitation can bring. Households did *not* recognize the health, and therefore the financial, benefits of constructing sanitation facilities. Where construction took place, it was more for reasons of social prestige, a luxury the poorest could not afford. The author has also visited with a provider of microcredit to supply water and sanitation in rural Karnataka, the NGO Mythri Sana Seva Samithi (MSSS).

MSSS has in the past had to do extensive education on the benefits to public health of adequate sanitation provision. MSSS sees signs of change here, partly because the problems open defecation causes are becoming more obvious as urbanization increases and partly because of the increasing recognition that cultural mores and modesty mean that women and girls only defecate in the open before or after the hours of daylight, making them vulnerable to attack and rape, shocking instances of which have been heavily covered in the media. MSSS also believes that the single biggest driver of change is that it is now compulsory for all primary schools to have at least a deep-drop sanitation facility, and with education on safe sanitation also being focused on children, the children are pressuring parents for the same facilities at home. MSSS, of course, is small and attempting to change practice only in one small area of a vast country, but Prime Minister Narendra Modi's emphasis on "toilets over temples" bodes well.[48]

Improving recognition of the benefits of sanitation and clean water do not, of course, make the capitalization of the loan any easier. Such capitalization requires the activity undertaken by the borrowers to be more profitable.

Mader argues that a lack of funding has meant that public utility providers were unable to lay mains pipes for sanitation or to deliver sufficient water for tap connections. This suggests to him that more *macro*finance is needed for upgrading systems, rather than more *micro*finance for extensions to individual households. He argues that water and sanitation are "network goods," that is, goods that generate significant benefits to the public for each additional household access, as well as to the individual (in the case of water and sanitation, through less spread of disease). They are also goods where significant economies of scale are possible, but only if there is mass, inclusive access. Thus collective, inclusive provision at the "systems" level is necessary, which requires macrofinancing, not individual microfinancing.

Having concluded that microfinance is not an effective solution to the lack of water and sanitation, Mader returns to the issue of whether it can be ethical to ask the poor to pay for public goods via microfinance. He argues: "Given the insight that resources with 'basic' or 'actual' public-goods characteristics will be underprovided unless collective

[48] See, for example, Amy Kazmin, "A New Broom Sweeps in India's Clean-up Drive," *Financial Times*, October 6, 2014.

action methods for their provision are found, the lack of safe water and sanitation in poor communities may be understood as resulting from too much *market* and too little *public* governance."[49]

If rights to health in rich countries have secured a public sector that has delivered sanitation, clean water, and healthcare reasonably well, it seems only reasonable for Mader to argue that the public sector should be strengthened in poor countries too, instead of being substituted for by microfinance. As he argues, a human right to water was codified in 2002 and is meant to be unconditional; the cost recovery approach of microfinance would seem to violate that unconditionality.

> Shifting the governance of vital goods from the public realm into the sphere of private interest (and capital markets in the case of microfinance) follows a cost-recovery paradigm which can be expected to exacerbate already existing inequalities in poor countries. Making microfinance loans a determinant for access leads to a micro-privatisation of public goods which then transfers the problem from the political level (where it might be remedied in a socially just way) to the private level, where one's capacity to pay is the main determinant. It should not be forgotten that the loan costs of microfinance—which even in India, a low-interest market, can exceed 60 percent per annum (Shridhar 2010)—increase the price for water and sanitation improvements for the poor by the factor of interest. In this way, the concept of self-help via microfinance makes the poor pay even more than they would otherwise have to.[50]

Microfinance cannot be the answer to delivering basic human rights and needs such as water and sanitation. Organizations such as MSSS carry out their work because they understand the need for sanitation, and the public good provided by it, to be great, and it is only through partial cost recovery through microfinance that they can get funding for their projects. But they know perfectly well that theirs is a sticking plaster solution to a problem that requires surgery.

The market cannot do everything (and, some would argue,[51] should not), and it does not function well here. In India, four hundred thousand children die a year of diarrhea.[52] India's rich can get clean water by buying bottled water or drilling private tube wells. The poor cannot afford these options and are left with no access to a clean water supply.

---

[49] Mader, "Making the Poor Pay," 33.

[50] Mader, "Making the Poor Pay," 34.

[51] See, for example, Debra Satz, *Why Some Things Should Not Be for Sale: The Moral Limits of Markets* (New York: Oxford University Press, 2010).

[52] See UNICEF India, The Children: Water, Environment and Sanitation, at http://www.unicef.org/india/children_2357.htm.

The rich can afford to install sanitation; over 50% of India's population still defecates in the open.

This is a failure of government. The likes of MSSS's attempts to remedy that failure are absolutely well intentioned, but they lack the resources and economies of scale to make more than a dent in the problem. To the extent that microfinance positions itself as a solution to public goods problems (I do not suggest MSSS argues that), it hinders rather than enhances development, by diverting attention and responsibility away from where the only real solutions can lie: with the state, either directly or on a delegated and regulated basis.

This chapter has looked at the macro impact of microfinance on development and found little to be positive about. The countries that have seen the most dramatic growth, and subsequent alleviation of poverty, over the past thirty to forty years, when microfinance has expanded exponentially globally, have not been the countries in which microfinance was expanding. Where microfinance has been expansive, it has been more closely correlated with booms and busts, which are inimical to development. Expanding microfinance where there is no effective demand may simply have redistributed poverty. Most microenterprises do not grow because they are too small and unprofitable and because, perhaps, for many growth is not their prime purpose. It is not clear that microfinance has necessarily *undermined* SME efforts, but it is likely to have diverted capital from them. Finally, the hopes that microfinance can be an effective solution to lack of water and sanitation seem misplaced: to fulfill a human right to water, the poor need, not credit to pay for it, but governments willing to invest in the infrastructure necessary to bring this service to all.

That microfinance does not have a significant positive macro impact on development does not, however, mean that it will cease being provided, given how profitable it has now become for some. And others with best intentions will continue to provide it because they believe it helps enough individuals, even though they are mistaken if they believe it creates a net benefit overall. Given the fact that it will continue to be offered in the near term, then, chapter 9 turns to summarizing all the themes arising in this book and asks: is it possible for microfinance be practiced ethically?

IV Making Microfinance More Ethical

'*Blanche Dubois*:I don't want realism, I want magic!... Yes, yes, magic! I try to give that to people. I misrepresent things to them. I don't tell the truth, I tell what ought to be the truth.'

—TENNESSEE WILLIAMS, A Streetcar Named Desire

9 Keeping the Good, Eliminating the Bad, Transforming the Ugly

HOW TO PRACTICE MICROFINANCE ETHICALLY

THIS BOOK BEGAN by describing the microfinance model and then examined the evidence for the claims of poverty alleviation and empowerment of poor women, and found that microfinance could not substantiate those claims. Certainly, with two hundred million borrowers, some are using their loans to improve their lives: but most are not, and evidence suggests that the suffering of those who do lose out, given that they tend to be the very poorest of borrowers, is out of proportion to the extra comfort and happiness gained by the somewhat less poor winners.

If that is so, why worry about the ethics of the practices of microfinance? If that is all that can be said for it, why not just walk away and stop funding this industry?

It is possible that development agencies and philanthropic donors will reduce funding for the industry. But the industry will not cease to exist overnight. The parts of it that are extremely profitable and whose social mission is now merely a part of history have no reason to exit. Microcredit has mutated from its old NGO days, and while new ways of servicing the poor might be possible, for microcredit there is no going back.

It matters not what the founders of microcredit intended to create or how we got to where we are. The issues that matter now are these: regardless of how unintended some of the consequences of microcredit's practices have been, how do we set about cleaning it up? Judging from the examination of the ethical outcomes of microfinance's practices over the past eight chapters, how can it be done better, be done ethically? Whether these ideas are taken up by individual MFIs through self-regulation or are imposed by a regulatory body, what do we need to do to ensure microfinance, where it continues to be practiced, is practiced ethically?

There are five principal areas that have emerged through this book, linked by a common thread. This chapter rehearses each, but to summarize, microcreditors ought to

1. Establish an ethical, nonexploitative interest rate and curtail lending above it.
2. Drop the use of group liability.
3. Tailor loan terms and conditions to the individual client and *specify* and implement serious client protection, including establishing credit bureaus.
4. Have a clear policy on what uses of loan capital are permissible, driven by the harm principle. Outlaw the use of harmful child labor (defined by a country's own laws) if not all child labor.
5. Be mindful of industry externalities. If there is no effective demand, increasing the supply of capital to create more petty trading businesses will only lower margins for all and redistribute the existing poverty. Do not let microcredit be used either by transnationals to shift distributional product risk onto those least able to bear it, or by governments to shift the onus to provide basic common goods from governments to the governed.

There is a common theme behind these five principles, which comes out more clearly when each is reiterated below. This is the need to replace the current opaqueness of the sector with regard to interest rates, loan collection policies, and loan use, with transparency about what is actually being practiced. Accountability to MIVs, donors, development agencies, and the borrowers themselves is not possible without transparency.

This might seem an overly optimistic wish list in a sector not known for the quality of its governance. Yet it might be that it is in the self-interest of even the most commercialized lenders to move in this direction, because these measures would reduce the chances of further repayment crises occurring. Many more of these might lead to a revulsion on the part of the public that would be exacerbated by the sense that it has been misled about the realities of microfinance. Loss of public support might not, of itself, sound overly threatening to some commercial MFIs: but it will matter when that public is also the taxpayer demanding accountability from the country's development agency.

So how could microfinance be practiced more ethically: can the five major areas of concern above be spelled out?

1. How to Charge a Nonexploitative Interest rate

We saw in chapter 3, table 3.1, just what microcredit interest rates actually are. Particularly outside Asia and particularly on smaller loans (usually those made to the poorest), they are commercial prime lending rates *times* a multiple, sometimes very many multiples, rather than prime *plus* a margin.

The offer of microcredit makes use of—exploits in its neutral sense—the desire for credit. So too does the offer of a Visa card to the affluent in developed countries, where the desire for convenient forms of payment is also made use of. So far, so uninteresting: this is exploitation in its broadest, and not morally pejorative, sense.

Following on from the definition given of wrongful exploitation in chapter 3, we can say that an interest rate is wrongfully exploitative when it takes advantage of a vulnerability of the borrower to the lender to derive a benefit from her, when that vulnerability itself arises from the borrower's low degree of local or global autonomy (or, in other versions, when taking advantage of that vulnerability is degrading to her, or the taking advantage of a vulnerability is itself seen as unfair).

Whichever nuance one prefers, microcredit at these rates is wrongfully exploitative. The borrower is undoubtedly vulnerable to the lender in a way the borrower in a developed country taking out a Visa card is not vulnerable to the credit card company. If I want a credit card for convenience but cannot get one, I can save, use my regular account, draw on an overdraft—I have tools available to me that the microcredit borrower does not. The classic microcredit borrower lacks access to financial services that would enable day-to-day money management, the building of savings, ordinary loans, or overdraft facilities. Her lack of access to formal financial services makes her vulnerable to small, unexpected financial needs becoming large-scale disasters; thus when she turns to microcredit, she is in a very poor negotiating position with regard to the terms and conditions on which she takes a loan.

The second requirement for wrongful exploitation—that the MFI derives, or intends to derive, a benefit from the rate it charges—is also met, through the profit garnered in the for-profit institution or the expansion/status/salaries achieved in the not-for-profit, where these are out of line with what could otherwise be earned by the individual or are disproportionate to the size of the MFI.

As we saw in chapter 3, that the MFI might be unable to offer the credit at a lower rate on a sustainable basis is irrelevant to whether the rate is wrongfully exploitative. When it comes to working out what rate must be offered the microcredit client that would *not* take advantage of her vulnerability, that would *not* exploit her, we need to look at interest rates from the other end of the telescope: not from the point of view of the MFI (and what it can realistically offer), but from the point of view of the borrower (and what she can realistically afford to pay). The terms on which microcredit would *not* on the face of it be wrongfully exploitative would be those offered to the financially included in her country: the cost of a regular bank account and savings account or an overdraft. Since the lending *is* unsecured, using formal prime rates might be too strict a benchmark: the regular rate for uncollateralized lending more likely approximates overdraft or credit card rates, albeit typically on a higher APR. The rate that would not take advantage of the poor's exclusion from financial services is the rate the nonpoor in any country borrow at without security.

It should be acknowledged that there is nothing *normative* about that rate. It is a function of the supply and demand for credit among all those in a society, all the financially included, just as high microfinance rates are a function of the supply and demand among the financially excluded. This is not a rate that is, in itself, morally superior—interest rates cannot be that—but it is a rate the use of which would not take advantage of a vulnerability that results from the borrower's exclusion from financial services. If it does not take advantage of that vulnerability, it does not wrongfully exploit her.

Once we see wrongful exploitation in microfinance as the taking advantage of a vulnerability that reflects a low degree of autonomy, the remedy—even if it is somewhat hypothetical—becomes clearer. This is to stop trying to assess any absolute level of interest rates as too high or to assess what a minimally low level of expenses or profits for the financial provider would be—all of which look at what is or is not exploitative from the point of view of the exploiter. Instead we should look at the issues from the point of view of the exploited. What would be the rate of interest the borrower would pay if she, individually, were *not* vulnerable, if she were *not* excluded from mainstream financial services, whether that exclusion be by dint of gender, culture, distance, or lack of formal collateral? What is the rate that would *not* exploit her by taking advantage of these vulnerabilities? This then becomes the rate—those of unsecured formal financial services in her country—at which she would not be wrongfully exploited. This might not be the rate she would *like* (we all prefer to borrow as cheaply as possible), but it would be the nonexploitative rate—without the imposition of group liability or compulsory savings.

Other attempts to provide a sense of what is a fair rate for a borrower to pay—the market rate or the cost of funds plus a margin[1]—fail to find a rate because either they fall foul of assuming that the market can set a normative rate or they focus on what is fair, in the sense of affordable, to the MFI, some rate at which it can at least break even. But if microfinance cannot be offered profitably or sustainably either by formal financial institutions developing deeper branch networks or by MFIs using newer, smartphone technology to cut costs, then it needs to be offered with a subsidy from government, aid agencies, or any other party prepared to tackle unjust vulnerability created for the world's poorest people by their exclusion from financial services—but only at the rates laid out above. Any higher rate wrongfully exploits the most vulnerable in our global society and, because the smallest loans bear the highest rates, wrongfully exploits the very poorest most.

If, at the end of all this, there is no party willing or able to offer microfinance at a local rate that does not wrongfully exploit, then, given the lack of evidence that microfinance is in fact of benefit to its borrowers, it were better not offered.

[1] Yunus has suggested the MFI's own cost of funds plus a margin of 15%. Muhammad Yunus, "Sacrificing Microcredit for Megaprofits," *New York Times*, January 14, 2011.

2. Ceasing the Use of Group Liability

Chapter 4 went into considerable detail about the perverse consequences the use of group liability can produce. Section 3 below will refresh the discussion in chapter 3 of what an MFI can do better to protect clients from overaggressive loan collection techniques by its own loan officers and agents—all the things an MFI can do differently and can be regulated to do differently, if necessary.

But no client protection measures can fully succeed if group liability is retained, because client protection measures only control the MFI and its officers. Group liability is destructive because it can turn the borrower's lending group into unsupervised, vigilante loan collection agents. If someone already on or around the poverty line is made to cover the loss of some other borrower, she *may* be pleased to see what she can do to help, or she may grab what she can to cover her loss, the last remaining assets of the defaulting borrower, literally the tin roof off her house. For the same reason, renewal of a loan should never be made dependent on others in the group having first paid back.

Group liability is not required to deliver MFIs the cost-effectiveness of lending in groups. Individual lending can take place within a group gathered to save time. The loss of the use of group liability *may* raise MFI costs somewhat, and *may* lead to a rise in default ratios, since the group no longer covers for individual default. But we saw in chapter 4 that there is evidence that individual lending can produce *better* repayment rates than group liability. There are also cases where group liability should, in theory, actually increase defaults.

MFIs may think that group liability takes the debt repayment problems away from them and passes them on to the group—as in the short term it does. However, there is a tipping point after which it is rational for an entire group to default en masse, and the credit problem then reverts to the MFI. This occurs when group members who can make their interest payments and would lose their 20% "compulsory savings" if they defaulted realize that likely defaults in the rest of the group are going to exceed the combination of their and the other nonstruggling members' total compulsory savings. At this point, since they can see that they are going to lose that 20% regardless of their own performance, it is rational for them to cease repayment and keep the outstanding loan balance, assuming that balance exceeds their compulsory savings. This pattern is only likely to occur when a serious bubble is building up in credit,[2] but that is exactly when the MFI needs to know about it (and with group liability it will not know until it is too late) because its own solvency may be at stake.

[2] Or where there is some general economic factor that is causing the quality of all loans to deteriorate simultaneously, such as a general rise in basic food prices, which reduces effective demand of the purchasers of the borrowers' goods, hitting all their sales.

If individual liability were implemented across the industry, as in developed countries, there would be an earlier, more persistent rise in loans past due payment, but as a credit bubble developed, this segment would begin to rise, acting as an early warning mechanism and signaling to the MFI to begin to curtail lending or raise its credit standards. Doing so then would deflate the bubble, prevent worse overindebtedness later on, and serve both borrowers' and MFIs' interests in the long term.

If ending the use of group liability turned out, in this way, to be in the interests of MFIs as well, that is all to the good. But it is principally the borrowers' interests that we are most concerned to protect here. If MFIs want to practice microfinance ethically, group liability has to go. But all the better if doing so also helps preserve the solvency of MFIs.

3. Establishing a Duty of Care: Individualized Loan Terms and Client Protection

Chapter 5 established the duty of care owed by microfinance institutions to borrowers. It was noted that financial institutions in general have the same duty of care to their borrowers when selling a potentially dangerous product (here, expensive debt) as other industries do. In finance, it has often not been made explicit because where the financial institution is at risk for the borrower's default, it is in its interest as well as that of the borrower to take steps to ensure that the borrower will not become overindebted by taking the loan, has some means of repayment, or the margins on the proposed business are recorded as likely to exceed the fully costed interest rates on the loan. We saw that group liability breaks down this coincidence of interest, by making other borrowers bear the risk of default rather than the MFI. But that did not mean that the duty of care had ceased to exist. It was just going unfulfilled.

To fulfill the duty of care to borrowers, to practice microfinance ethically, microfinance institutions need to allow more individualization of their loan offering, less of a one-size-fits-all approach, and to put in place far more serious client protection policies than exist at the moment. And as described in chapter 5, the duty of care requires establishing, before a loan is taken out, that the client has adequate means of repayment, that the margin on the projected business exceeds the interest rate on the loan or there are other sources of income that may do so, and that records are kept of all of this.

By increasing the individualization of loan terms, I mean an MFI recognizing that the standard weekly loan repayment terms, starting almost immediately a loan is disbursed, do not reflect the uncertain, variable cash flow of the borrower. The MFI needs to take into account the time it may take before a business can begin to turn a profit from which loan repayments can be made. Depending on the business proposed, longer gaps could be offered before the first payment was due. And most crucially, as we saw in chapter 7, offering the client a grace period of suspended repayments—or just not rolling over the loan—when there is a particular crisis, or when the harvest needs bringing in, could ease repayment difficulties and reduce the use of child labor among rural, subsistence family businesses.

To put in more serious client protection principles than exist at the moment, the industry needs to specify the Smart Campaign's client protection principles to a higher level than now exists. The principles themselves are perfectly reasonable: it is the absence of a suitably demanding specification of them that is the problem. And, of course, once fully specified, their actual implementation will need to be independently assessed.

The specification needs to cover three main areas: pricing, group liability, and monitoring of dropouts. Currently, to meet the CPP requirement under "Responsible Pricing," an MFI merely has to charge a rate in line with the market, operate at roughly the same efficiency ratio, and not charge excessive fees. What is excessive is not defined, but the worst part of this principle is considering any rate, so long as it is around or below the average, responsible. So in a market with rates of 100% interest, 70% would be responsible. There is no limit to how extortionate a rate need be to qualify as responsible, so long as there is someone charging an even higher one.

The defense of using market rates to define a responsible rate is that there is no industry-wide definition of usurious interest rates. Perhaps not: in which case, Smart could surely define one and perhaps set it from the point of view of the client whose aim it is to protect, rather than from the point of view of the industry (see my own suggestions in (1) above). And the rate needs to be transparent: a clear APR or EIR. The CPPs do say that to meet the standard, all costs must be disclosed, but it is not clear if that requires the calculation of an APR.

The other areas where the CPPs are underspecified are where they endorse the use of group liability and do not require the monitoring of dropouts. Coercion can thus still occur via the group; see section 2 above. Although implicit in the client protection principles, one point regarding dropouts is worth emphasizing. To fulfill a duty of care to borrowers, MFIs need to monitor their dropouts, trace what happens to them after dropping out, and ensure the burden of debt they took on is not exerting undue sacrifice if it has not been simply written off. And as we saw in chapter 6, MFIs would have a much better sense of how many of their clients are becoming overindebted if, when they measure default ratios, they measure defaults by individual, not by loan, so that if an individual has been unable to repay but the group's savings cover payments, it is still recorded as a default. Only by, over a long period, monitoring real default rates and numbers of dropouts, as well as those "successful" enough to stay in the program, can MFIs see where they are doing most good and most harm.

When it comes to implementing a set of much more fully specified set of Smart Campaign client protection principles, the industry as a whole will need to draw on the lessons from the experience of Indian MFIs through their various microfinance crises, to ensure that what they actually measure is practiced in reality on the ground, not just good practice as intended.

In 2011 an advisory company, M2i, launched a Code of Conduct Assessment (COCA) tool in India. This aimed to measure if MFIs' policies and systems in fact translated into ethical microfinance practice. But even it awarded high scores for mere board approval of a policy and continued to award high marks for implementation even while aware that an MFI being examined was lending to center leaders acting as agents, who were taking out multiple loans in the names of the rest of the group, paying the group some commission, and keeping all the money to become moneylenders themselves.

It was not just loan approval that was being poorly measured on the ground. Arunachalam observes M2i giving one MFI a full eleven points out of eleven on observance of the staff conduct code, while at the same time stating that "the internal audits were not found covering staff conduct issues adequately and explicitly."[3]

Arunachalam largely blames the 2010 Andhra Pradesh crisis on the reckless rate of growth leading up to it: he quotes Sriram on how microlending was going from small scale to industrial scale at a damaging pace.

> All was well for us, within the industry, when the base was small. There were several 100 percents in the microfinance sector. The growth rate was in excess of 100%, recovery was 100% and the sustainability indices quickly crossed 100 percent. Voila, we had found a magic mantra where the poor could be served, we could look good and put "eradication of poverty" on our mission statement and of course, lead a comfortable life. The alternative services that were funding the poor made us look like messiahs.
>
> The problem was that we were dealing with people and not processes and systems. . . . The question is whether the lender knows the absorption and repayment capacity of the borrower. It is impossible to know this if we are doing a group meeting in 20 minutes and moving on. It is impossible to address this when we have standardised products and offer a higher loan each cycle. Our credit officers are trained to be robots following a process mechanically and are prohibited to think. Therefore multiple lending is a problem of the MFIs. We clearly do not know our customers enough, and do not have time to know them.[4]

Arunachalam hopes that, this time around, regulatory architecture is taken seriously. "Otherwise . . . we will continue to have many wonderful proposals for self regulation that will not be implemented in real time. And crisis situations will again reappear."[5]

---

[3] Ramesh S. Arunachalam, *An Idea Which Went Wrong: Commercial Microfinance in India* (North Charleston, SC: Createspace Independent Publishing Platform, 2014), 175.

[4] M. S. Sriram, "What Is Wrong with Indian Microfinance?" *Forbes India*, May 5, 2010. at http:forbesindia.com/article/special/what-is-wrong-with-indian-microfinance/12962/1.

[5] Arunachalam, *Idea Which Went Wrong*, 178.

4. Permissible Uses of Loans and Child Labor

As chapter 7 explored, a few MFIs manage to be transparent on what uses of loans are allowed, and whether child labor is permissible. It is hard to see why *all* MFIs—and MIVs and development agencies—should not be explicit on their policies about this. Implementation on the ground may well be a more difficult matter: but if a loan officer does not know what he is supposed to keep an eye out for as he does his weekly rounds, there is not much hope of meeting an ethical standard.

Boards need to recognize that a transparent policy on permissible loan uses and use of child labor is a part of their corporate governance role. The policy needs to be transparent, so that the MFI can be held accountable for it: reporting by an MFI should include how many impermissible uses slipped through the net or got called something else, and the amounts of child labor used above whatever maximum threshold has been set. Donors and funders need the information to hold boards accountable to their own ethical standards: but first, of course, it would help if that standard were published!

5. Industry Externalities and Macro Impact

MFIs, MIVs, and other development funders need to be aware of the externalities they generate and their collective impact on development.

Chapter 8 reflected Bateman and Chang's powerful macro arguments that there is no evidence that microfinance en masse encourages economic development; and Banerjee and coauthors' work in chapter 2 also suggested that microfinance does not, overall, reduce individual poverty or empower women.

There are modest steps individual MFIs can take to mitigate the risk that they swamp a country or region with microloans where there is no effective demand. Countrywide credit bureaus and monitoring of total microcredit growth in an area could pick up early warning signals of overlending: but without an industry regulator to control how much credit each MFI supplies, this information is unlikely to overcome the incentives to grow as fast as possible when entering a new space in order to get unit costs down and secure profitability.

To seriously address this issue, microfinance firms need to consider their whole raison d'être. If providing credit in small lumps to individual borrowers does not promote job growth or development, could the capital be redirected to something that does? If microfinance is intended to help the poor raise themselves from poverty but fails to do so, might there be a better method, perhaps targeted subsidies or conditional cash transfers?

We have seen how the industry has changed its rationale, from being about development, to being about poverty alleviation, to now being about "financial inclusion." Access to savings accounts or even rudimentary checking accounts would be harmless and possibly helpful in smoothing uncertain income flows (provided the savings are safe). But the rhetoric of the microfinance industry in extolling the virtues of financial inclusion hide the fact that the small amount of financial services "inclusion" brings—some savings, some insurance—is being paid for, and made conditional on, old-fashioned, expensive microcredit. Until that changes and credit on much more reasonable terms is an add-on to a savings or checking product, the positive effects of the inclusion will be swamped by the cost of the credit.

The industry needs to do more than sing the praises of financial inclusion and savings while carrying on the same credit-based model as before. Over the longer term what might be more in the interests of borrowers and of development would be for the money that is supporting microfinance to move away from credit provision to support either grants and subsidies at the poorest end, or to support early stage SMEs at the less poor end. A few MFIs (e.g., Unitas) and individuals (e.g., Jeffrey Ashe) have moved on from microcredit, as a way of achieving financial inclusion, to self-help savings groups. Self-help groups, it will be recalled from chapter 1, operate within a community to pool savings, forming a pot from which members can borrow. Local community savings are indeed mobilized to provide credit in a community. High interest rates are often still charged, but at least the amount charged is paid back into the community's savings pot, rather than paying the wages of loan officers or for their expensive motorbikes or, cripplingly, their overseas head offices and staff. Self-help groups are perhaps unlikely to lead to the economic development of a country—they are too small—but they can provide access to financial inclusion with less risk (less, not none—self-help groups too have acted coercively in India) to borrowers than do MFIs.

Germany's ProCredit provides an example of an MFI going in the opposite direction—scaling up by ceasing to provide much conventional microcredit to clients and focusing on SME financing instead.

There are, then, options for the capital behind microcredit other than simply shrinking in size. If organizations wish to promote job growth and development, a focus on SME financing instead of microcredit may be more successful. If what is wanted is simply to promote savings to alleviate poverty through smoothing of consumption spending, that can be done through local savings in self-help groups. In the ideal world, both might be facilitated by subsidizing the spread of national banks or collective savings accounts such as post office savings, where the savings are mobilized to support SME lending: but that is probably a task too vast and uncommercial (at least for many years) for many backers of microfinance today.

6. Transparency for Accountability

Each of these five ways of improving the ethical balance in microfinance in practice involves increasing transparency—on interest rates, on coercive loan collection, on client protection generally, on loan uses and use of child labor, and on pooling individual impact to assess macro impact. The current lack of transparency makes holding the industry to account almost impossible—and note, the point about transparency applies to those funding MFIs too. MIVs cannot criticize MFIs for not publishing an ethics code or list of permissible loan uses if they do not do it themselves.

This lack of transparency in the industry suggests a low standard of governance. As the industry has shifted from being predominantly NGO-based to the commercialized mode, it has struggled with what sort of governance model it should have.

As it has become commercialized, the industry has tended to adopt the traditional, vertical corporate governance model of the for-profit sector, and although it may still declare a "social mission," the financial mission becomes dominant. One way of telling whether a mission statement is being taken seriously is seeing if it is being measured or not. In 2012, of six hundred MFIs who were reporting to MIX Market at that date, less than 20% consistently measured the poverty level of their clients, the number of enterprises they had financed, or the number of jobs created through the enterprises they had financed.[6]

The traditional, vertical corporate governance model focuses on the need to separate the directors from management, the need for independent audit and other committees, and the need for a strong, independently minded compliance function. It may be that commercialized MFIs have not all scored terribly well on even these factors,[7] but good governance is a wider concept than just these. Governance has best been described as "the system and processes concerned with ensuring the overall direction, effectiveness, supervision and accountability of a corporation."[8]

But whether the MFI is an NGO or a for-profit, one factor should determine the first priority that its governance model serves, and it should not be the type of corporation it is. It should be the fact that the MFI has a client base that is *vulnerable*. When the client base of any organization is by definition vulnerable, the paramount principle of its governance model has to be the protection of that client. Every other organizing principle after that, including the need to make a return, has to relate to how that vulnerability is protected and not taken advantage of. Each principle has to be transparent to ensure that that is so. Where the client base of an organization is vulnerable, as with microfinance,

---

[6] Micol Pistelli, "How Do We Improve Microfinance Governance? Start by Measuring It," CGAP blog, July 10, 2012.

[7] In the run-up to its flotation, the CEO of SKS, Vikrum Akula, would appear to have taken a Rs 1.636 crore loan (then approximately $350,000), interest free, from his company to buy shares in it at a price of Rs 10; SKS subsequently floated at Rs 980 and traded as high as Rs 1450. Had Akula sold all his shares in the offering acquired with the loan at launch (he in fact sold a portion), that would have netted him over $35 million. A higher standard of governance might not have allowed loans to directors to buy stock, especially in an organization that was supposed to be making loans to the poor in order to try to raise themselves from poverty, rather than to the CEO to enrich himself. See Ramesh S Arunachalam *Idea Which Went Wrong* 70–76..

[8] Chris Cornforth, The Governance of Public and Non-profit Organisations: What Do Boards Do? (London: Routledge, 2003).

the duty of care requires that protection of the client from harm (especially the harm in the offering of expensive debt) be the guiding source of the organization's governance. All five suggestions for improving the ethical balance of the practice of microfinance fall within the idea of good governance, with protection of the vulnerable as its central guiding principle.

The five suggestions detailed above for cleaning up the ethics of the practices of microfinance could all be taken as falling within the concept of good governance in the industry.

We are, of course, a long way away from being in the position where this is so. What might get us there?

The suggestions above go a lot further in their specification than the client protection principles of the Smart Campaign. Perhaps there could be a further draft of Smart's CPPs that drops group liability, specifies permissible loan and child labor use, monitors dropouts, and limits interest rates to prime plus a margin rather than prime times a multiple.

The difficulty, of course, is that very few MFIs are getting certified by Smart now, and if these ideas were incorporated, even fewer would qualify because so many charge excessive rates of interest. Compartamos, with its fully costed 195%, has been certified because it was not out of line with its peers. Under these proposals, it would lose that certification. For the sake of meaningful client protection principles, and for the sake of establishing the independence of Smart,[9] that might be no bad thing.

If the drive for a higher ethical standard of practice currently looks unlikely to come from within the industry, it could come from those who fund it: the MIVs and the development agencies behind them. However, the MIVs look unlikely, as they are also for-profit organizations. Requiring MFIs to slash interest rates while at the same time delivering the rates of return (on debt or equity) required to make the MIV its profit, too, is an impossible equation.

Development agencies could choose to fund only those MIVs that set these much higher client protection standards as investment criteria, but it might require the formation of a new, not-for-profit MIV to do so, as this approach would not sit well with a for-profit MIVs' shareholders.

There is another way in which this logjam could be broken. Individual countries could decide that they wish to take on the task of regulating microfinancc and holding it to higher standards. Or another repayment crisis, more severe than those that have gone before, might shrink the industry and development agency funding and encourage a new desire on the part of the industry that survives to adopt these higher standards in order not to experience the crisis again. And, of course, a severe repayment crisis could prompt regulation all by itself, as happened in Andhra Pradesh. Are further repayment crises possible, even likely? It seems so.

---

[9] SMART is part of Accion, which is a shareholder in Compartamos.

Bateman highlights Sri Lanka, Columbia, Lebanon, Cambodia, South Africa, and Bangladesh as in serious danger of a repayment crisis, but most especially Peru and Mexico.[10] In Peru, he notes, "A simply staggering $10.7 billion of microloans have been absorbed to date among only 4 million poor clients."[11] Mexico, particularly its southern region of Chiapas, has also been highlighted by consultant Daniel Rozas as posing the highest risk to the industry.

In three blogposts, Rozas explores the risks a repayment crisis in Chiapas would pose the industry as a whole.[12] He summarizes:

> In Chiapas, Mexico's poorest state of 5 million, there are some 40 MFIs operating. Multiple borrowing is rampant, with the average urban client in the state carrying 4–5 loans, while clients with as many as 7 loans are not unheard of. . . . The average microfinance loan size is 3.2% of per-capita GNI, but in impoverished Chiapas, that's 8.0% of the state's per capita income. Very roughly speaking, that translates to liabilities of at least 32% of a theoretical client's annual income owed in short-term loans (recognizing that the average microfinance client's income is likely to be below the state average). By comparison, loan sizes in Andhra Pradesh in 2010 were 11.5% of per capita GNI, while the rate of multiple borrowing in Chiapas is as bad or worse than was the case in Andhra Pradesh. Moreover, prevailing interest rates in Mexico are some 2–3 times higher than in India, which puts far greater stress on the clients' repayment capacity for the same amount of debt. Put together, these figures imply that the bubble in Chiapas is worse than was the case in Andhra Pradesh on the eve of the crisis.[13]

Rozas describes a situation that could spark a repayment crisis, and he believes that the fallout from one would be much worse than with Andhra Pradesh. Interest rates are much higher and the usual "client horror stories" would soon emerge. Combining these horror stories with Compartamos's high interest rates would provide sensational media coverage. Because Compartamos receives debt funding from IPC and IADB and has one of the biggest promoters of microfinance, Accion, as a significant equity holder, a repayment crisis would mean a PR nightmare for the whole sector.

But in Rozas's scenario, it gets worse. There is, of course, a large Mexican diaspora in the United States, and most Mexican immigrants come from the same sort of poor

---

[10] Milford Bateman, "The Rise and Fall of Muhammad Yunus and the Microcredit Model," International Development Studies Working Paper Series, January 2014.

[11] Bateman, "Rise and Fall," 21.

[12] Daniel Rozas, "What's Next: Another Repayment Crisis?" February 14, 2013; Daniel Rozas, "Worse Than Andhra Pradesh: The Damage of a Repayment Crisis in Chiapas," March 27, 2013; Daniel Rozas "Saving Chiapas, Saving Ourselves: How to Avoid a Repayment Crisis in Mexico," June 5, 2013, all blog posts on the Financial Access Initiative website at http://www.financialaccess.org/.

[13] Rozas, "What's Next," 2.

families that make up the MFIs' client base. Rozas concludes that a repayment crisis in Mexico would become a public outcry in the United States. As he observes:

> It's not difficult to imagine scenarios that would result in major rollbacks to USAID's microfinance funding, along with probable repercussions to IADB and the World Bank's efforts in the sector. Such a chain of events is also unlikely to go unnoticed in Europe. The result would put into question the core sources of funding for the sector not just in Mexico, but around the world. After all, DFIs are ultimately political entities susceptible to changing political winds, and if they were forced to change course, it's equally unlikely that private funders would be there to pick up the slack.[14]

The risk Rozas sees, then, is that a Mexican repayment crisis will degrade the reputation of the sector as an altruistic poverty-alleviator and expose its high interest rates and occasional coercive loan collection practices. A repayment crisis led to the virtual shutdown of microfinance in Andhra Pradesh, but local collapse would not be the end of it in Chiapas. The insiders—the development agencies, MIVs, MFIs—are not unaware of the ethical state of their industry. But the public is. The public still accepts the soft-focus hype of the industry's promotion of itself as "offering a hand, not a handout." The public is the taxpayers whose tax dollars support the development agencies. And the development agencies still provide 22% of the funding to the microfinance industry.[15]

This returns us to the all-encompassing theme of transparency and governance in microfinance and hence to the quotation at the start of this chapter. The worst excesses of microfinance hype might be in the past, but it was a serious failure of governance that permitted insiders to know that public claims about efficacy were exaggerated but to keep quiet so as not to disturb the marketing story and funding flow. Some in the industry think that the biggest danger facing it is skepticism, but the best way to counter skepticism is not, every time a claim for microcredit proves unfounded, to move the goalposts to the next aspiration, but rather to soberly, publicly, and transparently assess what went wrong with the last one.

In the ideal world, the industry would understand the threat of repayment crises and, from motives of self-interest, move to a higher set of ethical practices. Rozas believes that the industry got a second chance after Andhra Pradesh and that if it moved quickly to implement Smart certification for all, it could avoid wasting that chance. However, if the arguments I have put forward are correct, Smart certification will not be enough to implement the ethical practices needed to avoid a future crisis. Compartamos has, after all, been certified.

---

[14] Rozas, "Saving Chiapas," 2.

[15] MicroRate, *The State of Microfinance Investment 2013: Survey and Analysis of MIVs*, 8th ed., 10.

It would, of course, be unfortunate if the only means to get the industry to clean up its ethical act is another repayment crisis and the human cost that it will entail. The industry has the chance to raise itself to a better ethical standard. Perhaps some of the arguments in this book will help nudge it on the way, by demonstrating that acting ethically is not just the aspiration of many of those who support the industry, but a matter of self-interest, and that not making amends threatens its own survival.

It must be admitted that there is little evidence to support the optimistic hope that enlightened self-interest will lead the microfinance industry to make the ethical reforms that are necessary. Rather than conclude despondently, however, that the industry will reform only when larger crises have imposed much misery and suffering or that microfinance will be not so much regulated as banned or put out of existence by authorities, I shall end this chapter with a proposal. The proposal is made to the development agencies that have funded microfinance in the past, with USAID and DFID in mind in particular.

PROPOSAL TO DEVELOPMENT AGENCIES

The efforts toward self-regulation of the microfinance industry represented by the Smart Campaign go nowhere near far enough to prevent deeply unethical practices in the industry or the recurrence of repayment crises. The ethical issues microfinance raises are too engrained in its model—even the original one, let alone after commercialization—for tinkering at the edges to succeed. The protection to clients offered by the Smart Campaign may emerge from the best of intentions. There is no need to question that. What is needed, however, is independent regulation.

Much of microfinance is unregulated. Regulation that addressed the five areas of concern laid out in this chapter could do much to restore the ethical balance in microfinance. In particular it could protect the "losers" from microfinance while not preventing the very few "winners" from continuing to do well. If regulation could produce fewer losers in microfinance, it could help to shift microfinance's current, overall, "zero" impact on poverty to a modestly positive one. The method of achieving this would be to enshrine in regulation the principle of a duty of care on microfinance lender for microfinance borrower, with all the radical changes to microfinance's practices that this would entail.

Proper regulation in microfinance is restricted at present by the costs to national governments of designing appropriate, locally sensitive regulations, then training and paying local regulators to implement them. While microfinance operates differently in different countries, and local cultures must be respected in the design of local regulation, there is a common core to the problems posed by microfinance, which reflect the flaws inherent to a model that has been replicated globally.

The proposal to development agencies is that they kick-start the process of designing and implementing regulation, by switching some of the funds used already to support microfinance, to create an international forum to establish best regulatory practice. This should aim to provide a core set of regulations enshrining the duty of care for lending to the vulnerable, adapted for different countries' needs. The forum could comprise those with experience of regulating financial services industries, central bankers, existing supervisors where they exist, practitioners, consultants, economists, academics, and perhaps community leaders who have witnessed both the positive and negative impacts of microfinance.

Embedding a duty of care could mean, for example, MFIs being required to keep records of borrowers' income; of the margins predicted for a proposed business the loan is to fund; and certainly of the true interest rate on the loan, the APR or EIR after taking into account all fees, "compulsory savings," and flatline lending, which would be properly published. It would require individual lending without group liability, the follow-up of drop-outs, and the use of a non-exploititative interest rate. Once basic, local principles of regulation are worked out and legislated for as necessary, the proposal is that development agencies establish a training school or course that meets the need of ongoing training of local would-be regulators to implement these principles. The cost of this is currently a disincentive to countries providing it themselves. Once trained, the annual cost of regulatory salaries should be paid by a levy on the MFIs in the regulated country.

In addition to these principles of regulation, the regulators should require timely audited accounts and require the auditor to review the data quality and what is being sent to rating agencies and assessors. The regulators might consider the value of providing independent funding for institutions that currently provide public, freely available data on what MFIs charge and operational profitability (e.g., MIX Market, MF Transparency). This work is currently limited by lack of resources, but such data are extremely useful and important not only to regulators, but as a public good. Regulators could consider passing on the cost of this information through a levy on microfinance institutions. They might also consider making it a requirement of the audit that any MFI be rated by at least one rating agency, improving the free flow of useful and public information.

Development agencies could thus hope to reduce poverty, somewhat, by providing the training for a cadre of regulators to implement new regulation designed to prevent overindebtedness and the exacerbation of poverty while still allowing the reduction in poverty for those few whom microfinance helps.

This is, in one sense, a very modest proposal. It proposes that it is in the development agencies' power to help bring about not the enrichment and empowerment of millions, or the end of poverty, or even economic growth, but a rebalancing of the distribution of benefit and burdens in microfinance to relieve the losses and suffering of those who are at the worst end of it. Of course, to those who believe that the prevention of the accumulation of millions of small and not-so-small negatives is as important morally as the creation of high utility for a few successes, perhaps it is not so modest after all.

One ought to hold on to one's heart; for if one lets it go, one soon loses control of the head too.

—NIETZSCHE

10 Wider Lessons

WHAT WE CAN LEARN FROM MICROFINANCE FOR ANTIPOVERTY DEVELOPMENT EFFORTS

THIS BOOK BEGAN with a scathing quote from economists Banerjee and Duflo on how the "romantic idea of microcredit" led those involved with it to overlook the "3 Cs," credulity, cupidity, and corruption and thus not act to prevent the mass repayment crisis in Andhra Pradesh in 2010. In Part I, I traced how some of the ethical difficulties microcredit presents have been exacerbated by its commercialization, though some of them are intrinsic to its original model. Parts II and III unpicked the issues of exploitation, coercion, paternalism, and the unfulfilled requirements of a duty of care in microfinance, as well as exploring the distribution of its benefits and burdens and the complexities of ethical trading in the informal sector. Despite the challenges and sometimes contradictory nuances, in Part IV I have suggested ways in which microcredit could be practiced more ethically.

This final chapter serves as an epilogue. It stands back from the questions of why microfinance has ended up as it has and how to improve the ethics of its practice to ask whether there are wider lessons for development generally that we could learn from microfinance or, indeed, vice versa. For while some of what we can learn about microfinance is idiosyncratic to it, some of the mistakes it has made do have more general applicability.

I suggest that microfinance illustrates the dangers in five areas that can be applied more generally to development:

1. The dangers of hubris. Hubris can lead to a blindness to actual rather than intended results and impact, a failure to evaluate properly, and a failure to exit

what has become an unsuccessful intervention. Instead, excessive self-belief leads to self-perpetuation in the interests of the institutions rather than those they initially sought to serve.

2. The classic dangers posed by the principal-agent problem, leading to the risk of the hijacking of the development intention by private interests.
3. The dangers of not taking seriously enough the genuine paradox of trying to help others to help themselves.
4. The dangers posed to the whole project of development, despite the best of intentions, when there is insufficient transparency, feedback, and accountability.
5. The dangers, in focusing on micro solutions, of ignoring the macro picture.

1. Hubris

Particularly during its most evangelical phase in the middle of the first decade of this century, microfinance got carried away with the purity of its own good intentions, to the point of hubris. It did, at its peak, have an extraordinarily wide constituency to whom it delivered a strong feel-good factor, suiting many different types of agenda—liberal pro-poor altruism, self-help libertarianism, and empowerment feminism were all part of its constituency. Of course having a varied set of constituents all genuinely wanting an intervention to work is no substitute for its actually doing so.

Once a development intervention has succumbed to a blind belief in its own good intentions, participants in the industry can develop a weltanschauung where every new piece of information is interpreted in the light of that intent, and stray pieces of evidence that do not fit the narrative are excluded from consideration. Occasional critics (such as Milford Bateman in the case of microfinance) are dismissed for the flamboyance of their language rather than the substance of their argument.

Most people hold the beliefs that they do in a "web of belief"[1] where different beliefs interlock with each other. So if a new piece of information challenges one part of that system, there may be a choice of which belief to change. Faced with an RCT study of microfinance claiming that it had, overall, little impact, the conclusion that microcredit is less effective at relieving poverty than previously thought was only one possible conclusion. Another was to change the belief in the reliability of RCTs (deciding that they were not all they were cracked up to be) in order to hold onto the more important belief in the efficacy of microcredit. Microfinance practitioners have been guilty of this too, although the more RCT studies that come out showing the same negligible results, the harder the false belief in microfinance's efficacy is to sustain.

[1] The phrase comes from W. V. Quine and J. S. Ullian, *The Web of Belief* (New York: Random House, 1970).

When a group comes to forcefully believe in one particular thing, especially a belief with a moral content—be it a religion or a political party or a movement or other cause—the group often acts in a way to reinforce the common belief. In the mix of all the various beliefs held at one time, there can be no end of ways of reshaping secondary beliefs to ensure they fit with a central belief that is not to be challenged.[2] It does not have to be the case that there is bad faith in shifting other beliefs around to defend the most emotionally charged one, but taken to its extreme, such reshuffling verges on the delusional. This is not to suggest that advocates of microfinance went so far, even in its most evangelical phase. Hubris is a sufficient description.

One sure sign that hubris has set in is "moving the goalposts." Sometimes, of course, one discovers good things by accident, and if that occurs, the discovery can be celebrated. But if every time you find your intervention does not do what you had hoped, you now claim it does something else instead (as microfinance has in moving from development, to poverty alleviation, to financial inclusion), there is a real risk that you are in love with your intervention rather than its results.

There are two particular risks associated with hubris that microfinance demonstrates for development. The first is that it leads to poor evaluation, and evaluation of the wrong things; and the second is that, partly as a result of being in denial about its failures, a development intervention falls prey to self-perpetuation. In microfinance, too many founders are unwilling to look at overall results and exit, leaving the industry with a myriad of small, "zombie" MFIs that will never reach scale but whose founders cannot recognize that they have failed. They hobble on, charging cripplingly rates of interest, serving the interests of loan officers, staff, and executives, but not the poor.

HUBRIS AND EVALUATION

Microfinance is not the only development initiative to focus evaluation solely on where it believed its positive impact to be and not look at the downside. By not measuring dropouts or what became of them, microfinance did perhaps take this avoidance to an extreme. It was not just that microfinance was failing to evaluate negatives (at least until RCTs began to be used), but it was also careless about measuring the right *thing*.

We saw earlier that microfinance used the default ratio as a measure of success, that is, of clients' ability to repay, rather than the repayment rates among individuals, which group liability had hidden from sight. We also saw in chapter 9 MFI boards' willingness to be measured, in terms of client protection policies, by what code of conduct had been

[2] See, for example, Jonathan Glover's descriptions of the British Communist Party's struggle, after receiving the order from Moscow in 1939 to cease their support of the war against Hitler,to reconcile their deep belief that fighting Nazi Germany was correct, with the conflicting belief that the Soviet Union could do no wrong. Jonathan Glover, *Alien Landscapes? Interpreting Disordered Minds* (Cambridge, MA: Belknap Press of Harvard University Press, 2014), 150–151.

approved, rather than what code of conduct had actually been enforced. Microfinance, in short, has used tools that can only measure an overall result to make claims about individual results. It has measured its intent rather than reality.

Rigorous evaluation is of course costly and carries the risk that a program will be shown not to deliver all that was claimed for it, the result of which could be less funding in the future. So failing to look for unintended consequences or negative impact is a temptation to many development interventions. But a solution, perhaps involving more independent evaluations, needs to be found. Evaluation might be costly, but so is misallocating development dollars to projects that do not work.

Jonathan Morduch observes that microfinance has been especially poor at evaluating its social impact on different groups of borrowers, and he contemplates why this should be:

> The debates over the applicability of the vision—over the pros and cons of commercialization and subsidization—are neither mystical nor metaphysical; to the contrary, they involve largely straightforward technical questions. The underlying empirical questions (How great are the returns to capital for different groups below poverty lines? How high are the household impacts?) are answerable with the right data, but getting comprehensive data is complicated enough that independent researchers have had difficulty making headway on their own.[3]

So why has financial data been collated and analyzed by microfinance institutions, but not social data? As Morduch asks, "Why are we missing the data that practitioners and policymakers need to contextualize best practices, explore assumptions, and draw specific lessons for the wide variety of microcredit contexts?"

Costs are one explanation, but, as Morduch observes, "lack of clarity has yielded important benefits: it has helped microcredit to become popular quickly, riding a crest of success stories unchecked by hard numbers. It has also fostered a remarkable degree of consensus and goodwill for the movement, built on fuzzy measures of inputs and outcomes. Most microcredit institutions themselves have not been eager to collect sharper data for reasons described above, but it is likely that they would have with donor pressure and support."[4]

Morduch draws the lesson that incentives can work against good data collection in development, quoting Pritchett asking whether it "pays to be ignorant" for advocates of social programs.[5] He draws on Wildavsky's views that evaluation often suggests

---

[3] Jonathan Morduch, "The Knowledge Bank," in *Reinventing Foreign Aid*, ed. William Easterly (Cambridge, MA: MIT Press, 2008), 390.

[4] Morduch, "The Knowledge Bank," 391.

[5] Lant Pritchett, "It Pays to Be Ignorant: A Simple Political Economy of Rigorous Program Evaluation," *Journal of Policy Reform* 5, no. 4 (2002): 251–269.

innovation and change, which threatens the jobs of incumbents. Incumbents tend to dominate an organization's decision-making.[6] So evaluation finds itself with more enemies than friends. Less cynically, Morduch also suggests that "the antievaluation bent may emerge when staff members have strong and true beliefs in the worth of a project—and fear that formal statistical evaluations may fail to adequately measure the project's direct and indirect benefits."[7]

The lesson development can draw from microfinance, then, is that the stronger the faith of an intervention's proponents in its efficacy and indeed ethical good, the higher the risk that evaluation of it will be poor and the greater the need to ensure that evaluation takes place. For how else can a development agency choosing between different antipoverty interventions make a decision based on true cost-effectiveness?

Given our knowledge that, on average, microfinance does not enrich or empower, both development agencies and individual altruists will look harder at more effective interventions. Organizations such as International Initiative for Impact Evaluation (3ie) and the Abdul Latif Jameel Poverty Action Lab work at producing rigorous evidence-based assessments of interventions in agriculture, education, health, and more. At the individual charity level, Give Well in the United States and Giving What We Can in the United Kingdom do similar excellent comparative analysis of the charities and the interventions they implement. Their work, among others, may provide pointers to more cost-effective interventions. With microfinance having become a $100 billion industry, it matters that they do. A comparison of cost-effectiveness cannot be undertaken here, but one can only imagine what impact in reducing poverty such a sum funding mosquito nets or girls' education or vaccinations might have had.

HUBRIS AND SELF-PERPETUATION

Microfinance perhaps has more of an excuse than other interventions to switch from focusing on its clients' sustainability to its own, arguing that it could only grow to offer its goods on a mass-market scale if it was financially sustainable/profitable, for donor money would not reach so far. Vikram Akula at SKS and Carlos Danel at Compartamos have both defended the position that high profits and stock market flotations are the only ways to raise enough money to grow.

Microfinance, then, from starting out as a pro-poor intervention, became about the continuance of the MFIs themselves. As we saw in chapter 3, the focus switched from what interest rate the poor could actually afford to pay and still make a return on an enterprise, to what interest rate an MFI needed to charge to survive and then achieve a satisfactory profit.

---

[6] Aaron Wildavsky, "The Self-Evaluating Organisation," *Public Administration Review* 32, no. 5 (1972): 509–520.
[7] Morduch, "The Knowledge Bank," 384.

Without an identical commercial profit motive, development business nonetheless has the same tendency as microfinance to self-perpetuation. As Dichter observes, development did not begin with its own special jargon, institutions, and careers. It did not begin by seeking self-perpetuation and coveting contracts.[8] Nevertheless,

> Just as no commercial industry will voluntarily go out of business, so too has the dev biz taken on the self-perpetuating persona of the commercial corporate world. We still seek relevance and effectiveness . . . [but]. . . we will put our own survival ahead of our mission. . . . The speed with which resources shifted from development assistance in truly needy Africa to the newly independent states of Eastern Europe in the early 1990s is a sign of how market orientated, rather than need orientated, we have become. We too want to be where the action is. We want to keep our jobs, continue to develop our institutions, and to the extent possible publicize and justify what we do.

Microfinance is an extreme case study of hubris and self-perpetuation. But the lesson applies more widely for development: a good development strategy is one that seeks to put itself out of business through the recipient, rather than the development agency, becoming self-perpetuating. It is a reasonable test for any development intervention to pass.

2. The Dangers of the Principal-Agent Problem

Microfinance illustrates the classic principal-agent problem at several levels. The principal-agent problem is simply that the interests and actions of the principal (a development agency, MIV, or MFI) can never be known perfectly to the agent appointed to carry out the principal's policy (MIV, MFI, or MFI loan officer) and vice versa. The intent of the principal may very well be to serve the interests of the poor, but that may not be the goal, or the only goal, of the agent.

The principal has to take extreme care in setting the goals for his agent to ensure they reflect his aims as closely as possible. If he sets a high repayment rate as a measurable target for his agent, he cannot be surprised if coercion is used to achieve it, unless he has put in clear protections for clients that have (and are known to have) a higher priority than repayment. But of course measuring repayment is a lot more straightforward than measuring how it is achieved. The same applies to combining a high loan repayment target with a high loan disbursement requirement—it is all too easy for the agent to achieve both by making fresh loans to clients to repay the old ones that they are struggling with, thereby stacking up problems for the future.

---

[8] Thomas Dichter, *Despite Good Intentions: Why Development Assistance to the Third World Has Failed* (Amherst: University of Massachusetts Press, 2003), 110.

These issues can appear between development agency and MIV, MIV and MFI, and MFI and loan officer, so microfinance is rife with them. There are no easy solutions. Attempts to make the agent (still less the principal) responsible for actual outcomes fall foul of the difficulties of the time frame of their involvement (much shorter for the loan officer agent than his MFI principal), and all the other countervailing influences on the outcome apart from the credit.

At the extreme, the principal-agent problem can lead to private interests hijacking the development intervention, and this is clearly a risk beyond microcredit. Whenever a policy, no matter how well intentioned, requires contracting out to private companies to bring it to execution, those private agents may hijack the policy to serve their own interest. It is not unethical to allow those implementing a policy to make a profit, but if those agents have interests (such as their shareholders') other than the success of the development policy, the principal setting the policy needs to put sufficient checks in place to ensure those other interests do not end up swamping his own.

Microfinance, of course, began in the belief that it was possible to do well and do good at the same time. But microfinanciers have argued that growth and more lending (assumed to be a good thing) require high profits to raise equity and debt. High profits, high salaries, and high share valuations have been deemed necessary to attract investors and the right level of talent to run MFIs.

Of course, BRAC and Grameen exemplify institutions that have grown to serve millions without requiring such incentives, which suggests the arguments above are self-interested. But when funds intended for the common good are being translated into shares for individuals to make personal fortunes from, it is hard not to conclude that at least part of the microfinance industry has been hijacked for private interests.

It would matter less if the poor were doing well out of microcredit too, but, overall, that is not the case, and where the desire to achieve high share valuations has led to recklessly high growth and very high interest rates (to achieve a high price/earnings ratio), in turn leading to overindebtedness, the poor have not only not benefited, but been harmed.

Microfinance is a one case study: the hijacking of the principal's best intentions to serve private interests is a risk for any policy that provides a public good through private contractors. Again, it is not that public goods should only be provided by public bodies. But where a public good *is* provided by private contractors, as with water, energy, and deposit taking in developed countries, we regulate strictly. If private interests are to be allowed to execute a well-intentioned public policy, they require strict regulation while doing so.

3. The Dangers of the Paradox of Trying to Help People Help Themselves

Microfinance, as initially envisaged in the 1970s, seemed like the perfect case of actually helping people to help themselves: giving the poor something they previously lacked—access to credit—to enable them to lift themselves out of poverty. It seemed that this was one intervention that could answer John Stuart Mill's test for helping others while still respecting their autonomy. If

> the condition of anyone is so disastrous that his energies are paralyzed by discouragement, assistance is a tonic, not a sedative: it braces instead of deadening the active faculties: always provided that the assistance is not such as to dispense with self-help, by substituting itself for the person's own labour, skill, and prudence, but is limited to affording him a better hope of attaining success by those legitimate means. This accordingly is a test to which all plans of philanthropy and benevolence should be brought, whether intended for the benefit of individuals or classes, and whether conducted on the voluntary or on the government principle.[9]

David Ellerman argues helping people help themselves is the key paradox of development: "how can the helpers 'supply' help that actually furthers rather than overrides or undercuts the goal of the doers helping themselves."[10] (In Ellerman's terminology, the "helpers" are the providers of development assistance, the "doers" the recipients of it.) As he puts it, "If the helpers are supplying help that directly influences the doers, then how can the doers really be 'helping themselves'? Autonomy cannot be externally supplied. And if the doers are to become autonomous, then how can external helpers have any direct influence?"[11]

Ellerman calls the forms of help that undercut people's capacity to help themselves "unhelpful help." The "helping professions" are doctors, nurses, lawyers, psychologists, teachers, ministers, aid workers, social workers. All of these need to be in the paradoxical position of working to eliminate their own jobs. Those trying to help must not create dependence on them or the doer will never self-help (although it perpetuates the job for the helper). "In spite of the 'helping self-help' rhetoric, helpers are often driven by their own organizational imperatives to use 'giving-fish' strategies that tend to perpetuate the continuing need for helpers rather than 'learn-how-to-fish' strategies that will foster the doers' autonomy—and that will, by the same token, remove the source of income for the helpers."[12]

Ellerton believes that autonomy-respecting assistance needs a new approach, one where instead of the helper providing the motivation in a carrot-and-stick approach, the helper starts by finding a doer who is *already* motivated and just needs some external help to help himself.

---

[9] J. S. Mill, *Principles of Political Economy and Chapters on Socialism*, Book V.11 (Oxford: Oxford University Press World's Classics, 1994), 355.

[10] David Ellerman, Helping People Help Themselves: From the World Bank to an Alternative Philosophy of Development Assistance (Ann Arbor: University of Michigan Press, 2005), 4.

[11] Ellerman, *Helping People Help Themselves*, 4.

[12] Ellerman, *Helping People Help Themselves*, 8.

One can see why Ellerton initially thought that microfinance could provide a rare case of such a model. Recall Yunus did, originally, find someone to help who was already motivated—the basket-weaving Begum, who was an existing entrepreneur who could be helped by cutting the price at which she was effectively borrowing. And one of the lessons for microfinance, discussed in the previous chapter, is that it looks to stand a much greater chance of being successful helping people become entrepreneurial if that is what they have already been motivated to choose—undercutting the cost of borrowing for existing entrepreneurs, not trying to turn everyone into one. The evidence from Banerjee and coauthors is indeed that microfinance works best where it serves a "doer" who is already motivated, who is, in their terms, a "gung-ho" entrepreneur.

But sadly, as we saw in chapter 1, Yunus's original model for microfinance is not how most of it has come to be practiced, including by Grameen Bank itself. Most microcredit loans are taken out by "reluctant entrepreneurs"; most microloans are rolled onto the next cycle. There are very few graduates. Dependence is created, and the only jobs that are perpetuated are those of the MFI's employees.

The village savings and loans groups and the ROSCAs, where the emphasis is on a small group saving each week with just a few at a time borrowing, and the money coming from and staying in the community, stand a better chance of being helpful help. They will not do a great deal to alleviate poverty and will not lead to development, but they do not do the harm of microcredit, and being able to smooth consumption when on the poverty line is a genuine good.

For a brief moment, then, a wider lesson for development that could have been drawn from microfinance seemed to be that those economists who looked to achieve development through finding rare ways to help people help themselves had a point: it was a paradox, but by seeking out existing motivated clients, having a time-limited engagement and providing the only missing ingredient (credit), development could be fostered. Unfortunately microfinance then became a one-size-fits-all solution extended to those without any actual motivation to be entrepreneurs, and little overall poverty alleviation or development followed. It may be that if microfinance shrank back to that original model, it could achieve a better balance of results. But until then, its lesson for development is only to illustrate how easily the best-intentioned self-help strategy can fall foul of development's central paradox.

4. The Dangers of a Lack of Transparency, Feedback, and Accountability

Microfinance suffers from a high degree of lack of transparency, poor feedback from its clients, and a lack of accountability to them. We saw in chapter 7 that there have been moves to increase transparency, but they have not yet gone nearly far enough. To reiterate the argument made there: it is not enough for the Smart Campaign to state that interest rates should be transparent; an APR is needed. It is not enough to aim to monitor effectiveness in achieving client outcomes if dropouts are not also monitored and counted. And it is not enough for an MFI to claim to lend responsibly, but have no list of impermissible loan uses or a policy on child labor.

Microfinance needs transparency in each of these areas not only to avoid deceiving its supporters and donors as to its efficacy and ethical worth, but also to avoid deceiving itself on these points. The risk of continuing the deception is that when the problems manifest themselves in a repayment crisis, that crisis is worse than it would have been if the underlying, growing indebtedness had been addressed earlier, and the time required by borrowers or indeed donors to forgive the deception will be long.

In its lack of transparency, microfinance illustrates a common problem for development. In the nonideal real world, implementing an intervention will always run the risk of some fraud, some corruption, some unforeseen consequences of dubious ethical value. Those trying to implement their intervention will always ask themselves: should I report this small-scale fraud to my donors and risk their losing faith in my project, or do I sweep it under the carpet, hope I never get found out, and preserve the public image? What this calculation misses, of course, is the common good that would be achieved if everyone *were* transparent, reducing bribery, fraud, and corruption.

In microfinance, as in development generally, it is seldom in anyone's interest to be the first mover to be transparent with regard to the flaws and frauds that occur along the way. The fear that one who did so would lose funding to the rest is too strong, and the risk if all do so together is that a particular intervention might not be funded after the declaration. So opaqueness remains.

Microfinance is like many other development interventions in having poor feedback (unsurprisingly, if dropouts are not monitored) and being accountable not to those it seeks to help, but rather to overseas donors or shareholders. Some MFIs could argue that they are exceptions to this; Grameen in particular can argue that it is owned by its borrowers and that borrowers sit on its board. But the legal ownership structure of Grameen is disputed, and while borrowers have indeed sat on its board, quite how much control they have exercised is moot. Nonetheless, one could concede this exception and still apply the point about lack of accountability to clients very generally.

The distinctiveness of development aid compared to commercial markets or democratic politics has been noted by many authors.[13] In commercial markets, the consumer's choice of what and how much he buys gives suppliers much of the feedback they need about how to maximize their offering, and the client-supplier contract ensures accountability. In the domestic politics of democracies, it is the voters who consume their government's services, give feedback politically, and hold their government to account at the ballot box. None of this is true for overseas development aid: the donors or voters who

[13] Easterly emphasizes the point in his introduction to *Reinventing Foreign Aid*, 1–43, and also quotes Ritva Reinikka, "Donors and Service Delivery," Bertin Martens, "Why Do Aid Agencies Exist?" and Jakob Svensson, "Absorption Capacity and Disbursement Constraints," all in his volume.

vote for development aid to be given are not the recipients of it, and the actual recipients have few means of expressing how happy or otherwise they are with what is provided.

Microfinance arguably provides a partial solution to this in being offered commercially: in theory a borrower could choose between MFIs with different interest rates or schedules for repayment. In theory, some of the feedback mechanisms of the marketplace could apply. But the emergence of "best practices" and the sustainability requirement have meant that, within countries, the product offered has historically largely been a standard, Grameen-style replicator. Mobile telephone technology and an increase in individual lending have improved that lack of choice a little, but the poor feedback loops and lack of accountability are still problematical.

5. The Dangers of Ignoring the Macro While Focusing on the Micro

We do not really know what will finally trigger development out of stagnancy: it is suspected that it is a myriad of different things, and the supply of capital *may* be one of them, but supplying one element without the context of the rest may have the impact of pushing on a string. And the historic lesson, seen in chapter 8, is that entrepreneurship creates capital—not that capital creates entrepreneurship.

Microfinance put the cart before the horse. In now-developed countries, early formal finance for the poor came from savings, family, and thrift: access to credit *followed* savings and was used for consumption. Microfinance got this the wrong way round and put credit first: only now is it turning to building self-sufficiency through using the savings of its members.

Here microfinance should take a lesson from development economics. Economic development did not depend on credit being available for the poor. Rather, it was the process of development that created jobs, which generated a need for financial services to provide savings facilities, which then permitted consumption. The lesson from development for microcredit is that it is neither necessary nor sufficient, at any rate for the purposes of development. In taking this lesson on board, microfinance also needs to learn the other lesson from chapter 8—that if it practices where there is no effective demand, poverty will not be alleviated, just redistributed. For microfinance to have a role in development, it needs to funnel its credit into enterprises large enough to export to a market outside the immediate, poor neighborhood where there *is* some effective demand. That alone is unlikely to be enough for development, but at least business could then grow without acting to the detriment of others, as it may do where effective demand is absent.

6. Final Remarks

This book has looked at how we could make microfinance "work". It has produced ideas as to how we could practice microfinance more *ethically*—by getting rid of group liability;

by charging nonexploitative interest rates (prime plus a margin, not times a multiple); by introducing detailed client protection measures; by establishing permissible uses of loan capital and child labor; by looking at its overall impact on an economy, the sum of all its activities, rather than just individual MFIs' efforts; and by regulating it.

Practicing microfinance more ethically is an improvement on practicing it unethically, but in itself will not make microfinance "work" in terms of alleviating poverty or promoting economic development. As the repayment crises of recent years have acted to roll back some of the hubris of the sector, and segments of the industry have begun to face up to the reality of microfinance's limited impact (if not in all of its publicity materials), the industry has begun to fragment. Grameen-style replicators are not quite the monolith they once were.

As we have seen, some, like ProCredit, have moved out of traditional microfinance to focus on the SME sector. Others have started over with a focus on providing savings through ROSCAs and village savings and loans groups, without the need for external capital that requires a profit from the activity it supports. Both routes are plausible, and both are considerably more cautious than traditional microfinance about what they can achieve.

But the bulk of microfinance today is either straightforwardly commercial or offered under the "financial inclusion" banner, where the offer of savings alongside credit is supposed to make the offering as a whole more likely to alleviate poverty. At the margin, it may (assuming the savings are not the "compulsory savings" of microcredit), but that is very much at the margin. It will be nothing like enough to make microfinance work for the poor.

Several major reasons have emerged through this book as to why microfinance does not achieve its original intention of getting capital to the poor to help them start their own businesses and work their own way out of poverty. One is that credit has been offered to all on the assumption that everyone can become an entrepreneur, with no evidence for that view and some evidence suggesting precisely the opposite. A second major "macro" reason has been that offering credit to build businesses in locations where there is no effective demand is doomed to failure. Nothing can make microfinance work in these areas. And then there is the question of the rate at which most microfinance is offered, at multiples of formal rates.

Microfinance can improve its chances of working by shrinking, offering credit only to actual entrepreneurs in places where there is effective demand. This would substantially reduce the amount on offer and go a way toward ensuring that too many entrepreneurs are not financed who begin a race to the bottom with their businesses. But this still leaves the problem that credit in poor countries often cannot be offered sustainably without charging rates that are multiples of the formal sector. Although a few can make a turn on money borrowed at such rates, most cannot, and their continued repayment and borrowing is not a sign of successful loan use but hides a wealth of complexity of multilayered borrowings, sacrifice, and loss of assets.

The position of commercialized microfinance is difficult, outside of areas where high population density, loan size, or new technology has genuinely reduced the unit cost of making a loan. In those areas, it is possible to be commercialized and have rates that approach those of the formal sector. But for most MFIs, including NGOs that aim only at sustainability, the high unit cost of lending requires charging rates only the most desperate borrowers—the poorest—would choose to pay.

Microfinance has made a Faustian bargain. In exchange for sustainability, and with it the chance to reach out to a mass market, it has given away a critical component of its ability to help people to help themselves. It lost control of the price at which that help is offered. The price is set by the cost of making the loan plus a profit margin, rather than being set by what price the borrower can afford while making a profit herself. The commitment to sustainability brought a vast array of support in terms of grants, donations, and debt and equity capital, at the cost of undermining the very goal microfinance set out with. And although there has been some overt personal profit maximization by microfinanciers, generally this erosion of the original goal has come about with the best of intentions.

It is not always wrong to make a profit from the poor. If credit were being offered at close to formal rates and under terms and conditions that allowed the borrower to make good use of it, the MFI offering credit would not be acting unethically if it also made a profit. By making its offer close to formal rates, the MFI would not be taking advantage of the vulnerability of the borrower and so would not exploit her. So making a profit while serving the poor is not *necessarily* unethical. But in market structures where rates that are multiples of the formal sector's rates are required just to break even, and the borrower's exclusion from the formal sector means she has to take whatever rate is offered, the vulnerability of the borrower *is* taken advantage of in charging those rates, and the borrower is exploited. In markets with high loan costs per unit, the decision to become sustainable trades development agency / MIV / donor support for an MFI's ability to set a nonexploitative interest rate.

The different retellings of the Faustian fable differ in whether, at the end, Faust loses his soul to the devil. The final chapter for microfinance has yet to be written, and different outcomes remain possible. It could abandon the ground of individual lending to the poor and move to a simpler provision of savings facilities, probably with subsidy. It could focus on funding small- to medium-sized enterprises. Those who still have the best of intentions for microfinance and want to keep its current lending profile could introduce self-regulation that includes caps on interest rates to margins over prime rates, not multiples of it. Subsidies now being thin on the ground, that regulation would force many out of business, and it is a rare industry that will introduce such strong self-regulation. The signs are that the nods in the direction of self-regulation will not be detailed enough to tackle the issue. If not, then for all the good intentions, that portion of microfinance which does not migrate to SMEs or savings-based models will require external regulation to ensure that microfinance is practiced ethically and without exploitation.

Bibliography

Abraham, Ronald, Felipe Kast, and Dina Pomeranz. "Insurance through Savings Accounts: Evidence from a Randomized Field Experiment among Low-Income Micro-entrepreneurs in Chile." Unpublished paper, 2011.

Akula, Vikram. *A Fistful of Rice: My Unexpected Quest to End Poverty through Profitability*. Boston: Harvard Business School Press, 2010.

Alexander, Lawrence A. "Zimmerman on Coercive Wage Offers." *Philosophy and Public Affairs* 12, no. 2 (1983): 160–164.

Alexander-Tedeschi, Gwendolyn, and Dean Karlan. "Microfinance Impact: Bias from Drop-outs." Financial Access Initiative and Innovations for Poverty Action, 2006.

Anderson, Joel. "Disputing Autonomy: Second-Order Desires and the Dynamics of Ascribing Autonomy." *Nordic Journal of Philosophy* 9, no. 1 (2008): 7–26.

Anderson, Scott. "Coercion." In *The Stanford Encyclopedia of Philosophy*, ed. Edward N. Zalta, Spring 2006 ed. http://plato.stanford.edu/archives/spr2006/entries/coercion/.

Anderson, Scott. "The Enforcement Approach to Coercion." *Journal of Ethics and Social Philosophy* 5, no. 1 (2010): 1–31.

Anderson, Scott. "Of Theories of Coercion, Two Axes, and the Importance of the Coercer." *Journal of Moral Philosophy* 5 (2008): 394–422.

Anderson, Scott. "On the Immorality of Threatening." *Ratio* 24, no. 3 (2011): 229–242.

Angelucci, Manuela, Dean Karlan, and Jonathan Zinman. "Microcredit Impacts: Evidence from a Randomized Microcredit Program Placement Experiment by Compartamos Banco." *American Economic Journal: Applied Economics* 7, no. 1 (2015): 151–182.

Armendáriz, Beatriz, and Jonathan Morduch. *The Economics of Microfinance*. Cambridge, MA: MIT Press, 2007.

Arneson, Richard. "Broadly Utilitarian Theories of Exploitation and MultiNational Clinical Research." In *Exploitation and Developing Countries: The Ethics of Clinical Research*, ed. Jennifer Hawkins and Emmanuel Ezekiel. Princeton, NJ: Princeton University Press, 2008: 142–174.

Arneson, Richard. "Egalitarianism and Responsibility." *Journal of Ethics* 3, no. 3 (1999): 225–247.

Arneson, Richard. "Exploitation." In *Encyclopaedia of Ethics*, ed. Lawrence C. Becker. New York: Garland, 1992: 350–352.

Arneson, Richard. "Joel Feinberg and the Justification of Hard Paternalism." *Legal Theory* 11 (2005): 259–284.

Arneson, Richard, "Mill versus Paternalism." *Ethics* 90, no. 4 (1980): 470–489.

Arneson, Richard. "Paternalism, Utility and Fairness." *Revue Internationale de Philosophie* 170 (1989): 409–437.

Arneson, Richard. "What's Wrong with Exploitation?" *Ethics* 91, no. 2 (1981): 202–227.

Arnold, Denis. "Coercion and Moral Responsibility." *American Philosophical Quarterly* 38, no. 1 (2001): 53–67.

Arnold, Denis. "Exploitation and the Sweatshop Quandary." *Business Ethics Quarterly* 13, no. 2 (2003): 243–256.

Arnold, Denis. "Sweatshops and Respect for Persons." *Business Ethics Quarterly* 13, no. 2 (2003): 221–242.

Arnold, Denis, and Norman Bowie. "Respect for Workers in Global Supply Chains: Advancing the Debate over Sweatshops." *Business Ethics Quarterly* 17, no. 1 (2007): 135–145.

Arun, Thankom, David Hulme, Imran Martin, and Stuart Rutherford. "Finance for the Poor: The Way Forward?" In *Microfinance: A Reader*, ed. David Hulme and Thankom Arun. New York: Routledge, 2010: 7–16.

Arunachalam, Ramesh S. *An Idea Which Went Wrong: Commercial Finance in India*. North Charleston, SC: Createspace Independent Publishing Platform, 2014.

Arunachalam, Ramesh S. *The Journey of Indian Microfinance: Lessons for the Future.* Chennai: Aapti Publications, 2011.

Ashta, Arvind, Saleh Khan, and Philipp Otto. "Does Microfinance Cause or Reduce Suicides? Policy Recommendations for Reducing Borrower Stress." Work in progress paper, 2011. Available at SSRN: http://ssrn.com/abstract=1715442 or http://dx.doi.org/10.2139/ssrn.1715442.

Asia Microfinance Analysis and Benchmark Report. MIX Market, Microfinance Information Exchange, 2009.

Attanasio, Orazio, Britta Augsburg, Ralph de Haas, Emla Fitzsimmons, and Heike Harmgart. "The Impacts of Microfinance: Evidence from Joint-Liability Lending in Mongolia." *American Economic Journal: Applied Economics* 7, no. 1 (2015): 90–122.

Augsburg, Britta, Ralph de Haas, Heike Harmgart, and Costas Meghir. "The Impacts of Microcredit: Evidence from Bosnia and Herzegovina." *American Economic Journal: Applied Economics* 7, no. 1 (2015): 183–203.

Ball, Terence. "Two Concepts of Coercion." *Theory and Society* 5, no. 1 (1978): 97–112.

Ballantyne, Angela. "Benefits to Research Subjects in International Trails: Do They Reduce Exploitation or Increase Undue Inducement?" *Developing World Bioethics* 8, no. 3 (2008): 178–191.

Banerjee, Abhijit. "Microcredit under the Microscope: What Have We Learnt in the Last Two Decades, What Do We Need to Know? *Annual Review of Economics* 5 (2013): 487–519.

Banerjee Abhijit, Pranab Bardhanm, Esther Duflo, Erica Field, Dean Karlan, Asim Khwaja, Dilip Mookherjee, Rohini Pande, and Raghuram Rajan. "Help Microfinance, Don't Kill It." *Indian Express*, November 26, 2010.

Banerjee, Abhijit, Emily Breza, Esther Duflo, and Cynthia Kinnan. "Do Credit Constraints Limit Entrepreneurship? Heterogeneity in the Returns to Microfinance." Preliminary, 2014.

Banerjee Abhijit, Esther Duflo, Rachel Glennerster, and Cynthia Kinnan. "The Miracle of Microfinance? Evidence from a Randomized Evaluation." *American Economic Journal: Applied Economics* 7, no. 1 (2015): 22–53.

Banerjee, Abhijit, Dean Karlan, and Jonathan Zinman. "Six Randomized Evaluations of Microcredit: Introduction and Further Steps." *American Economic Journal: Applied Economics* 7, no. 1 (2015): 1–21.

Basu, Ranajoy, consulting ed. *Microfinance: A Practitioner's Handbook*. London: Globe Law and Business, 2013.

Bateman, Milford, ed. *Confronting Microfinance: Undermining Sustainable Development*. Sterling, VA: Kumarian Press, 2011.

Bateman, Milford. "Confronting Microfinance Myths and Legends in the Western Balkans." *Indian Microfinance Business News*, August 22, 2011.

Bateman, Milford. "The Rise and Fall of Muhammad Yunus and the Microcredit Model." International Development Studies Working Paper Series, January 2014.

Bateman, Milford. *Why Doesn't Microfinance Work? The Destructive Rise of Local Neoliberalism*. London: Zed Books, 2010.

Bateman, Milford, and Ha-Joon Chang. "Microfinance and the Illusion of Development: From Hubris to Nemesis in Thirty Years." *World Economic Review* 1 (2012): 13–36.

Bateman Milford, and Ha-Joon Chang. "The Microfinance Illusion." University of Jurag Dobrila Pula, and University of Cambridge, 2009. Unpublished paper available at http://hajoonchang.net/2009/03/05/the-microfinance-illusion.

Becker, Lawrence C., ed. *Encyclopedia of Ethics*. 1st ed. New York: Garland, 1992.

Becker, Lawrence C., and Charlotte B. Lawrence, eds. *Encyclopedia of Ethics*. 2nd ed. New York: Routledge, 2001.

Benditt, Theodore. "Threats and Offers." *Personalist* 58, no. 4 (1977): 328.

Bentham, Jeremy. *An Introduction to the Principles of Morals and Legislation*. Ed. J. H. Burns and H. L. A. Hart. London: Athlone Press, 1970.

Bentham, Jeremy. *In Defence of Usury*. Gloucester: Dodo Press, 2008.

Berman, Mitchell N. "The Normative Functions of Coercive Claims." *Legal Theory* 8, no. 1 (2002): 45–89.

Berofsky, Bernard. "Identification, the Self, and Autonomy." *Social Philosophy and Policy* 20, no. 2 (2003): 199–200.

Bloom, G. F. "A Reconsideration of the Theory of Exploitation." *Quarterly Journal of Economics* 55, no. 3 (1941): 413–442.

Blume, Jonas, and Julika Bieyer. "Microfinance and Child Labour." Employment Working Paper No. 89, Internation Labour Office, 2011.

Brune Lasee, Xavier Gine, Jessica Goldberg, and Dean Yang. "Commitments to Save: A Field Experiment in Malawi." Impact Evaluation Series 50, Policy Research Working Paper No. 5748, World Bank Development Research Group, 2011.

Buchanan, Allen. "Medical Paternalism." *Philosophy and Public Affairs* 7, no. 4 (1978): 214–234.

Buchanan, Allen. "Exploitation, Alienation, and Injustice." *Canadian Journal of Philosophy* 9, no. 1 (1979): 121–139.

Butt, Daniel. "Microfinance, Non-ideal Theory, and Global Distributive Justice." In *Microfinance, Rights and Global Justice*, ed. Tom Sorrell and Luis Cabrera. New York: Cambridge University Press (2015): 63–83.

Cabrera, Luis, and Tom Sorrell, eds. *Microfinance, Rights and Global Justice*. New York: Cambridge University Press, 2015.

Cane, Peter. "Negligence in Civil Law." In *The New Oxford Companion to Law*, ed. Peter Cane and Joanne Conaghan. Oxford: Oxford University Press, 2008: 828–829.

Carr, Craig. "Coercion and Freedom." *American Philosophical Quarterly* 25, no. 1 (1988): 59–67.

Carse, Alisa L., and Margaret O. Little. "Exploitation and the Enterprise of Medical Research." In *Exploitation and Developing Countries: The Ethics of Clinical Research*, ed. Jennifer Hawkins and Ezekiel Emmanuel. Princeton NJ: Princeton University Press, 2008: 206–245.

Chakravarty, Anuradha, and Soma Chaudhuri. "Strategic Framing Work(s): How Microcredit Loans Facilitate Anti-Witch-Hunt Movements." *Mobilization* 17, no. 2 (2012): 175–194.

Chang, Ha-Joon. *23 Things They Didn't Tell You about Capitalism*. London: Allen Lane, 2011.

Chen, Greg, Stephen Rasmussen, and Xavier Reille. " Growth and Vulnerabilities in Microfinance." Focus Note No. 61, CGAP, 2010.

Christman, John. "Constructing the Inner Citadel: Recent Work in the Concept of Autonomy." *Ethics* 99, no. 1 (1988): 109–124.

Christman, John. *The Politics of Persons: Individual Autonomy and Socio-historical Selves*. Cambridge: Cambridge University Press, 2009.

Christman, John, and Joel Anderson, eds. *Autonomy and the Challenges to Liberalism: New Essays*. Cambridge: Cambridge University Press, 2005.

Cohen, G. A. "The Labour Theory of Value and the Concept Of Exploitation." *Philosophy and Public Affairs* 8, no. 4 (1979): 338–360.

Cohen, G. A. "Nozick on Appropriation." *New Left Review* 150 (1985): 89–105.

Coleman, Brett E. "Microfinance in Northeast Thailand: Who Benefits and How Much?" ERD Paper Series No. 9, Asian Development Bank, April 2002.

Collins, Daryl, Jonathan Morduch, Stuart Rutherford, and Orlanda Ruthuen. *Portfolios of the Poor: How the World's Poor Live on $2 a Day*. Princeton, NJ: Princeton University Press, 2010.

Conly, Sarah. "Seduction, Rape and Coercion." *Ethics* 115 (2004): 96–121.

Conroy Anne, Malcolm Blackie, Alan Whiteside, Justin Malewezi, and Jeffrey Sachs. *Poverty, Aids and Hunger: Breaking the Poverty Trap in Malawi*. Basingstoke: Palgrave Macmillan, 2009.

Copestake, James, Martin Greeley, Susan Johnson, Naila Kabeer, and Anton Simanowitz. *Money with a Mission*. Vol. 1, *Microfinance and Poverty Reduction*. Institute of Development Studies, 2005.

Cornforth, Chris. *The Governance of Public and Non-profit Organisations: What Do Boards Do?* London: Routledge, 2003.

Counts, Alex. *Give Us Credit*. New York: Times Books, 2006.

Crépon, Bruno, Florencia Devoto, Esther Duflo, and William Parienté. "Estimating the Impact of Microcredit on Those Who Take It Up: Evidence from a Randomized Evaluation in Morocco." *American Economic Journal: Applied Economics* 7, no. 1 (2015): 123–150.

Crocker, L. "Marx's Concept of Exploitation." *Journal of Social Issues* 28 (1972): 201–215.

Crossley, David. "Paternalism and Corporate Responsibility." *Journal of Business Ethics* 21 (1999): 291–302.

Cull, Robert, Asli Demirüç-Kunt, and Jonathan Mordoch. "Microfinance Meets the Market." *Journal of Economic Perspectives* 23, no. 1 (2009): 167–192.

Daley-Harris, Sam, ed. *Pathways out of Poverty: Innovations in Microfinance for the Poorest Families*. Bloomfield, CT: Kumarian Press, 2002.

Daley-Harris, Sam, and Awimbo Anna, eds. *New Pathways out of Poverty*. Sterling, VA: Kumarian Press, 2011.

Darwall, Stephen. "Two Kinds of Respect." *Ethics* 88, no. 1 (1977): 36–49.

Darwall, Stephen. "The Value of Autonomy and Autonomy of the Will." *Ethics* 116 (2006): 263–284.

Debes, Remy. "Dignity's Gauntlet." *Philosophical Perspectives* 23, no. 1 (2009): 45–78.

De Marneffe, Peter. "Avoiding Paternalism." *Philosophy and Public Affairs* 34, no. 1 (2006): 68–94.

Demirgüç-Kunt, Asli, Leora Klapper, and Georgios Panos. " The Origins of Self-Employment." Development Research Group, World Bank, 2007.

de Soto, Hernando. *The Mystery of Capital: Why Capitalism Triumphs in the West and Fails Everywhere Else*. New York: Basic Books, 2000.

de Soto, Hernando. *The Other Path: The Invisible Revolution in the Third World*. New York: Harper and Row, 1989.

D'Espallier, Bert, Isabelle Guérin, and Roy Mersland. "Women and Repayment in Microfinance: A Global Analysis." *World Development* 39, no. 5 (2011): 758–772.

Dichter, Thomas. "The Chicken and Egg Dilemma in Microfinance: An Historical Analysis of the Sequence of Growth and Credit in the Economic Development of the 'North.'" In *What's Wrong with Microfinance?*, ed. Thomas Dichter and Malcolm Harper. Rugby: Practical Action Publishing, 2007: 179–192.

Dichter, Thomas. *Despite Good Intentions: Why Development Assistance to the Third World Has Failed*. Amherst: University of Massachusetts Press, 2003.

Dichter, Thomas, and Malcolm Harper, eds. *What's Wrong with Microfinance?* Rugby: Practical Action Publishing, 2007.

Dowla, Asif, and Dipal Barua. *The Poor Always Pay Back: The Grameen II Story*. Bloomfield, CT: Kumarian Press, 2006.

Duflo, Esther, Abhijit Banerjee, Rachel Glennerster, and Cynthia Kinnan. "The Miracle of Microfinance? Evidence from a Randomized Evaluation." NBER Working Paper No. 18950, May 2013. Available at http://www.nber.org/papers/w18950.

Dupas, Pascaline, and Jonathan Robinson. "Saving Constraints and Microenterprise Development: Evidence from a Field Experiment in Kenya." NBER Working Paper No. 14693, 2009.

Duvendack, Maren, Richard Palmer-Jones, James Copestake, Lee Hooper, Yoon Loke, and Nitya Rao. " What Is the Evidence of the Impact of Microfinance on the Well-being of Poor People?" London: EPPI-Centre, Social Science Research Unit, Institute of Education, University of London, 2011.

Dworkin, Gerald. "Compulsion and Moral Concepts." *Ethics* 78, no. 3 (1968): 227–233.

Dworkin, Gerald, ed. *Mill's "On Liberty": Critical Essays*. Lanham, MD: Rowman & Littlefield, 1997.

Dworkin, Gerald. "Moral Paternalism." *Law and Philosophy* 24, no. 3 (2005): 305–319.

Dworkin, Gerald. "Paternalism." In *Encyclopedia of Ethics*, ed. Lawrence C. Becker and Charlotte B. Becker. 2nd ed. New York: Routledge, 2001.

Dworkin, Gerald. "Paternalism." In *The Stanford Encyclopedia of Philosophy*, ed. Edward N. Zalta, Summer 2010 ed. http://plato.stanford.edu/archives/sum2010/entries/paternalism/

Dworkin, Gerald. "Paternalism, Some Second Thoughts." In *Paternalism*, ed. Rolf Sartorius. Minneapolis: University of Minnesota Press, 1983: 105–111.

Dworkin, Gerald. *The Theory and Practice of Autonomy*. Cambridge: Cambridge University Press, 1988.

Easterly, William. *The Tyranny of Experts: Economists, Dictators and the Forgotten Rights of the Poor*. New York: Basic Books, 2013.

Ebejer James M., and Michael J. Morden. "Paternalism in the Marketplace: Should a Salesman Be His Buyer's Keeper?" *Journal of Business Ethics* 7 (1988): 337–339.

Edmundson, William A. "Comments on Richard Arneson's 'Joel Feinberg and the Justification of Hard Paternalism.'" *Legal Theory* 11 (2005): 285–291.

Edmundson, William A. "Is Law Coercive?" *Legal Theory* 1 (1995): 81–111.

Edmundson, William A. *Three Anarchical Fallacies*. Cambridge: Cambridge University Press, 1998.

Ellerman, David. *Helping People Help Themselves: From the World Bank to an Alternative Philosophy of Development Assistance*. Ann Arbor: University of Michigan Press, 2005.

Elster, John. "Exploitation, Freedom and Justice." In *Exploitation*, ed. Kai Nielsen and Robert Ware. Atlantic Highlands, NJ: Humanities Press, 1997: 27–48.

Elster, John. "Exploring exploitation." *Journal of Peace Research* 15, no. 1 (1978): 3–17.

Emran, Shahe, and Joseph Stiglitz. "On Selective Indirect Tax Reform in Developing Countries." *Journal of Public Economics* 89, no. 4 (2005): 599–623.

Faraizi, Aminul, Taskinur Rahman, and Jim McAllister. *Microcredit and Women's Empowerment: A Case Study of Bangladesh*. London: Routledge, 2011.

Fedder, Marcus. "Microfinance from an Investor's Perspective." In *Microfinance: A Practitioner's Handbook*, consulting ed. Ranajoy Basu. London: Globe Law and Business, 2013.

Feinberg, Joel. *The Moral Limits of the Criminal Law*. Vol. 1, *Harm to Others*. New York: Oxford University Press, 1984.

Feinberg, Joel. *The Moral Limits of the Criminal Law*. Vol. 3, *Harm to Self*. New York: Oxford University Press, 1986.

Feinberg, Joel. *The Moral Limits of the Criminal Law*. Vol. 4, *Harmless Wrongdoing*. New York: Oxford University Press, 1988.

Feinberg, Joel. "Noncoercive Exploitation." In *Paternalism*, ed. Rolf Sartorius. Minneapolis: University of Minnesota Press, 1984: 201–236.

Ferguson, James. *The Anti-politics Machine: "Development," Repoliticization, and Bureaucratic Power in Lesotho*. Minneapolis: University of Minnesota Press, 1994.

Fernando, Jude L. "Microcredit and the Empowerment of Women: blurring the boundary between development and capitalism." In *Microfinance: Perils and Prospects*, ed. Jude L. Fernando. New York: Routledge, 2006: 1–42.

Fernando, Jude L., ed. *Microfinance: Perils and Prospects*. New York: Routledge 2006.

Fowler, Mark. "Coercion and Practical Reason." *Social Theory and Practice* 8, no. 3 (1982): 329–355.

Frankena, William. "The Ethics of Respect for Persons." *Philosophical Topics* 14, no. 2 (1986): 149–167.

Frankfurt, Harry R. "Coercion and Moral Responsibility." In *Essays on Freedom and Action*, ed. Ted Honderich, 65–86. London: Routledge and Kegan Paul, 1973.

Frankfurt, Harry R. "Freedom of the Will and the Concept of a Person." *Journal of Philosophy* 68, no. 1 (1971): 5–20.

Frey, R. G., and Christopher Morris, eds. *Violence, Terrorism and Justice*. Cambridge: Cambridge University Press, 1991.

Fuchs, Alan. "Autonomy, Slavery and Mill's Critique of Paternalism." *Ethical Theory and Moral Practice* 4, no. 3 (2001): 231–251.

Gert, Bernard, and Charles Culver. "Paternalistic Behaviour." *Philosophy and Public Affairs* 6, no. 1 (1976): 45–57.

Gewirth, Alan. "Economic Rights." *Philosophical Topics* 14, no. 2 (1986): 169–193.

Ghate, Prabhu. "Learning from the Andhra Pradesh Crisis." In *What's Wrong with Microfinance?* ed. Thomas Dichter and Malcolm Harper. Rugby: Practical Action Publishing, 2007: 163–176.

Glover, Jonathan. *Alien Landscapes? Interpreting Disordered Minds*. Cambridge, MA: Belknap Press of Harvard University Press, 2014.

Glover, Jonathan. *Choosing Children*. Oxford: Oxford University Press, 2006.

Glover, Jonathan. "It Makes No Difference Whether or Not I Do It." *Proceedings of the Aristotelean Society Supplementary* 49 (1975): 171–90.

Goetz, Anne Marie, and Rina Sen Gupta. "Who Takes the Credit? Gender, Power and Control over Loan Use in Rural Credit Programs in Bangladesh." *World Development* 24 (1996): 45–63.

Gonzalez, Adrian. "Efficiency Drivers of Microfinance Institutions (MFIs): The Case of Operating Costs." *Microbanking Bulletin* 15 (Autumn 2007).

Gonzalez, Adrian. "Microfinance, Incentives to Repay, and Overindebtedness: Evidence from a Household Survey in Bolivia." PhD diss., Ohio State University, 2008.

Goodin, Robert E. "Exploiting a Situation and Exploiting a Person." In *Modern Theories of Exploitation*, ed. Andrew Reeve. London: Sage, 1987: 166–200.

Goodin, Robert E. *Political Theory and Public Policy*. Chicago: University of Chicago Press, 1982.

Goodin, Robert E. *Protecting the Vulnerable: A Reanalysis of Our Social Responsibilities*. Chicago: University of Chicago Press, 1985.

Goodin, Robert E. *Utilitarianism as a Public Philosophy*. Cambridge: Cambridge University Press, 1995.

Gorr, Michael. *Coercion, Freedom and Exploitation*. New York: Lang, 1989.

Gorr, Michael. "Toward a Theory of Coercion." *Canadian Journal of Philosophy* 16, no. 3 (1986): 383–406.

Grammling, Mattias. "Cross-Borrowing and Over-indebtedness in Ghana: Empirical Evidence from Microfinance Clientele and Small Enterprises." Technical draft for discussion, ProCredit Holding, Frankfurt am Main, 2009.

Graves, Steven M. "Landscapes of Predation, Landscapes of Neglect: A Location Analysis of Payday Lenders and Banks." *Professional Geographer* 55, no. 3 (2003): 303–317.

Guérin, Isabelle, Solène Morvant-Roux, and Magdalena Villarreal, eds. *Microfinance, Debt and Over-indebtedness: Juggling with Money*. New York: Routledge, 2014.

Guérin Isabelle, Marc Roesch, Venkatasubramanian, and Santosh Kumar. "The Social Meaning of Over-indebtedness and Credit Worthiness in the Context of Poor Rural South India Households (Tamil Nadu)." RUME Working Paper Series 2011–1, Institute de recherche pour le développement, Paris, 2011.

Gunderson, Martin. "Threats and Coercion." *Canadian Journal of Philosophy* 9, no. 2 (1979): 247–259.

Guyer, Paul. "Kant on the Theory and Practice of Autonomy." *Social Philosophy and Policy Foundation* 20, no. 2 (2003): 70–98.

Hall, David, and Emanuele Lobina. *Water as a Public Service*. A report commissioned by Public Services International, 2006.

Hanlon, Joseph, Armando Barrientos, and David Hulme. *Just Give Money to the Poor: The Development Revolution from the Global South*. Sterling, VA: Kumarian Press, 2010.

Hansard HC Debate February 8, 1861, vol. 161, cols. 262–267.

Hare, R. M. "What Is Wrong with Slavery?" *Philosophy and Public Affairs* 8, no. 2 (1979): 103–121.

Harper, Malcolm. "The Commercialization of Microfinance: Resolution or Extension of Poverty?" In *Confronting Microfinance: Undermining Sustainable Development*, ed. Malcolm Harper. Sterling, VA: Kumarian Press, 2011; 49–63.

Harper, Malcolm, ed. *Confronting Microfinance: Undermining Sustainable Development*. Sterling, VA: Kumarian Press, 2011.

Harper, Malcolm. "Some Final Thoughts." In *What's Wrong with Microfinance?* ed. Thomas Dichter and Malcolm Harper. Rugby: Practical Action Publishing, 2007: 257–259.

Harper, Malcolm. "What's Wrong with Groups?" In *What's Wrong with Microfinance?* ed. Thomas Dichter and Malcolm Harper. Rugby: Practical Action Publishing, 2007: 35–48.

Harper, Malcolm, Lalitha Iyer, and Jane Rosser. "Doing Well versus Doing Good." In *Whose Sustainability Counts? BASIX's Long March from Microfinance to Livelihoods*, ed. Malcolm Harper, Lalitha Iyer, and Jane Rosser. Sterling, VA: Kumarian Press, 2011: 219–237.

Harper, Malcolm, Lalitha Iyer, and Jane Rosser, eds. *Whose Sustainability Counts? BASIX's Long March from Microfinance to Livelihoods*. Sterling, VA: Kumarian Press, 2011.

Hashemi, Syed, Sidney Ruth Schuler, and Ann Riley. "Rural Credit Programs and Women's Empowerment in Bangladesh." *World Development* 24, no. 4 (1996): 635–653.

Hawkins, Jennifer, and Ezekiel Emmanuel, eds. *Exploitation and Developing Countries: The Ethics of Clinical Research*. Princeton, NJ: Princeton University Press, 2008.

Haworth, Alan. "Local Alcohol Issues in Zambia." In *Moonshine Markets: Issues in Unrecorded Alcohol Beverage Production and Consumption*, ed. Alan Haworth and Ronald Simpson. New York: Brunner-Routledge, 2004: 41–66.

Haworth, Alan, and Ronald Simpson, eds. *Moonshine Markets: Issues in Unrecorded Alcohol Beverage Production and Consumption*. New York: Brunner-Routledge, 2004.

Hayek, Friedrich. *The Constitution of Liberty*. London: Routledge and Kegan Paul, 1960.

Hazarika, Gautam, and Sudipta Sarangi. "Household Access to Microcredit and Child Work in Rural Malawi." *World Development* 36, no. 5 (2008): 843–859.

Herman, Barbara. *The Practice of Moral Judgement*. Cambridge, MA: Harvard University Press, 1996.

Hill, Thomas E., Jr. *Autonomy and Self-Respect*. Cambridge: Cambridge University Press, 1991.

Hill, Thomas E., Jr. "Humanity as an End in Itself." *Ethics* 91, no. 1 (1980): 84–99.

Hill, Thomas E., Jr. *Respect, Pluralism and Justice: Kantian Perspectives*. Oxford: Oxford University Press, 2000.

Holmstrom, Nancy. "Exploitation." *Canadian Journal of Philosophy* 7, no. 2 (1977): 353–369.

Hooker, Brad. *Ideal Code, Real World*. Oxford: Clarendon Press, 2002.

Hulme, David. "Is Microdebt Good for Poor People?" In *What's Wrong with Microfinance?* ed. Thomas Dichter and Malcolm Harper. Rugby: Practical Action Publishing, 2008: 19–22.

Hulme, David. "The Story of the Grameen Bank: From Subsidized Microcredit to Market Based Microfinance." In *Microfinance: A Reader*, ed. David Hulme and Thankom Arun. London: Routledge, 2009: 163–170.

Hulme, David, and Thankom Arun, eds. *Microfinance: A Reader*. London: Routledge, 2009.

Hulme, David and Paul Mosley. 'Microenterprise Finance: Is There a Conflict Between Growth and Poverty Alleviation?' *World Development* 26, 5 (1998): 783–990

Hulme, David, and Paul Mosley. *Finance against Poverty: Effective Institutions for Lending to Small Farmers and Microenterprises in Developing Countries*. London: Routledge, 1996.

Hulme, David, and Paul Mosley. "Finance for the Poor or Poorest? Financial Innovation, Poverty and Vulnerability." Discussion Papers in Development Economics Series G, vol. 4, 1996.

Hummel, Agatha. "The Commercialization of Microcredit and Local Consumerism: Examples of Over-indebtedness from Indigenous Mexico." In *Microfinance, Debt and Over-indebtedness*, ed. Isabelle Guérin, Solène Morvant-Roux, and Magdalena Villarreal. New York: Routledge, 2014: 253–271.

Islam, Tazul. *Microfinance and Poverty Alleviation*. Aldershot: Ashgate, 2007.

Kabeer, Naila. "Between Affiliation and Autonomy: Navigating Pathways of Women's Empowerment and Gender Justice in Bangladesh." *Development and Change* 42, no. 2 (2011): 499–528.

Kabeer, Naila. "Conflicts over Credit: Re-evaluating the Empowerment Potential of Loans to Women in Rural Bangladesh." *World Development* 29, no. 1 (2001): 63–84.

Kabeer, Naila. "Is Microfinance a 'Magic Bullet' for Women's Empowerment? Analysis of Findings from South Asia." In *Microfinance and Women's Empowerment: A Critical Assessment*, ed. S. Rajagopalan. Hyderabad, India: Icfai University Press, 2009: 59–82.

Kabeer, Naila. "Resources, Agency, Achievements: Reflections on the Measurement of Women's Empowerment." *Development and Change* 30, no. 3 (1999): 435–464.

Kabeer, Naila, Simeon Mahmood, and Jairo Guillermo Isaza Castro. "Strategies and the Challenge of Development and Democracy in Bangladesh." IDS Working Paper No. 343, 2010.

Kabeer, Naila, Simeen Mahmood, and Sakiba Tasheen. "Does Paid Work Provide a Pathway to Women's Empowerment? Empirical Findings from Bangladesh." IDS Working Paper No. 375, 2011.

Kalichman, Seth, Leickness Simbayi, Michelle Kaufman, Demetria Cain, and Sean Jooste. "Alcohol Use and Sexual Risks for HIV/AIDS in Sub-Saharan Africa: Systematic Review of Empirical Findings." *Society of Prevention Research* 8, no. 2 (2007): 141–151.

Karim, Lamia. "Demystifying Micro-credit: The Grameen Bank, NGOs, and Neoliberalism in Bangladesh." *Cultural Dynamics* 20, no. 1 (2008): 5–29.

Karim, Lamia. *Microfinance and Its Discontents: Women in Debt in Bangladesh*. Minneapolis: University of Minnesota Press, 2011.

Karlan, Dean, and Jacob Appel. *More Than Good Intentions: How a New Economics Is Helping to Solve Global Poverty*. New York: Dutton, 2011.

Karlan, Dean, and Jonathan Zinman. "Expanding Credit Access: Using Randomized Supply Decisions to Estimate the Impacts." *Society for Financial Studies* 23, no. 1 (2009): 433–464.

Karlan, Dean, and Jonathan Zinman. "Microcredit in Theory and Practice: Using Randomized Credit Scoring for Impact Evaluation." *Science* 332 (2011): 1821–1826.

Karnani, Aneel. *Fighting Poverty Together: Rethinking Strategies for Business, Governments and Civil Society to Reduce Poverty*. New York: Palgrave Macmillan, 2001.

Karnani, Aneel. "Microfinance Misses Its Mark." *Stanford Social Innovation Review*, Summer 2007.

Karnani, Aneel. "Undermining the Chances of Sustainable Development in India with Microfinance." In *Confronting Microfinance: Undermining Sustainable Development*, ed. Milford Bateman. Sterling, VA: Kumarian Press, 2011: 83–95.

Khan, N., and E. Stewart. "Institution Building and Development in Three Women's Village Organisations: Participation, Ownership and Autonomy." Unpublished paper, BRAC Research and Evaluation Division, Dhaka.

Kleinig, John. *Paternalism*. Manchester: Manchester University Press, 1983.

Kohn, Doris, ed. *Microfinance 3.0: Reconciling Sustainability with Social Outreach and Responsible Delivery*. Heidelberg: Springer, 2013.

La Porta, Rafael, and Andrei Schleifer. "The Unofficial Economy and Economic Development." NBER Working Paper No. 14520, December 2008.

Lascelles, David, Sam Mendelson, and Daniel Rozas. *Microfinance Banana Skins 2014: Facing Reality*. Centre for the Study of Financial Innovation, 2014.

Latif, Muhammad Abdul. "Programme Impact on Current Conception in Bangladesh." *Bangladesh Development Studies* 22, no. 1 (1994): 27–61.

Ledgerwood, Joanna. *Microfinance Handbook: An Institutional and Financial Perspective*. Washington, DC: World Bank, 1999.

Leleux, Benoît, and Dinos Constantiou, eds. *From Microfinance to Small Business Finance: The Business Case for Private Capital Investments*. Basingstoke: Palgrave Macmillan, 2007.

Leleux, Benoit, and Dinos Constantiou 'An analysis of Microfinance Business Models' in *From Microfinance to Small Business Finance: The Business Case for Private Capital Investments*. eds. Benoit Leleux and Dinos Constantiou. Basingstoke: Palgrave Macmillan, 2007: 49–79.

Logar, Tea. "Exploitation as Wrongful Use: Beyond Taking Advantage of Vulnerabilities." *Acta Analytica* 24, no. 4 (2010): 329–346.

Maddocks, William. "How Can Microfinance Programs Help the Struggle against Social Problems Such as Begging, Child Labor, Prostitution, Violence against Women, Criminality, Gangs, and Drug Addiction?" Commissioned paper for the Global Microcredit Summit, Valladolid, 2011.

Mader. Phil "Making the Poor Pay for Public Goods via Microfinance: Economic and Political Pitfalls in the Case of Water and Sanitation." MPIfG Discussion Paper No. 11/14.

Maes, Jan, and Larry Reid. *State of the Microcredit Summit Report 2012*. Washington, DC: Microcredit Summit Campaign, 2012.

Malpas, Jedd, and Norelle Lickiss. *Perspectives on Human Dignity*. Dordrecht: Springer, 2007.

May, Thomas. "The Concept of Autonomy." *American Philosophical Quarterly* 31, no. 2 (1994): 133–144.

Mayer, Robert. "Sweatshops, Exploitation and Moral Responsibility." *Journal of Social Philosophy* 38, no. 4 (2007): 605–619.

Mayer, Robert. "What's Wrong with Exploitation?" *Journal of Applied Philosophy* 24, no. 2 (2007): 7–150.

Mayoux, Linda. "Tackling the Downside: Social Capital, Women's Empowerment and Microfinance in Cameroon." *Development and Change* 32, no. 3 (2001): 435–464.

Mayoux, Linda, Margaret Jiri, and Marinela Cerqueira. *Microfinance for Urban Poverty Reduction: Sustainable Livelihoods Project, Angola*. London: One World Action, 2002.

McCloskey, H. J. "Coercion: Its Nature and Significance." *Southern Journal of Philosophy* 18, no. 3 (1980): 335–353.

McKernan, Signe-Mary. "The Impact of Microcredit Programs on Self-Employment Profits: Do Noncredit Program Aspects Matter?" *Review of Economics and Statistics* 84, no. 1 (2002): 93–115.

Mele, Alfred. "History and Personal Autonomy." *Canadian Journal of Philosophy* 23, no. 2 (1993): 271–280.

Meyers, C. D. "Moral Duty, Individual Responsibility, and Sweatshop Exploitation." *Journal of Social Philosophy* 38, no. 4 (2007): 620–626.

Meyers, C. D. "Wrongful Beneficence: Exploitation and Third World Sweatshops." *Journal of Social Philosophy* 35, no. 3 (2004): 319–333.

Mill, John Stuart. *The Collected Works of John Stuart Mill*. Gen. ed. John M. Robson. 33 vols. Toronto: University of Toronto Press; London: Routledge & Kegan Paul, 1963–1991.

Miller, David. "Exploitation in the Market." In *Modern Theories of Exploitation*, ed. Andrew Reeve. London: Sage, 1987: 149–165.

Miller, Franklin G., and Alan Wertheimer. "Facing Up to Paternalism." *Hastings Center Report* 37, no. 3 (2007): 24–34.

MIX Microfinance World. Sub-Saharan Africa Microfinance Analysis and Benchmarking Report 2010, Microfinance Information Exchange.

Montgomery, Richard. "Disciplining or Protecting the Poor? Avoiding the Social Costs of Peer Pressure in Micro-credit Schemes." *Journal of International Development* 8, no. 2 (1996): 289–305.

Morduch, Jonathan. "The Knowledge Bank." In *Reinventing Foreign Aid*, ed. William Easterly. Cambridge, MA: MIT Press, 2008: 377–397.

Morduch, Jonathan. "The Microfinance Schism." In *Microfinance: A Reader*, ed. David Hulme and Thankom Arun. London: Routledge, 2009: 17–35.

Morduch, Jonathan. "The Role of Subsidies in Microfinance: Evidence from Grameen Bank." *Journal of Development Economics* 60, no. 1 (1999): 229–248.

Morgenbesser, Sidney, Patrick Suppes, and Morton White, eds. *Philosophy, Science, and Method: Essays in Honor of Ernest Nagel*. New York: St. Martin's Press, 1969.

Morojele, Neo, Millicent Kachieng'a, Matsobane Nkoko, Kgaogelo Moshia, Evodia Mokoko, Charles Parry, Mwansa Nkowane, and Shekar Saxena. "Perceived Effects of Alcohol Use on Sexual Encounters among Adults in South Africa." *African Journal of Drugs and Alcohol Studies* 3 (2004): 1–21.

Mosley, Paul. "The Use of Control Groups in Impact Assessments for Microfinance." Working Paper No. 19, International Labour Office, Geneva, 1998.

Murray, Michael J., and David F. Dudrick. "Are Coerced Acts Free?" *American Philosophical Quarterly* 32, no. 2 (1995): 109–123.

Nelson, William. "Kant's Formula of Humanity." *Mind* 117, no. 465 (2008): 85–106.

Neuhouser, Frederick. "Jean-Jacques Rousseau and the Origins of Autonomy." *Inquiry* 54, no. 5 (2011): 478–493.

Nielsen, Kai, and Robert Ware, eds. *Exploitation*. Atlantic Highlands,NJ: Humanities Press, 1997.

Latin America and Caribbean Benchmarks Report 2009, MIX Market, Microfinance Information Exchange.

Nozick, Robert. *Anarchy, State and Utopia*. Oxford: Blackwell, 1974.

Nozick, Robert. "Coercion." In *Philosophy, Science, and Method: Essays in Honor of Ernest Nagel*, ed. Sidney Morgenbesser, Patrick Suppes, and Morton White. New York: St Martin's Press, 1969: 440–472.

Nussbaum, Martha C. *Creating Capabilities: The Human Development Approach*. Cambridge, MA: Belknap Press of Harvard University Press, 2011.

O'Neill, Onora. "Autonomy: The Emperor's New Clothes." *Proceedings of the Aristotelian Society Supplementary Volumes* 77 (2003): 1–21.

O'Neill, Onora. *Autonomy and Trust in Bioethics*. Cambridge: Cambridge University Press, 2002.

O'Neill, Onora. "Between Consenting Adults." *Philosophy and Public Affairs* 14, no. 3 (1985): 252–277.

O'Neill, Onora. *Bounds of Justice*. Cambridge: Cambridge University Press, 2000.

O'Neill, Onora. *Constructions of Reason: Explorations of Kant's Practical Philosophy*. Cambridge: Cambridge University Press, 1989.

O'Neill, Onora. *Faces of Hunger: An Essay on Poverty, Justice and Development*. London: Allen & Unwin, 1986.

O'Neill, Onora. "Paternalism and Partial Autonomy." *Journal of Medical Ethics* 10 (1984): 173–178.

O'Neill, Onora. *Towards Justice and Virtue*. Cambridge: Cambridge University Press, 1996.

O'Neill, Onora. "What Are the Offers *You* Can't Refuse?" In *Violence, Terrorism and Justice*, ed. R. G. Frey and Christopher Morris. Cambridge: Cambridge University Press, 1991: 170–195.

Oshana, Marina. "How Much Should We Value Autonomy?" *Social Philosophy and Policy* 20, no. 2 (2003): 99–126.

Øverland, Gerhard. "Pogge on Poverty: Contribution or Exploitation?" *Journal of Applied Philosophy* 30, no. 4 (2013): 319–334.

Pagés, Carmen, ed. *The Age of Productivity: Transforming Economies from the Bottom Up*. Washington, DC: Inter-American Development Bank; New York: Palgrave Macmillan, 2010.

Parfit, Derek. "Another Defence of the Priority View." *Utilitas* 24 (2012): 399–440.

Parfit, Derek. "Equality and Priority." *Ratio* 10, no. 3 (1997): 202–221.

Parfit, Derek. *Reasons and Persons*. Oxford: Clarendon Press, 1984.

Parry, Gereaint, Asif Quershi, and Hillel Steiner, eds. *The Legal and Moral Aspects of International Trade*. London: Routledge, 1998.

Pink, Thomas. "Thomas Hobbes and the Ethics of Freedom." *Inquiry* 54, no. 5 (2011): 541–563.

Pitt, Mark, and Shahidur Khandker. "The Impact of Group-Based Credit Programs on Poor Households in Bangladesh: Does the Gender of Participants Matter?" *Journal of Political Economy* 106, no. 5 (1998): 958–996.

Powers, Penny. "Persuasion and Coercion: A Critical Review of Philosophical and Empirical Approaches." *HEC Forum* 19, no. 2 (2007): 125–143.

Prahalad, C. K. *The Fortune at the Bottom of the Pyramid.* Upper Saddle River, NJ: Wharton School Publishing, 2006.

Prior, Franceso, and Antonio Argandona. "Credit Accessibility and Corporate Social Responsibility in Financial Institutions: The Case of Microfinance." *Business Ethics* 18, no. 4 (2009): 349–363.

Pritchett, Lant. "It Pays to Be Ignorant: A Simple Political Economy of Rigorous Program Evaluation." *Journal of Policy Reform* 5, no. 4 (2002): 251–269.

Quine, W. V., and J. S. Ullian. *The Web of Belief*. 2nd ed. New York: Random House, 1978.

Rahman, Aminur. *Women and Microcredit in Rural Bangladesh: An Anthropological Study of the Rhetoric and Realities of Grameen Bank Lending*. Boulder, CO: Westview Press, 1999.

Rajagopalan, S., ed. *Microfinance and Women's Empowerment: A Critical Assessment*. Hyderabad, India: Icfai University Press, 2009.

Rajbanski, Ram, Meng Huang, and Bruce Wydick. "Measuring Microfinance: Cognitive and Experimental Bias—with new Evidence from Nepal." Working paper, 2012.

Ramalingam, Ben. *Aid on the Edge of Chaos: Rethinking International Co-operation in a Complex World*. New York: Oxford University Press, 2013.

Raz, Joseph. *From Normativity to Responsibility*. Oxford: Oxford University Press, 2011.

Raz, Joseph. *The Morality of Freedom*. Oxford: Clarendon Press, 1986.

Raz, Joseph. *Value, Respect and Attachment*. Cambridge: Cambridge University Press, 2001.

Reed, Larry, with Jesse Marsden, Amanda Ortega, Camille Rivera, and Sabina Rogers. *Resilience: The State of the Microcredit Campaign Report*. Microcredit Summit Campaign, 2014.

Reeve, Andrew, ed. *Modern Theories of Exploitation*. London: Sage, 1987.

Reidy, David A., and Walter J. Riker. *Coercion and the State*. Dordrecht: Springer, 2008.

Reiman, Jeffrey. "Exploitation, Force and the Moral Assessment of Capitalism: Thoughts on Roemer and Cohen." In *Exploitation*, ed. Kai Nielsen and Robert Ware. Atlantic Highlands, NJ: Humanities Press, 1997: 154–188.

Rhyne, Elisabeth. *Mainstreaming Microfinance: How Lending to the Poor Began, Grew and Came of Age in Bolivia*. Sterling, VA: Kumarian Press, 2001.

Rhyne, Elisabeth. *Microfinance for Banking and Investors: Understanding the Opportunities and Challenges of the Market at the Bottom of the Pyramid*. New York: McGraw-Hill Professional, 2009.

Riddell, Roger. *Does Foreign Aid Really Work?* Oxford: Oxford University Press, 2007.

Riley, Jonathan. *Mill on Liberty*. New York: Routledge, 1998.

Ripstein, Arthur. "Authority and Coercion." *Philosophy and Public Affairs* 32, no. 1 (2004): 2–35.

Robinson, Joan. *An Essay on Marxist Economics*. London: Macmillan, 1964.

Robinson, Marguerite. "Supply and Demand in Microfinance." In *Microfinance: A Reader*, ed. David Hulme and Thankom Arun, 45. New York: Routledge, 2010: 45–64.

Roemer, John E. *A General Theory of Exploitation and Class*. Cambridge, MA: Harvard University Press, 1982.

Roemer, John. "Should Marxists Be Interested in Exploitation?" In *Exploitation*, ed. Kai Nielsen and Robert Ware. Atlantic Highlands, NJ: Humanities Press, 1997: 122–153.

Roemer, John. "What Is Exploitation? Reply to Reiman." In *Exploitation*, ed. Kai Nielsen and Robert Ware. Atlantic Highlands, NJ: Humanities Press, 1997: 189–196.

Roethlisberger, Fritz, and William Dickson. *Management and the Worker.* Cambridge MA: Harvard University Press, 1939.

Rolfe, Robert, Douglas Woodward, Andre Ligthelm, and Paulo Guimaraes. "The Viability of Micro-enterprise in South Africa." Paper presented at the conference "Entrepreneurship in Africa," Whitman School of Management, Syracuse University, Syracuse, New York April 1–3, 2010.

Ronzoni, Miriam. "The Global Order: A Case of Background Injustice? A Practice-Dependent Account." *Philosophy and Public Affairs* 37, no. 3 (2009): 229–256.

Roodman, David. "Does Compartamos Charge 195% Interest?" *Microfinance Open Book Blog*, January 31, 2011. Available at http://blogs.cgdev.org/open_book/2011/01/compartamos-and-the-meaning-of-interest-rates.php.

Roodman, David. "Due Diligence: An Impertinent Inquiry into Microfinance." Center for Global Development Brief, January 2012.

Roodman, David. "Grameen Bank Portfolio Keeps Deteriorating." *Microfinance Open Book Blog*, April 16, 2012. Available at http://blogs.cgdev.org/open_book/2012/04/grameen-bank-portfolio-continues-deteriorating.php.

Roodman, David, and, Jonathan Morduch. "The Impact of Microcredit on the Poor in Bangladesh: Revisiting the Evidence." Working Paper No. 174, Centre for Global Development.

Rosenberg, Richard. "Microcredit Interest Rates." CGAP Occasional Paper No. 1, Center for Global Development, 2002.

Rosenberg, Richard, Scott Gaul, William Ford, and Olga Tomilova. "Microcredit Interest Rates and Their Determinants: 2004–2011." In *Microfinance 3.0: Reconciling Sustainability with Social Outreach and Responsible Delivery*, ed. Doris Kohn. Heidelberg: Springer, 2013: 69–104.

Rosenberg, Richard, Adrian Gonzalez, and Sushma Narain. " The New Moneylenders: Are the Poor Being Exploited by High Microcredit Interest Rates?" CGAP Occasional Paper No. 15, Center for Global Development, 2009.

Rosenburg, Richard, and Jessica Schicks. "Too Much Microcredit? A Survey on the Evidence of Over-indebtedness." CGAP Occasional Paper No. 19, Center for Global Development, 2011.

Rowland-Serdar, Barbara, and Peregrine Schwartz-Sen. "Empowering Women: Self, Autonomy, and Responsibility." *Western Political Quarterly* 44, no. 3 (1991): 605–624.

Roy, Ananya. *Poverty Capital: Microfinance and the Making of Development*. London: Routledge, 2010.

Rutherford, Stuart. *The Poor and Their Money*. Oxford: Oxford University Press, 2001.

Rutherford, Stuart, with Md Maniruzzaman, S. K. Sinha, and Acnabin and Co. "Grameen II—the First Five Years: 2001–2006." Grameen II Briefing Notes for MicroSave.

Ryan, Alan. *The Philosophy of John Stuart Mill*. Basingstoke: Macmillan, 1998.

Ryan, Cheyney C. "The Normative Concept of Coercion." *Mind* 89 (1980): 481–498.

Sample, Ruth. *Exploitation: What It Is and Why It Is Wrong*. Lanham, MD: Rowman & Littlefield, 2003.

Sandberg, Joakim. "Mega-interest on Microcredit: Are Lenders Exploiting the Poor?" *Journal of Applied Philosophy* 29, no. 3 (2012): 169–185.

Sartorius, Rolf, ed. *Paternalism*. Minneapolis: University of Minnesota Press, 1984.

Satz, Debra. *Why Some Things Should Not Be for Sale: On the Limits of the Market*. New York: Oxford University Press, 2010.

Schicks, Jessica. "Developmental Impact and Coexistence of Sustainable and Charitable Microfinance Institutions: Analysing BancoSol and Grameen Bank." *European Journal of Development Research* 19, no. 4 (2007): 551–568.

Schneewind, Jerome B. *The Invention of Autonomy: A History of Modern Moral Philosophy*. Cambridge: Cambridge University Press, 1997.

Schuler, Sidney Ruth, and Syed Hashemi. "Credit Programmes, Women's empowerment and Contraceptive use in rural Bangladesh." *Studies on Family Planning* 25, no. 2 (1994): 65–76.

Schwartz, Justin. "What's Wrong with Exploitation?" *Noûs* 29, no. 2 (1995): 158–188.

Sen, Amartya. *Development as Freedom*. Oxford: Oxford University Press, 1999.

Sensat, Julius. "Exploitation." *Noûs* 18, no. 1 (1984): 21–38.

Sherratt, Lesley "Is exploitation permissible in microcredit?" in *Microfinance, Rights and Global Justice*, ed. Tom Sorrell and Luis Cabrera. New York: Cambridge University Press (2015): 105–128

Siegel, Andrew. "Kantian Ethics, Exploitation and Multinational Clinical Trials." In *Exploitation and Developing Countries: The Ethics of Clinical Research*, ed. Jennifer Hawkins and Ezekiel Emmanuel. Princeton, NJ: Princeton University Press, 2008: 175–205.

Simanowitz, Anton. "Challenges to the Field and Solutions: Overindebtedness, Client Drop-outs, Unethical Collection Practices, Exorbitant Interest Rates, Mission Drift, Poor Governance Structures, and More." In *New Pathways out of Poverty*, ed. Sam Daley-Harris and Anna Awimbo. Sterling, VA: Kumarian Press, 2011: 53–120.

Simanowitz, Anton, and Katharine Knotts. *The Business of Doing Good: Insights from One Organisation's Journey to Deliver on Good Intentions*. Rugby: Practical Action Publishing, 2015.

Sinclair, Hugh. *Confessions of a Microfinance Heretic: How Microfinance Lost Its Way and Betrayed the Poor*. San Francisco: Berrett-Koehler, 2012.

Sinha, Frances, with Ajay Tankha, Reddy L. Raja, and Malcolm Harper. *Microfinance Self-Help Groups in India: Living Up to Their Promise?* Rugby: Practical Action Publishing, 2009.

Skorupski, John. *John Stuart Mill: The Arguments of the Philosophers*. London: Routledge, 1989.

Skorupski, John. *Why Read Mill Today?* London: Routledge, 2007.

Smillie, Ian. *Freedom from Want: The Remarkable Success Story of BRAC, the Global Grassroots Organization That's Winning the Fight against Poverty*. Sterling, VA: Kumarian Press, 2009.

Snyder, Jeremy. "Exploitation and Demeaning Choices." *Politics, Philosophy and Economics* 12, no. 4 (2013): 345–360.

Snyder, Jeremy. "Exploitation and Sweatshop Labor: Perspectives and Issues." *Business Ethics Quarterly* 20, no. 2 (2010): 187–213.

Snyder, Jeremy. "Needs Exploitation." *Ethical Theory and Moral Practice* 11, no. 4 (2008): 389–405.

Steiner, Hillel. "Exploitation, a Liberal Theory Amended, Defended and Extended." In *Modern Theories of Exploitation*, ed. Andrew Reeve. London: Sage, 1987: 132–148.

Steiner, Hillel. "A Liberal Theory of Exploitation." *Ethics* 94, no. 2 (1984): 225–241.

Stewart Ruth, Carina van Rooyen, Kelly Dickson, Mabolaeng Majoro, and Thea de Wet. "What Is the Impact of Microfinance on Poor People? A Systematic Review of the Evidence from Sub-Saharan Africa." Technical report, EPPI-Centre, Social Science Research Unit, University of London, 2010.

Stewart Ruth, Carina van Rooyen, Marcel Korth, Admire Chereni, Natalie Rebelo Da Silva, and Thea de Wet. " Do Micro-credit, Micro-savings and Micro-leasing Serve as Effective Financial Inclusion Interventions Enabling Poor People, and Especially Women, to Engage in Meaningful Economic Opportunities in Lower and Middle Income Countries?" Technical report, EPPI-Centre, Social Science Research Unit, Institute of Education, University of London, 2012.

Stiglitz, Joseph. *Making Globalization Work*. London: Penguin, 2006.

Stoll, David. *El Norte or Bust! How Migration Fever and Microcredit Produced a Financial Crash in a Latin American Town*. Lanham, MD: Rowman & Littlefield, 2013.

Sub-Saharan Africa Microfinance Analysis and Benchmarking Report 2010. MIX Market, Microfinance Information Exchange.

Sunstein, Cass R., and Richard H. Thaler. "Liberal Paternalism Is Not an Oxymoron." *University of Chicago Law Review* 70, no. 4 (2003): 1159–1202.

Tarozzi, Alessandro, Jaikishan Desai, and Kristin Johnson. "The Impacts of Microcredit: Evidence from Ethiopia." *American Economic Journal: Applied Economics* 7, no. 1 (2015): 54–89.

Taylor, James Stacey. "Autonomy, Duress and Coercion." *Social Philosophy and Policy* 20, no. 2 (2003): 127–155.

Taylor, James Stacey, ed. *Personal Autonomy: New Essays on Personal Autonomy and Its Role in Contemporary Moral Philosophy*. Cambridge: Cambridge University Press, 2005.

Ten, C. L., ed. *Mill's "On Liberty": A Critical Guide*. Cambridge: Cambridge University Press, 2008.

Todd, Helen, ed. *Cloning Grameen Bank: Replicating a Poverty Reduction Model in India, Nepal and Vietnam*. London: IT Publications, 1996.

Todd, Helen. *Women at the Center: Grameen Bank Borrowers after One Decade*. Dhaka: Westview Press, 1996.

Tooley, Michael. "Personhood." In *A Companion to Bioethics*, Second ed. Helga Kuhse and Peter Singer. Oxford: Blackwell, 1998: 129–139.

Tronto, Joan. *Moral Boundaries: A Political Argument for an Ethic of Care*. New York: Routledge, 1994.

Valdman, Mikhail. "Exploitation and Injustice." *Social Theory and Practice* 34, no. 4 (2008): 551–572.

Valdman, Mikhail. "A Theory of Wrongful Exploitation." *Philosopher's Imprint* 9, no. 6 (2009): 1–14.

Von der Pfordten, Dietmar. "On the Dignity of Man in Kant." *Philosophy* 84, no. 3 (2009): 371–391.

Wall, Steven. "Freedom as a Political Ideal." *Social Philosophy and Policy* 20, no. 2 (2003): 307–334.

Walt, S. "Comment on Steiner's Liberal Theory of Exploitation." *Ethics* 94, no. 2 (1984): 242–247.

Walzer, Michael. "Political Action: The Problem of Dirty Hands." *Philosophy and Public Affairs* 2, no. 2 (1973): 160–180.

Waterfield, Chuck. 2011. "Is Transparency Enough? What Is Fair and Ethical When It Comes to Prices in Microfinance?" October 11, 2011. Available at http://www.mftransparency.org/wp-content/uploads/2012/06/MFT-RPT-501-EN-Is-Transparency-Enough-What-is-Fair-and-Ethical-in-pricing.pdf.

Weinhardt, Lance, and Michael Carey. "Does Alcohol Lead to Sexual Risk Behaviour?" *Annual Review of Sex Research* 11 (2001): 125–157.

Weir, Sharon, Charmaine Pailman, Xoli Mahlalela, Nicol Coetzee, Farshid Meidany, and Ties Boerma. "From People to Places: Focusing AIDS Prevention Efforts Where It Matters Most." *AIDS 17*, no. 8 (2003): 95–903.

Wertheimer, Alan. *Coercion*. Princeton, NJ: Princeton University Press, 1987.

Wertheimer, Alan. "Coercion." In *Encyclopedia of Ethics*, ed. Lawrence C. Becker and Charlotte B. Becker. 2nd ed. New York: Routledge, 2001: 245–248.

Wertheimer, Alan. *Exploitation*. Princeton, NJ: Princeton University Press, 1996.

Wertheimer, Alan. "Exploitation." In *The Stanford Encyclopedia of Philosophy*, ed. Edward N. Zalta, Fall 2008 ed. http://plato.stanford.edu/archives/fall2008/entries/exploitation.

Wertheimer, Alan. "Exploitation in Clinical Research." In *Exploitation and Developing Countries: The Ethics of Clinical Research*, ed. Jennifer Hawkins and Ezekiel Emmanuel. Princeton, NJ: Princeton University Press, 2008: 63–104.

Westen, Peter, and H. L. A. Hart. "'Freedom' and 'Coercion': Virtue Words and Vice Words." *Duke Law Journal* 1985, nos. 2–4 (1985): 541–593.

Wildavsky, Aaron. "The Self-Evaluating Organisation." *Public Administration Review* 32, no. 5 (1972): 509–520.

Wilkinson, Stephen. *Bodies for Sale: Ethics and Exploitation in the Hunan Body Trade*. London: Routledge, 2003.

Wilson, Kim, Malcolm Harper, and Matthew Griffith, eds. *Financial Promise for the Poor: How Groups Build Microsavings*. Sterling, VA: Kumarian Press, 2010.

Wolff, Jonathan. *Ethics and Public Policy: A Philosophical Inquiry*. London: Routledge, 2011.

Wolff, Jonathan. "The Ethics of Competition." In *The Legal and Moral Aspects of International Trade*, ed. Geraint Parry, Asif Quershi, and Hillel Steiner. London: Routledge, 1998: 82–96.

Wolff, Jonathan. "Fairness, Respect and the Egalitarian Ethos." *Philosophy and Public Affairs* 27, no. 2 (1998): 97–122.

Wolff, Jonathan. "Marx and Exploitation." *Journal of Ethics* 3 (1999): 105–120.

Wolff, Jonathan, and Avner De-Shalit. *Disadvantage*. Oxford: Oxford University Press, 2007.

Wood, Allen. " Autonomy as the Ground of Morality." O'Neil Memorial Lectures, University of New Mexico, March 1999.

Wood, Allen. "Exploitation." In *Exploitation*, ed. Kai Nielson and Robert Ware. Atlantic Highlands, NJ: Humanities Press, 1997: 2–26.

Wood, Allen. "Human Dignity, Right and the Realm of Ends." Keynote lecture, 2007. Available at www.stanford.edu/~allenw/webpapers/keynote2007.doc.

Wright, Graham. "Dropouts and Graduates: Lessons from Bangladesh." *Microbanking Bulletin* 6 (2001): 14–16.

Wright, Katie. "The Darker Side to Microfinance: Evidence from Cajamarca, Peru." In *Microfinance: Perils and Prospects*, ed. Jude L. Fernando. New York: Routledge, 2006.

Young, Iris Marion. *Responsibility for Justice*. New York: Oxford University Press, 2011.

Young, Robert. "John Stuart Mill, Ronald Dworkin, and Paternalism." In *Mill's "On Liberty,"* ed. C. L. Ten. Cambridge: Cambridge University Press, 2008: 209–227.

Young, Robert. *Personal Autonomy: Beyond Negative and Positive Liberty*. London: Croom Helm, 1986.

Yunus, Muhammad. *Banker to the Poor: Micro-lending and the Battle against World Poverty*. New York, N.Y.: PublicAffairs, 1999.

Yunus, Muhammad, with Alan Jolis. *Banker to the Poor: The Autobiography of Muhammad Yunus*. Rev. ed. New York: PublicAffairs, 2003.

Zimmerman, David. "Coercive Wage Offers." *Philosophy and Public Affairs* 10, no. 2 (1981): 121–145.

Zimmerman, David. "More on Coercive Wage Offers: A Reply to Alexander." *Philosophy and Public Affairs* 12, no. 2 (1983): 165–171.

Zimmerman, David. "Taking Liberties: The Perils of 'Moralizing' Freedom and Coercion in Social Theory and Practice." *Social Theory and Practice* 28, no. 4 (2002): 577–609.

Zimmerman, Matt. "The Ethics of Price Gouging." *Business Ethics Quarterly* 18, no. 3 (2008): 347–378.

Zimmerman, Matt. "Sweatshops, Choice and Exploitation." *Business Ethics Quarterly* 17, no. 4 (2007): 89–727.

Zwolinski, Matt. "Structural Exploitation." *Social Philosophy and Policy* 29, no. 1 (2012): 154–179.

Index

Notes and tables are indicated by "n" and "t" following page numbers.